COLLECTED ESSAYS ON AMERICANISM

Third Edition

DAVID CLAIRE JENNINGS

Collected Essays on Americanism

Published by Southern Heart Publishing Co.
Author's website: www.davidclairejennings.com

ISBN-13: 978-0-9974601-7-9
ISBN-10: 0-9974601-7-2

Also by David Claire Jennings:

After Bondage and War
Hanna's Promise: A Story of Grace and Hope
The American: A Man's Life
Slaves, Saints and Soldiers
The Goodness of Alzheimer's

Table of Contents

Introduction

Writing is a solitary process. Some do it anyway because they have to, hoping they can connect with another and reverse the solitude someday. They hope it will make another human feel something, learn something, believe something or make some small difference in their lives.

For so many years I wrote essays, long before I wrote novels, before I went back to school to study history and study it further on my own. Before that I wrote technical manuals and instructions. Inexplicably, few read those, while they are needed for some practical purpose. But essays – narrations of ideas – have always been at the heart of my writing, even when infused within my characters and their stories in my novels.

Whether we believe the divine account or man's scientific tentative determinations, the Earth formed from the cosmos, likely in one momentous event, many eons ago. For myself, both ideas of creation work and are compatible. I believe that God created it, that He is ageless and timeless and we cannot know His purpose.

Man began sometime thereafter in the northeastern region of the African continent and the fertile crescent there. The color of his skin was black for God's or nature's good reasons. Man's population spread quickly to what is now the Middle East nearby.

We understand man propagated and formed family units and then groups for socialization and banded together for cooperation and survival. He became tribal. He spread across the vast distances of land and some believe he crossed large bodies of water even in early times.

The tribes fought for dominance and the stronger, cleverer, or benefactors of good circumstance from any manner of things, grew to mighty early civilizations in Egypt, Greece, Rome and Arabia. Ideas of philosophy, divine deity and mortal monarchy changed the lives of both the meek and the powerful.

Most agree that as a result of a brief climatic change – an ice age – men, women and children of Asia crossed a temporary, propitious land bridge over the Bering Strait, maybe some thirteen thousands of years ago, and came to what is now North America. They settled in warmer areas, the ice age dissipated and the bridge dissolved. We believe the earliest major settlement was near what is now Clovis, New Mexico. We call them the Clovis people. They spread down the thread and spine connecting North and South America. That thread of Central America brought mighty Inca and Mayan civilizations into the northwestern regions of South America.

Centuries later the western European highly developed civilizations - now nations - began to cross the Atlantic Ocean and around Africa and South America on frightful voyages of exploration for riches and treasures and future needs for more land. What some did to others is what we call history.

The Spaniards came to America as the first Europeans, followed by the Dutch, the French and the British. In our part of the hemisphere, the British dominated and formed the basis for our future country – our laws and our Christianity.

It is about what followed after that, our country we call the United States, or simply America, that has occupied my thoughts for all the years of my late maturity.

So here then are my essays, with some more recent in my years as an old student with passion for history and its people, and finally as a novelist of some years with a compulsion to understand humanity and its creation.

Some, the most early, are not so well written – it was before my depth of reverence for the English language grew to its present appreciation - and maybe weakly compelling, while a few show a spark of intelligence with profundity and maybe wisdom.

There is a little bit of memoir, some painful but honest and personal. Some are now outdated but reflect what I saw at the time. They are my own words.

They are topically grouped in sections – society, bureaucracy, history, law, politics, economics, and literature as art. Each section contains a number of essays. They are eclectic in topic and without particular order within each category, with a few humorous and some naïve, but most with a serious intent. The whimsical and sardonic ones are channeling P.J. O'Rourke for anyone who has read and enjoyed his books. I must thank my teachers in classes, the knowledge from many books and myself for my life's experience.

I noted that Charles Krauthammer has been a newspaper correspondent and astute political commentator for many years and has recently compiled some of his columns (essays) into a book titled *Things That Matter*. I read it and enjoyed it. At first I did not like him very much, but have come to admire him as the acquired taste that he is. When his mind is tuned in, he is brilliant. When it is not, he bullshits effectively. While I do not have his credentials or celebrity; he was a doctor who became a writer, while I was an engineer who has done the same.

With my first novel *After Bondage and War* published in June and October 2015, my second novel *Hanna's Promise: A Story of Grace and Hope* published in May 2016 and *The American: A Man's Life* published December 2016, my 19th century historical fiction trilogy is complete. An anthology titled *Slaves, Saints and Soldiers* has been published in 2017 to offer the three-books under one cover. There have been non-fiction books written and published during this period also.

I have only reviewed these old essays now to compile them and correct them for typographical errors, punctuation errors and the like. Whatever it was, it was what I wrote at the time. For whatever value that has now, it has.

A comment about this third edition:

This edition has been expanded to eighty seven essays. Since the second edition, two have been added to Section 3 – History and nine have been added to Section 7 – now named Literature as Art. These last add more thoughts about writing and additional exegesis as appreciation for renowned American writers who have inspired my writing.

Enjoy them if you may.

David Claire Jennings

Section 1 – Society

The Goodness of Alzheimer's

Published in 2014, re-published in 2016

Preface

I first published this work as a pamphlet in 2014 with the belief it might be passed around and provide some comfort and solace to a caregiver or any person concerned or worried about Alzheimer's. Nothing has changed me in that wish or belief or any feeling I felt and shared in that earlier work.

But now I am publishing it as an e-book to distribute it to all the online sites where interested readers can easily acquire it. To do that it is necessary for the reader to pay 99 cents. I had wished to offer it free but that would have disqualified it from one or more of the important outlets.

My darling wife's illness has progressed much further in the two years since that pamphlet was printed. We used to notice changes in her over a span of 3 to 6 months, now it is 1 to 2. The regression is accelerating. It is simply a matter of recognizing and accepting a paradigm shift, adjusting to the new reality, while continuing to live with her in the present.

We know exactly how it will end if she does not pass away for some other thing. Just as a child living in reverse, she will unlearn how to walk, unlearn how to eat and swallow, and finally unlearn how to breathe. Her natural moment of death from Alzheimer's will be just as it is the moment we are born.

It is not a burden. It is not difficult to bear – not in the least. The love remains now as it was before and will be until she leaves for her next life. My hope and belief is that I will join her again someday. As we have learned in Ecclesiastes, to everything there is a season. As some leaves fall and others grow in their place, so too with the generations of flesh and blood, one dies and another is born.

In the Beginning

Life is difficult. My good son read me that from his insights of M. Scott Peck's "The Road Less Traveled". That sounds so simple, so basic, so obvious. But to truly embrace and accept that life is difficult is hard. And life has constant but differing challenges. Alzheimer's disorder or disease is only one of these and not the worst. It takes a long time to understand it and accept it. It takes even longer to see its goodness. I will try to save you some worry and time, help you understand it better, and reduce the fears you may have that it may happen to you or your loved one.

Alzheimer's Nature

What I believe it isn't. - Years ago, I watched one of those sensitive and touching movies produced by Hallmark I sometimes enjoy. It was the story of an elderly couple who lived by themselves in a beautiful woodsy place in a nice home much like a luxurious log cabin.

The wife developed most noticeable memory loss. She was fully cognizant, knew just what was happening, and what it portended for her future. It was her husband who was in denial. She was a bright woman, and early in her illness, she decided to move to a home on her own volition and spare her husband hardship. Her husband was saddened, disagreed, and didn't want her to go. He reluctantly agreed and set her free because he loved her. He visited her often and watched her decline. Toward the end she developed a friendship, and something of a romance, with a fellow patient she knew to be much like her. Her husband viewed this and was further saddened. Eventually, he accepted this also. She ultimately viewed this stranger that came to visit her as someone from her past where they may have shared love. Maybe it was her father, but it was a person who must have mattered. He became something like a dear friend. The husband accepted this too.

This tender story disturbed me. It was unrealistic in that it was not the true nature of the disorder. It may be for some, but I tend to doubt it. It was tender, but sad and hopeless. It doesn't have to be like this. I don't think it is the nature of the illness either. The woman could not have had the awareness, cognizance, or insight as portrayed. The husband could not have left it all in her hands. He was intelligent too.

What I believe it is - Years ago, I watched "The Incredible Life of Benjamin Button", portrayed very sensitively by Brad Pitt. It was a fantasy about a man who lived his life backwards. He was born an old man and died a baby. The story progressed and showed his life from a very old man, to an elderly man, to a middle aged man, to a young energetic and adventurous man, to a boy, and finally an infant - all the stages of life in reverse. Throughout his whole life there was a lady friend who started out as a girl and ended as an old woman. When their lives crossed together, around age 30, they had a brief passionate time as boyfriend and girlfriend. At the end, she cradled him in her arms and they felt the mother-infant bond of love. For the infant Benjamin, awareness was vague but love was felt and shared.

The man that wrote this was portraying the nature of Alzheimer's. And I believe this is its nature. But their story was different and not as good as ours. There was only a brief time they were at the same age. They could not live throughout their lives with matching roles, at each age, as we do. The roles constantly changed as their lives moved in opposite directions. Also, and very important, the Alzheimer's patient has generally lived most of a conventional full life and then, in a relatively brief span, lived a similar life again in reverse.

I have seen this up close and personal. I have watched my wife go from a forgetful older adult to regressive personalities of a young woman, to a petulant teenage adolescent, to a young girl and now maybe something like a 5 or 6 year old child. It has taken me time to adjust. There is anger to deal with, as well as love, both ways between us.

The Mechanics and Emotions of Care

When the close-by and emotionally invested caregiver engages, it can often go like this:

"Come here we need to change your wet pants."

"No, I don't need to, they aren't wet".

"Yes they are but you don't understand. Come here now please."

"No. Go to hell. You're stupid."

"No I'm not . You're too stupid to know I'm trying to help you."

"I don't want you to talk to me anymore. Shut up. I'm leaving."

She goes upstairs to her bedroom and slams the door. I have not been successful or handled this with the best parenting skill needed. After a few minutes, I go to her room and ask how she is feeling.

"I'm OK. Where have you been? I haven't seen you in so long. Have you been at work?"

"No. I have been right around, but missed you and wanted to see you."

"I'm so happy to see you again."

"I have a good idea. Let's both get out of our wet pants. We will feel better."

"Oh. OK. If you think so."

From there things get better.

She is in another room talking to my son in a rare lucid moment of self-reflective insight.

She tells him "Maybe he should leave me. I wouldn't blame him." My son tells me what she said. Here was a rare moment when she did feel psychic pain and suffered but, unlike us, it would only last for a moment. I asked my son to bring her to me. I held her cheeks gently so that we could look at each other's eyes.

"I love you. I have always loved you. I will love you forever. I will never leave you."

Her faced contorted in a twisted smile. Tears ran down her cheeks.

"Really? You do feel that way? You holler at me and I thought you didn't love me. That is wonderful and makes me happy."

"Let me tell about the night we got married. It was a long time ago. Forty-two years. We have been married and together most of our lives. It was close to Christmas and a candlelight service on a Friday night. There were poinsettias all around the church. The lights were dim and the candlelight was warm. It was beautiful. When I saw you coming down the aisle in your beautiful Spanish lace wedding gown, I couldn't believe how lucky I was to have you for my wife. You were so beautiful, I had all I could do to keep from crying right then."

"That's nice. I love you."

From there things get better.

A good loving dog can be helpful. One with high emotional intelligence and empathy can serve as a good arbitrator. When you are toe to toe, and nose to nose, hollering as loud as you can at each other, both frustrated because you cannot communicate, the dog will run right to you. She will bark as loud as she can to tell you she is upset her loved ones are fighting. You will reset.

When you are standing together in a long hug and smooching, the dog will run right to you. She will get all excited, furiously wag her tail, look at you both and approve. She will want you to pick her up so she can get in on the love fest. She will lick both your faces and be happy for her and you.

A good home-aid can be helpful. She will be skilled at quickly modifying uncooperative behavior. She won't be emotionally invested and can be more effective to get done the difficult necessary chores that are so hard for you. Maybe it's about getting your spouse to shower and look after her hygiene. You have tried to get her to agree and help her to shower. She has petulantly refused. You have fought her and tried every scheme you could think of. She doesn't want water on her body or her hair. You have given up and tried a few days later. It was the same and you repeat. It has been 3-4 weeks. Finally she agrees and you help her shower.

A good home-aid can get this done skillfully every week and save you the struggle. She will paint her finger nails. They will have a little girlfriend time together. Your loved one may read her children's books or show her companion pictures. It will be good for everyone.

The Understanding and Hope

While the caregiver may have full knowledge of the past and can project some vision for the future, and live in that context, the patient cannot. The patient has no choice. She can only live in the moment, right now. There is no past and there is no future. There is no other reality.

When long term and short term memory is gone, that is only the beginning. Outside loved ones cannot know the fallout and consequence of that, and where it goes from there. The patient's whole reality changes without the benefit of her memory. She may remember a few things, correctly or distorted. She may bring them up like a routine at the very same time each day. At the supper table she may say every day-

"How are your Mom and Dad? I have not seen them in a long time."

"They passed away a long time ago but lived a full and good life. Now it is you and me that are the old ones."

"I always liked your mother and wonder if she liked me."

"Mom always loved you. She was so happy I found such a smart and ladylike woman like you."

"That's nice."

From there things get better.

The Goodness, Acceptance and Peace

She will know you and close loved ones right to the end. Even if she may mix up some names, she will know who you are. But most of the time, the memories of less close ones, like old friends or co-workers, will be gone. That is not the most important thing for you to concern yourself with. You must understand, cherish and preserve your new relationship.

There will always be an end to life and we all know that. But Alzheimer's is hardly the end. It can be a beautiful transition. The patient feels no pain unlike so many terminal illnesses. If their feelings are hurt, they forget and forgive a moment later. Most of us cannot do that so easily. That is a blessing. They can be happy, and generally are, in their altered world.

If the caregiver can learn to join the patient and live in the moment, if only when he is with her, they will be together and happy all the way to the end. I think that may be the key. I have discovered this, have tried it, and we both are very happy together, as before, but in a new way. And our life together can be just as rewarding, loving, and rich as it was before. I understand and accept that we are living in a different way. That is OK. It is still good.

The Conclusion

I often can't behave in the best way that I should but recognize I am human. I am so far from a saint. However, I must do the things necessary for her health, safety and comfort, whether she agrees or fights me. That is my responsibility in the role as her parent. The lessons I have learned have made it better for both me and my dearest wife. Our life is still rich, fulfilling and loving. With a touch of humor and poignancy, I hope this has been hopeful and helpful.

For now, don't worry too much about the future. Enjoy to its fullest the wonderful life in the stage you are living in. Future stages can be just as rewarding. And at the end, if this terminal illness should become part of your life, know that it will be much better than other, more painful terminal illnesses. You will learn how to make lemonade from lemons.

The American Dream

Originally written in 2014

Forward

I didn't write this story. I found it in a cigar box. As I have studied our American society and history, I have learned much about the good, the bad, and the ugly. There is a lot to regret and many shameful chapters. But once in a while, we discover the good and are reminded of what makes life worth living.

Immigration is a very contentious issue and has always been so in our history. Without going into this politically charged topic - that is not my purpose here - read this simple story and remember the true source of our greatness and American spirit. It is heartening. I am proud of the Padron family and they make me proud of my country.

The Story of "THE LITTLE HAMMER"

In 1962, I arrived in Miami, an unknown city in a foreign land. I had to start from zero. At first, I received $60 monthly, as government aid given to Cuban refugees. I was thirty-six years old, strong, and in good health. Every time I cashed that check, I felt like a burden on the country that had taken me in. For many days, I looked for a job and did not find one. Every night, I went home and thought of the future. I was determined to do something so that I could support my family.

One day, Raul Fernandez, a friend who worked in the Cuban Refugee Office asked if I had any carpentry skills. I said I did. He gave me a gift – a small hammer – which he asked me to put to good use. The hammer made me feel I had the necessary tool to become self-sufficient and not depend on a government hand-out.

During the days, I worked as a gardener. At nights, I did carpentry with the hammer.

My dream was to save enough money to open a factory to make great cigars, like the ones we used to smoke in Cuba. Through a lot of sacrifice and hard work, I managed to save $600 – money I made working with the hammer. With that, I made my dream come true and opened Padron Cigars in 1964.

I still have the hammer as a reminder of how we started. More than 40 years later … the hammer is still here and so is Padron Cigars, the brand the hammer helped build.

Jose Orlando Padron

As a boy, my father would show me a small, old hammer and tell me how it changed his life. We, his children, grew up hearing the story of el martillito, the little hammer. It became a tradition which we now tell our children. The hammer represents the dedication and hard work that went into building Padron Cigars. It reminds us of our roots and humble beginnings. It stands for tenacity, integrity, perseverance, loyalty, commitment to quality … and much more. The hammer helped lay the foundation for what we are today. The hammer has a deep meaning for the Padron family. This is why we are sharing the story with you.

Jorge Padron

This is an American story; one of courage, hard work and integrity.

Celebrating White History

Originally written in 2012

In 2006 Edie and I took a wonderful 21-day, motor coach excursion covering over 3,300 miles of the UK. We departed from London and went to Oxford, Stratford, Coventry, Kenilworth, Wedgewood, York, Durham, Jedburgh, Edinburgh, St. Andrews, Dundee, Perth, Pitlochry, Laggan (in the Highlands), Isle of Skye, Loch Lomond, Glasgow, Grasmere, Manchester, Anglesey, Caernarvon, Chester, Ludlow, Liangollen, Liandrindod Wells, Caerphilly, Cardiff, Tintern Abbey, Bath, Glastonbury, Dunster, Exmoor, Torquay, St. Ives, Plymouth, Salibury, Lymington, Yarmouth, Isle of Wight, Portsmouth, Winchester and back to London.

Our driver, Jim Burke, was a stereotypical Scot, standing 5 foot 6 at 200 pounds and cranky but with sardonic wit and pride. He insisted we refer to him as a motor coach driver, not a bus driver. The way he spoke of his bus reminded me of Scotty in Star Trek.

Our Tour Director, Steve Tormey, was a smooth talking Welshman; tall and handsome with gray hair and bushy black eyebrows; very well spoken and charming. As we departed from London, Steve asked us all where we were from. We answered Australia, New Zealand, Canada and the US. Steve said "Well you have all come home now, haven't you? Welcome home". This struck a nostalgic, sentimental chord with all of us. I have never thought of myself as a European American or a white American; just an American with pride in my country and its history. This was the first moment of my life when I felt my heritage strike my heart.

In the Isle of Skye, there was a lady folksinger who entertained us in the lobby of our old hotel. She said "Half of me is Irish and half of me is Scottish; so I really want a drink, but I don't want to pay for it!" At my request she sang the old Irish song "Carrickfergus". Steve Tormey sat next to us nipping his single malt and singing along in his beautiful Welsh voice. Carrickfergus is on the coast of Northern Ireland in Ulster. The sad melancholy lyrics:

I wish I was in Carrickfergus, only for nights in Ballygrand

I would swim over the deepest ocean, the deepest ocean for my love to find

But the sea is wide and I cannot swim over and neither have I wings to fly

If I could find me a handsome boatman to ferry me over to my love and die

My childhood days bring back sad reflections of happy times I spent so long ago

My boyhood friends and my own relations have all passed on now like melting snow

But I'll spend my days in endless roaming, soft is the grass, my bed is free

Ah to be back in Carrickfergus on that long road down to the sea

And in Kilkenny it is reported there are marble stones as black as ink

With gold and silver I would support her, but I'll sing no more now till I get a drink

I'm drunk today and I'm seldom sober, a handsome rover from town to town

Ah, but I'm sick now, my days are numbered so come all ye young men and lay me down

Scotch-Irish (or Scots-Irish) Americans are the descendants of an estimated 250,000 Presbyterian and other Protestant dissenters from the Irish province of Ulster who immigrated to North America primarily during the colonial era. Some scholars also include the 150,000 Ulster Protestants who immigrated to America during the early 19th century, and their descendants. Most of the Scotch-Irish were descended from Scottish and English families who colonized Ireland during the Plantation of Ulster in the 17th century. While an estimated 36 million Americans (12% of the total population) reported Irish ancestry in 2006, and 6 million (2% of the population) reported Scottish ancestry, an additional 5.4 million (1.8% of the population) identified more specifically with Scotch-Irish ancestry. People in Great Britain or Ireland that are of a similar ancestry usually refer to themselves as Ulster Scots, with the term *Scotch-Irish* used only in North America.

American descendants of this heritage include John Wayne, Elvis Presley, John McCain, Ulysses S. Grant, George S. Patton, Andrew Jackson and, of course, countless others.

Because of the close proximity of the islands of Britain and Ireland, migrations in both directions had been occurring since Ireland was first settled after the retreat of the ice sheets. Gaels from Ireland colonized current South-West Scotland as part of the Kingdom of Dal Riata, eventually replacing the native Pictish culture throughout Scotland. These Gaels had previously been named Scoti by the Romans, and eventually the name was applied to the entire Kingdom of Scotland.

The origins of the Scotch-Irish lie primarily in the Lowlands of Scotland and in northern England, particularly in the border country on either side of the Anglo-Scottish border, a region that had seen centuries of conflict. In the near constant state of war between England and Scotland during the Middle-Ages, the livelihood of the people on the borders was devastated by the contending armies. Even when the countries were not at war, tension remained high, and royal authority in one or the other kingdom was often weak. The uncertainty of existence led the people of the borders to seek security through a system of family ties, similar to the clan system in the Scottish Highlands. Known as the Border Reivers, these families relied on their own strength and cunning to survive, and a culture of cattle raiding and thievery developed.

Scotland and England became unified under a single monarch with the Union of the Crowns in 1603, when James VI, King of Scots, succeeded Elizabeth I as ruler of England. In addition to the unstable border region, James also inherited Elizabeth's conflicts in Ireland. Following the end of the Irish Nine Years' War in 1603, and the Flight of the Earls in 1607, James embarked in 1609 on a systematic plantation of English and Scottish Protestant settlers to Ireland's northern province of Ulster. The Plantation of Ulster was seen as a way to relocate the Border Reiver families to Ireland to bring peace to the Anglo-Scottish border country, and also to provide fighting men who could suppress the native Irish in Ireland.

The first major influx of Scots and English into Ulster had come in 1606 during the settlement of East Down onto land cleared of native Irish by private landlords chartered by James. This process was accelerated with James's official plantation in 1609, and further augmented during the subsequent Irish Confederate Wars. The first of the Stuart Kingdoms to collapse into civil war was Ireland where, prompted in part by the anti-Catholic rhetoric of the Covenanters, Irish Catholics launched a rebellion in October. In reaction to the proposal by Charles I and Thomas Wentworth to raise an army manned by Irish Catholics to put down the Covenanter movement in Scotland, the Parliament of Scotland had threatened to invade Ireland in order to achieve "the extirpation of Popery out of Ireland" (according to the interpretation of Richard Bellings, a leading Irish politician of the time). The fear this caused in Ireland unleashed a wave of massacres against Protestant English and Scottish settlers, mostly in Ulster, once the rebellion had broken out. All sides displayed extreme cruelty in this phase of the war. Around 4000 settlers were massacred and a further 12,000 may have died of privation after being driven from their homes. In one notorious incident, the Protestant inhabitants of Portadown were taken captive and then massacred on the bridge in the town. The settlers responded in kind, as did the British-controlled government in Dublin, with attacks on the Irish civilian population. Massacres of native civilians occurred at Rathlin Island and elsewhere. In early 1642, the Covenanters sent an army to Ulster to defend the Scottish settlers there from the Irish rebels who had attacked them after the outbreak of the rebellion. The original intention of the Scottish army was to re-conquer Ireland, but due to logistical and supply problems, it was never in a position to advance far beyond its base in eastern Ulster. The Covenanter force remained in Ireland until the end of the civil wars but was confined to its garrison around Carrickfergus after its defeat by the native Ulster Army at the Battle of Benburb in 1646. After the war was over, many of the soldiers settled permanently in Ulster. Another major influx of Scots into Ulster occurred in the 1690s, when tens of thousands of people fled a famine in Scotland to come to Ireland.

Just a few generations after arriving in Ireland, considerable numbers of Ulster-Scots emigrated to the North American colonies of Great Britain throughout the 18th century (between 1717 and 1770 alone, about 250,000 settled in what would become the United States). According to Kerby Miller, *Emigrants and Exiles: Ireland and the Irish Exodus to North America* (1988), Protestants were one-third the population of Ireland, but three-quarters of all emigrants leaving from 1700 to 1776; 70% of these Protestants were Presbyterians. Other factors contributing to the mass exodus of Ulster Scots to America during the 18th century were a series of droughts and rising rents imposed by often absentee English and/or Anglo-Irish landlords.

During the course of the 17th century, the number of settlers belonging to Calvinist dissenting sects, including Scottish and Northumbrian Presbyterians, English Baptists, French and Flemish Huguenots, and German Palatines, became the majority among the

Protestant settlers in the province of Ulster. However, the Presbyterians and other dissenters, along with Catholics, were not members of the established church and were consequently legally disadvantaged by the Penal Laws, which gave full rights only to members of the Church of England/Church of Ireland. Those members of the state church were often absentee landlords and the descendants of the British aristocracy who had been given land by the monarchy. For this reason, up until the 19th century, and despite their common fear of the dispossessed Catholic native Irish, there was considerable disharmony between the Presbyterians and the Protestant Ascendancy in Ulster. As a result of this many Ulster-Scots, along with Catholic native Irish, ignored religious differences to join the United Irishmen and participate in the Irish Rebellion of 1798, in support of Age of Enlightenment-inspired egalitarian and republican goals.

Scholarly estimate is that over 200,000 Scotch-Irish migrated to the Americas between 1717 and 1775. As a late arriving group, they found that land in the coastal areas of the British colonies was either already owned or too expensive, so they quickly left for the hill country where land could be had cheaply. Here they lived on the frontiers of America. Early frontier life was extremely challenging, but poverty and hardship were familiar to them. The term hillbilly has often been applied to their descendants in the mountains, carrying connotations of poverty, backwardness and violence; this word having its origins in Scotland and Ireland.

The first trickle of Scotch-Irish settlers arrived in New England. Valued for their fighting prowess as well as for their Protestant dogma, they were invited by Cotton Mather and other leaders to come over to help settle and secure the frontier. In this capacity, many of the first permanent settlements in Maine and New Hampshire, especially after 1718, were Scotch-Irish and many place names as well as the character of Northern New Englanders reflect this fact. The Scotch-Irish brought the potato with them from Ireland (although the potato originated in South America, it was not known in North America until brought over from Europe). In Maine it became a staple crop as well as an economic base. From 1717 to the next thirty or so years, the primary points of entry for the Ulster immigrants were Philadelphia, Pennsylvania, and New Castle, Delaware. The Scotch-Irish radiated westward across the Alleghenies, as well as into Virginia, North Carolina, South Carolina, Georgia, Kentucky, and Tennessee. The typical migration involved small networks of related families who settled together, worshipped together, and intermarried, avoiding outsiders.

This story of my heritage is long but so is the history of my ancestors. It is full of pain, suffering, cruelty, fighting and the quest for freedom. It is the story of our American history. In our 21st century society, our history is neglected. It will never be celebrated as a federal holiday, or with a monument on the National Mall or by a month long celebration of our heritage and culture.

Most of us know the stories of our founding fathers. Their lives are well documented and are fairly well represented on our National Mall. But most of them were born here. George Washington and Thomas Jefferson were born in Virginia. John Adams and Benjamin Franklin were born in Massachusetts. They were British subjects and later our first American citizens.

This story is not about them. It is about the throngs of European immigrants that came over and specifically those from the U.K. It is about my proud heritage. It is not racist. Sorry Al and Jesse; it's not about you. It's about me.

A Sociologist Studies Working Class Saloons in Chicago

Originally written in 2014

This document is about a study conducted by a sociologist named Royal Melendy in 1900. While the writer's demeanor is academic and a bit stuffy, the most interesting aspect of the article is that the sociologist came to the study with a preconceived notion but completed it with a surprising, and completely different, conclusion.

The introductory summary titled "A Sociologist Studies Working-Class Saloons in Chicago"[1] sets the tone for the article titled "Royal Melendy - Ethical Substitutes for the Saloon, 1900"[2] as quoted here entirely as follows:

Progressive temperance reformers believed that saloons seduced customers into lives of drunkenness, crime, and debauchery. Many progressives also believed social problems such as saloons should be studied scientifically. Sociologist Royal Melendy investigated saloons in a working-class neighborhood of Chicago as part of an "Ethical Subcommittee" set up to study "the liquor problem," as he put it. Venturing out from a progressive social settlement house in an industrial district of the city, Melendy discovered that saloons met major needs of working people. His study, excerpted below revealed the gap between the realities of working-class life and the assumptions and preconceptions of many progressives.[3]

The first thing Melendy learned was that "The popular conception of the saloon as a "place where men and women revel in drunkenness and shame," or "where sotted beasts gather nightly at the bar," is due to exaggerated pictures, drawn by temperance lecturers and evangelists, intended to excite the imagination with a view to arousing public sentiment."[4]

Referring to the saloon as an institution, he further determined that "It is a part of the neighborhood, which must change with the neighborhood; it fulfills in it the social functions which unfortunately have been left to it to exercise."[5] He further considered that "In some sections of the city it has the appearance of accomplishing more for the laboring classes from business interests then we from philanthropic motives...."[6] Melendy concluded that it is a workingman's club and serves a common ground for ethnicity, occupation, or political affiliation. It is also a place for assistance in finding employment and acts as a labor bureau, without a feeling of accepting charity. It is a place of friendship. He said that "Untrammeled by rules and restrictions, it surpasses in spirit the organized club. That general atmosphere of freedom, that spirit of democracy, which men crave, is here realized....."[7]

His understanding deepens with his statements: "This is the working man school. He is both scholar and teacher".[8] and "I believe it is true that all the charity organizations in Chicago combined are feeding fewer people than saloons".[9]

Certainly Royal Melendy was drawn to the conclusion that the saloon is a positive good. Certainly progressives reading his report would reject it and require further study.

This paper was especially enjoyable to write due to its topic and outcome. It is not often that one can get legitimate academic license to describe the way in which progressives have often believed that they are the better ones by providing their brand of loving-kindness, tolerance, and goods and services to their neighbors based on their assumptions. As Royal Melendy learned, it is an arrogant and naive belief that we know best how to do good and that our solutions are needed in every case.

Notes

1. Michael P. Johnson, *Reading the American Past, Selected Historical Documents, Volume 2: From 1865, Fifth Edition* (New York: Bedford/St. Martin's, 2012), 105.

2. Ibid., 105

3. Ibid, 105

4. Ibid, 105

5. Ibid, 105

6. Ibid, 105

7. Ibid, 106

8. Ibid, 107

9. Ibid, 107

Bibliography

Johnson, Michael P. *Reading the American Past, Selected Historical Documents, Volume 2:*

From 1865, Fifth Edition, New York: Bedford/St. Martin's, 2012.

Who Will Take Care of the Poor?

Originally written in 2011

If you don't believe that the government should take care of the poor, you must be mean spirited, selfish and totally lacking in compassion for those less fortunate. At least that is the guilt-driven view of Liberals.

Recently I was explaining the limited role of government from a Libertarian point of view to a Liberal. We were discussing the whole gamut of the concepts of rights, entitlements, obligations, individuality, and liberty. When I explained that caring for the poor is not the business of government, I was accused of not believing in Christian charity. Au contraire, mon ami! That's precisely my point.

What did Jesus teach? I think he said we are our brothers' keepers. Those of us who are blessed with so much are chastened to help those with so little. We are expected to help the poor and helpless. But Jesus meant us as individuals; not Caesar. In today's society that means charity should come from friends, family, churches, soup kitchens, food banks, the Salvation Army, the Rescue Mission and other charitable non-profit organizations, privately financed organizations funded by individuals, fraternal organizations, wealthy individuals and corporations who want to give. If anyone wants to give, no one will stop them. That is Christian charity.

When the government does it, it is not charity. It is feckless bureaucrats doling out OPM (other people's money) based on laws passed by possibly well-meaning politicians. The problem is that we as individuals do not get to decide. It is coerced charity and that is robbery.

So don't you dare characterize those of us who believe in liberty as lacking compassion for the poor just because we don't buy into the nonsense that what government does is charity. I don't believe that even their motives are pure. They are using OPM to establish their base of dependent, entitled voters for their reelections. So actually this isn't just robbery; its robbery with evil, selfish motives.

There is absolutely no expectation that government policy will change this far into our history. This is about presenting an uncomfortable principle. It is about setting aside emotion, rejecting incorrect initial premises and applying the rational mind to objective reality.

The views expressed here are not politically correct and will offend the sensibilities of the progressive mainstream and its media. That is my mission.

An Honest Conversation About Race

Originally written in 2013

Note: Anyone choosing to read this article may decide at the middle of it that the conclusion is known. If the topic is of interest to the reader, please read it to the end. It is written in a circle and ends where it begins.

I have met a few first generation citizens and immigrants from African countries like Sudan. My son has met and worked with immigrants from Nigeria and Kenya as graduate students. They are truly wonderful people. One, named Dut, is in my history class along with his younger cousin who is preparing to take her citizenship tests.

My new friend, in such a short time, has taught me so much. We have had many simple and profound discussions about people and life. He told me that storytelling is important in African life. One day he will return to Africa and tell a story about an old man with white hair that he once made a human connection with.

These are affable, friendly, religious, and inquisitive people who are very happy to be here. They do not carry any crippling baggage of victimhood or anything like that. Dut became an American citizen a couple years ago.

They have come to our country following the traditional path of immigrants like the Irish and Italians in the 18th century. But I have learned that their test for citizenship is more difficult now than it used to be. You are not just asked how many states there are; you have to have knowledge of our history and government structure.

In any case, it appears that Dut, and others like him, in our modern time will be likely better advantaged than their 18th century white predecessors. I welcome him, and all others like him,

31

with open arms and affection as new Americans with all the attending rights and privileges that affords. Certainly Dut will be occasionally profiled for the color of his skin, but I believe his struggle to thrive in America will encounter less hardships than his predecessors.

Eric Holder, our Attorney General, and others have asked us to have an honest conversation about race; this in the aftermath of the tragic death of Trayvon Martin and the acquittal of George Zimmerman.

I cannot know what is in his heart or mind but I think Eric Holder and others are being disingenuous and really mean to have the same conversation about race that we have been having for 50 years.

Let us have an honest conversation about race. This must begin with our history- where we began to where we are.

Slavery-
- Our history shows about 140 years of slavery, forced upon blacks by whites, as British colonies.

- Then we fought a war for independence and formed a government still permitting slavery in order to form a union of mostly northern abolitionists and mostly southern slaveholders. Slavery in new territories would be decided in the future.

- Economically motivated, as are all events in history, slavery continued as a practice under the new government for about 85 more years. At this point, it had existed about 225 years.

- Early federalism gave way to nationalism. Nationalism yielded to sectionalism as regional economic motivations became conflictive and diverged. Slavery was the rallying issue.

- Finally we fought a great war where 600,000 to 700,000 Americans died to preserve the Union and ultimately settle this fundamental issue. This was an immense loss of life; but was unavoidable and was required. While the closing chapter was profoundly sad; the issue of slavery was resolved.

Racism-

- What followed the Civil War was a failed reconstruction and about 100 years of bitterness and increased intense racism, forced upon blacks by whites, before genuine efforts commenced in the early 1960's to at least provide a legal basis for civil rights by legislation.

- Society and culture would take much longer.

- Before that, free men of color had limited suffrage and were segregated from whites in all institutions.

- Blacks were overtly and openly persecuted in southern society and covertly persecuted in northern society.

- Without equal citizenship, a few determined blacks managed to thrive and excel; even under those conditions. They founded their own institutions and created their own successes.

Redress and Reform-

- In the 50 years since the 1960's much has been done to provide restitution for our earlier history and opportunity for blacks to achieve an equal place in our society.

- Cultural shifts in attitude, as well as government programs, have shown and given much positive benefit and progress.

- Efforts to legislate and fund the elimination of the underlying issues of poverty and education have not been completely successful. For decades drug use, crime and imprisonment have been disproportionately prevalent in black sub-culture and society.

- Many, many more blacks have risen, thrived and succeeded in this era.

At present we are looking back at 225 years of slavery, 100 years of racism, and 50 years of reform. This much is historically true.

Blacks have, after way too many years of sinful, shameful, and exploitive treatment, at long last, arrived at a starting point where they are advantaged relative to our 18th century white immigrants.

But the official Civil Rights establishment today abides by the positions of its inception as though not much has changed. The old dialog perpetuates the careers of the race baiters like Al Sharpton and, to a lesser degree, Jesse Jackson. They cannot ever let the old civil rights movement end. Their careers depend upon it. They have the full support of the old-school white civil rights era "believers" to keep them viable.

I can never forget Martin Luther King, Jr.'s great and historic words when he said (to paraphrase him), judge a man not by the color of his skin, but by the content of his character. I try to do this. By this measure, I cannot give Al Sharpton high marks. Dred Scott and Frederick Douglas are heroes to me, while Al Sharpton is not.

So many older white liberals and black activists are mentally stuck in the 1960's either unconsciously or by intent. Their views are fully formed and they cannot or will not adjust to the visible amount of change that has occurred. Younger people lack that intense background and may be more open minded and racially blind, or at least less obsessed with what is the past.

Looking at the sweep of our history, recent minor setbacks like voter ID requirements established in one state or another, as permitted under Article I., Section 4, may disaffect some poor voters but are truly trivial and inconsequential. Despite political motivation, there may be some benefit to all from this initiative. But this gives the "movement" something to grab onto. It desperately needs anything to keep the "movement" going.

The "movement" has taught young blacks that they are victims or if not that, at least that their lot in life is not their fault. Everything is not their fault and, by extension their responsibility.

Some of the pop culture and entertainment media has fostered bad behavior, bad attitude, and resentment toward civil society. This sends the wrong message and is very harmful to progress. It cannot help but foster fear, distrust, suspicion, and prejudice between the races when we encounter each other as strangers in public. On occasion, these feelings are warranted.

At this juncture, the "movement" is now holding the progress of African Americans back. They are hurting them. They have preached victimhood and entitlement to blacks and guilt to whites for so long that it is in our DNA from generation to generation.

Well the truth about race is that the civil rights era is over. Fifty more years of the same will not see any significant improvement. The crippling DNA will only become more embedded. The battles for blacks to rise must now be fought from within. The solutions are now internal. Very little more can be solved from external effort. The Age of Civil Rights must give way to a new Age of Civil Responsibility.

The voices of the Age of Civil Responsibility are beginning to speak forcefully but few are listening. Dr. Ben Carlson, Dr. Bill Cosby, David Webb, Allen West, Thomas Sowell, and others are trying to give new voice to the racial issue. As model examples of success, they are suggesting in essence, that a new era must replace the old era. This might just be an honest conversation about race.

In the area of education, new public and private schools all over the country are experimenting with new magnet concepts and methods to motivate young black students. Many are proving very successful and are raising achievement and performance levels to national standards. But when a black youth defends his culture by condemning education as being white, his mother and father need to talk to him. This is ignorance and is self-destructive.

That is why old-school Bill Cosby is telling them to pull their pants up, drop their attitude, learn to speak English, learn respect and manners, get an education and assimilate into society. His message is harsh but cannot be excluded in an honest conversation about race. Otherwise, don't blame the white man. You have no one to blame but yourself.

However, these new racial equal opportunity advocates are not welcome at the table as participants in an honest conversation about race. More specifically, they are not welcome at NAACP conferences. The traditionalists of the "movement" will not allow their voices to be heard. In their view, after 50 years of advance, there is still so much to be done that it must be tweaked for another undefined span of time.

Our President has been perfectly positioned, even historically poised, to be transformational on the issue of race but has remained silent for political expedience. He has made a few expected, traditional platitudes to insure his political base, but nothing more.

If someone considers these views themselves racist, it is apparent who they are and where they are coming from. Their motives are suspect. It's not true, not helping, and attempted misdirection. Without good faith, no productive conversation is possible.

The time has come to evaluate precisely where we are and renew our efforts in a new direction. This, I believe, would be the beginning of the first honest conversation about race.

There are two honest conversations we need to have about race. The first is this agreement about our progress as a society and the next step needed in that regard. The second is about our feelings and how we perceive each other as individuals when we encounter one another as strangers.

The way I understand the Trayvon Martin - George Zimmerman story is the following: George saw a stranger going through his neighborhood who he thought looked, dressed and walked suspiciously. Rightly or wrongly, he made it his business to follow him. Trayvon noticed a man following him suspiciously and, perhaps out of fear, decided to turn back and confront George. Likely angry words led to the scuffle where Trayvon knocked George to the ground and beat him. George responded, perhaps out of both fear and anger, took out his handgun and killed Trayvon. The jury acquitted George. A tragic misjudgment on the part of both men is the best way to characterize this horrific event.

How can we change the perceptions that cause events like this to occur? If fear is at the root of it just as much as hatred, the assumptions we make (profiling) cannot stop until the fear goes away. The feelings are valid. I have experienced them myself when a passing on the street begins with wary, suspicious expressions, but ends with a smile and a pleasant polite exchange. Fear is replaced by the warmth of a human connection. On other occasions, the confrontation can be very bad. A family member was ruthlessly beaten and hospitalized for being guilty of walking on the street of his own neighborhood in his city. It wasn't reported in the news.

Both races bear equal responsibility and need to change these feelings. There is that word "responsibility" again. One side cannot fix the problem for the other.

Critical thinking is not criticizing people and things. It's analyzing and understanding causes and effects of events. It's about the influences and the whys and wherefores sought by an inquisitive mind.

But the solution to the problem of post-1960's racism cannot come from the mind. As a problem at the human level, the answers have always resided in the heart. The issues have always been emotional - fear, resentment, anger, guilt, suspicion, mistrust. Until these feelings can be replaced, and behavior modified by all parties, with respect for the other, belief in common humanity, manners, courtesy, trust, optimism, and kindness, no change is possible.

The end of racism will take a long time. In the meantime, I will never forget my friend Dut.

Race vs. Class

Originally written in 2008

I respect Bob Schieffer as a journalist for his integrity and forthright manner. However, on Face the Nation this Sunday morning, he annoyed and disappointed me with one of his questions to the panel. As a journalist, he is trained and conditioned, as are all his colleagues, to ask questions that spark controversy or evoke a desired response.

I can't quote him exactly, but he asked the black member of the panel if he thought the black community expects President Obama to look out for their interests. The panelist responded, just as he was primed to respond, that the black community has many needs that they would hope Obama will address.

Schieffer asked the wrong question. I wish I had been the panelist and could have responded as follows:

Your question is typical of contemporary journalism. You direct questions and key them to the respondent in a manner that is not quite racist but still continues to foster divisiveness. The racial issue will never go away as long as questions like this continue to be asked.

My President will not allow himself to be entrapped by questions like these because they pit black against white and vice versa. They foster attitudes of entitlement and resentments against attitudes of entitlement. Obama knows this. He is very intelligent and fair-minded with genuine noble aspirations. Maybe I'm naive, but I think he is the real deal and I trust him. He steadfastly talks about uniting us all as Americans.

He writes about the issues of poverty, unemployment, health care, education, affirmative action and welfare (both of the poor and the corporate type). These issues are colorblind. He frames his core values around class; meaning the poor, lower working class, middle class and rich. He is brilliant at finding the common ground of conflicting views and proceeding from that positive position.

He has dealt with racial issues in his early life and has evolved to become more like Abraham Lincoln and Martin Luther King, Jr.; not like one-issue proponents like Al Sharpton, Jeremiah Wright and Jesse Jackson. His focus is on individual responsibility, work ethic, and taking charge of one's future; with a safety net to level the playing field when necessary.

He says the core issues of class need to be addressed to lift us all up. I believe Obama's goal is the same as mine – that we can become truly colorblind. I don't expect to see this in my lifetime but hope that it becomes an "absolute" before the next century. A good place to start would be for journalists to follow the President's lead and stop focusing on what divides us but instead what unites us – the common ground.

Acting in Good Faith

Originally written in 2010

Whether you are religiously devout or secular, the ideals of honor, virtue and morality apply. I have heard from the religious right that there is no moral compass, and therefore no morality, without religious belief. I reject that assertion.

Once again, here are John Adams' words to Benjamin Rush in his letter of February 6, 1805-

"Is the present state of the national republic enough? Is virtue the principle of our government? Is honor? Or is ambition and avarice, adulation, baseness, covetousness, the thirst for riches, indifference concerning the means of rising and enriching, the contempt of principle, the spirit of party and of faction the motive and principle that governs?"

These questions and concerns are more relevant today than ever.

Capitalism has been criticized as an immoral institution operating only for self-interest and not to the benefit of all. That is not entirely true. A case has even been made for the morality of pure capitalism. I don't think it is either entirely moral or immoral; it is an economic system. The question is, does capitalism work for all of us. I believe that it does when it operates in good faith? In the many cases where it doesn't, it does not serve the interest of all. Bernie Madoff, Kenneth Lay, Jeff Skilling, Andrew Fastow, George Soros- the list goes on.

Fairly and reasonably, the same argument applies to the government as any other institution. When it operates in good faith, it is moral and serves the interests of all. I don't see much evidence of this today. In my view, Dick Cheney, George W. Bush,

Don Rumsfeld, Barack Obama, Nancy Pelosi and many others have not acted with honor or virtue and in good faith. Do you see how this 'politics without parties' thing works out for me?

To a degree, the same metric can be applied to the media.

I have been searching for contemporary persons of honor and virtue in business, government and the media. They are hard to find and it is very difficult to be certain. I think I have found two or three in the private sector. For their private philanthropy, my candidates would be Bill and Melinda Gates, Warren Buffett and Ted Turner.

What do you think?

Man's Rights

Originally written in 2011

The time for turning back 100 years of entrenched progressivism in our society has passed. Our Federal government has demonstrated clearly that it has no will to diminish the concentration of power and money in Washington, DC. The recent bipartisan bill to increase the debt limit, despite the influence of the Tea Party, has proven that our entrenched Washington establishment (both parties) is unwilling and unable to sever the "Gordian knot" of collectivist-altruism.

Congratulations to Standard and Poor's for appropriately downgrading the credit rating of our treasury from AAA to AA+. There is a 1 in 3 chance it will be downgraded again within 6 months and still our legislators will likely not take necessary action.

How did we come to this? The founding principles of individual rights thrived for the first 120 years of our history. The long and steady assault on our personal freedoms probably began during the Wilson administration (1913-1921). Collectivist-altruism began creeping into our politics and society as it has invariably done around the world.

We often concern ourselves about the separation of church and state and vigorously debate the issue on both sides. We do not concern ourselves about the separation of the economy and the state. So here we are and here we will stay. What is lost is lost forever.

Perhaps the following will lend a perspective of what has changed and a hint of what we could have been. This is an excerpt from "The Virtue of Selfishness: A New Concept of Egoism" by Ayn Rand. The book is non-fiction and a collection of her essays with contributions from Nathaniel Branden. The essay is titled **"Man's Rights"**.

"Consider the curious fact that never has there been such a proliferation, all over the world, of two contradictory phenomena: of alleged new "rights" and of slave labor camps.

The "gimmick" was the switch of the concepts of rights from the political to the economic realm.

The Democratic Party platform of 1960 summarizes the switch boldly and explicitly. It declares that a Democratic Administration "will reaffirm the economic bill of rights which Franklin Roosevelt wrote into our national conscience sixteen years ago."

Bear clearly in mind the meaning of the concept of "rights" when you read the list which the platform offers:

1. The right to a useful and remunerative job in the industries or shops or farms or mines of the nation.

2. The right to earn enough to provide adequate food and clothing and recreation.

3. The right of every farmer to raise and sell his products at a return which will give him and his family a decent living.

4. The right of every businessman, large and small, to trade in an atmosphere of freedom from unfair competition and domination by monopolies at home and abroad.

5. The right of every family to a decent home.

6. The right to adequate medical care and the opportunity to achieve and enjoy good health.

7. The right to adequate protection from the economic fears of old age, sickness, accidents and unemployment.

8. The right to a good education.

A single question added to each of the above eight clauses would make the issue clear: *At whose expense?*

Jobs, food, clothing, recreation, homes, medical care, education, etc. do not grow in nature. These are man-made values – goods and services produced by men. *Who* is to provide them?

If some men are entitled *by right* to the products of the work of others, it means that those others are deprived of rights and condemned to slave labor.

Any alleged "right" of one man, which necessitates the violation of the rights of another, is not and cannot be a right.

No man can have a right to impose an unchosen obligation, an unrewarded duty or an involuntary servitude on another man. There can be no such thing as *"the right to enslave."*

A right does not include the material implementation of that right by other men; it includes only the freedom to earn that implementation by one's own effort.

Observe, in this context, the intellectual precision of the Founding Fathers: they spoke of the right to the *pursuit of happiness*; it *does not* mean that others must make him happy.

The right to life means that a man has the right to support his life by his own work (on any economic level, as high as his ability will carry him); it does *not* mean that others must provide him with the necessities of life.

45

The right to property means that a man has the right to take the economic actions necessary to earn property, to use it and to dispose it; it does *not* mean that others must provide him with property.

The right of free speech means that a man has the right to express his ideas without danger of suppression, interference or punitive action by the government. It does *not* mean that others must provide him with a lecture hall, a radio station or a printing press through which to express his ideas.

Any undertaking that involves more than one man, requires the *voluntary* consent of every participant. Every one of them has the *right* to make his own decision, but none has the right to force his decision on the others.

There is no such thing as "a right to a job" – there is only the right of free trade, that is: a man's right to take a job if another man chooses to hire him. There is no "right to a home", only the right of free trade: the right to build a home or to buy it. There are no "rights to a 'fair' wage or a 'fair' price" if no one chooses to pay it, to hire a man or to buy his product. There are no "rights of consumers" to milk, shoes, movies or champagne if no producers choose to manufacture such items (there is only the right to manufacture them oneself). There are no "rights" of special groups, there are no "rights of farmers, of workers, of businessmen, of employees, of employers, of the old, of the young, of the unborn".

There are only the *Rights of Man* – rights possessed by every individual man and by *all* men as individuals.

Property rights and the right of free trade are man's only "economic rights" (they are, in fact, *political* rights) – and there can be no such thing as "an economic bill of rights." But observe that the latter have all but destroyed the former.

Remember that rights are moral principles which define and protect a man's freedom of action, but impose no obligations on other men. Private citizens are not a threat to one another's rights or freedom. A private citizen who resorts to physical force and violates the rights of others is a criminal – and men have legal protection against him."

Also, you may wish to read "The Makers and the Takers" in this blog.

Charity and the Government

Originally written in 2011

Charity is the voluntary act of helping others in need. It is a moral act exemplified in our Judeo-Christian ethic and in the tenets of the teachings of Jesus as described in the bible. As Americans, "Christian charity" is in our core DNA. We enjoy the reputation of being the most generous people in the world. Rightfully, we are admonished to help the poor, downtrodden, helpless and needy. This is an individual, personal decision.

If I meet you on the street and hold a gun to your face demanding a dollar to give to the homeless man on the sidewalk, what would happen to me? I would be arrested! This "coerced charity" is not charity; it is robbery and it is illegal.

In my view, it is the dark side of human nature that decides what others should give. It is easy to decide that others are not being generous enough with their property and should give more; and to make that pompous decision indignantly. These individuals invariably are resentful of the lack of generosity of others. You know who they are. You can connect the dots and see where I am going with this; right?

Nathaniel Branden is a psychotherapist best known today for his work in the psychology of self-esteem from a humanistic perspective and a former associate of Ayn Rand. In 1958, Branden established The Nathaniel Branden Institute (NBI) as an educational organization to spread the philosophical principles of Objectivism, the philosophy of Ayn Rand. Barbara Branden was his first wife, collaborator and lecturer whose lecture series included The Art of Thinking.

Once, when Barbara Branden was asked by a student: "What will happen to the poor in an Objectivist society?" She answered: "If you want to help them, you will not be stopped." This clipped, succinct response, offered without embellishment or apology, reminds me of Howard Roark and John Galt, Ayn Rand's two heroic fictional characters in her novels.

In her essay, "Collectivized Ethics", Rand writes "This is the essence of the whole issue and a perfect example of how one refuses to accept an adversary's premises as the basis of discussion. Only individual men have the right to decide when or whether they wish to help others; society – as an organized political system – has no rights in the matter at all."

The following is an excerpt from "The Virtue of Selfishness: A New Concept of Egoism" by Ayn Rand. The book is non-fiction and a collection of her essays with contributions from Nathaniel Branden. The essay is titled **"The Nature of Government"**.

"If physical force is to be barred from social relationships, men need an institution charged with the task of protecting their rights under an *objective* code of rules.

This is the task of a government – its basic task, its only moral justification and the reason why men need a government.

A government is the means of placing retaliatory use of physical force under objective control –i.e., under objectively defined laws.

The fundamental difference between private action and government action – a difference thoroughly ignored and evaded today – lies in the fact that a government holds a monopoly on the legal use of physical force. It has to hold such a monopoly, since it is the agent of restraining and combating the use of force; and for that very same reason, its actions have to be rigidly defined, delimited and circumscribed; no touch of whim or caprice should be permitted in its performance; it should be an impersonal robot, with the laws as its only motive power. If a society is to be free, its government has to be controlled.

Under a proper social system, a private individual is legally free to take any action he pleases (so long as he does not violate the rights of others), while a government official is bound by law in every official act. **A private individual may do anything except that which is legally *forbidden*; a government official may do nothing except that which is legally *permitted*.**

This is the means of subordinating "might" to "right". This is the American concept of "a government of laws and not of men".

The nature of the laws proper to a free society and the source of its government's authority are both to be defined from the nature and purpose of a proper government. The basic principle of both is indicated in The Declaration of Independence" "to secure these [individual] rights, governments are instituted among men, deriving their just powers from the consent of the governed . . . "

Since the protection of individual rights is the only proper purpose of a government, it is the only proper subject of legislation: all laws must be based on individual rights and aimed at their protection. All laws must be *objective* (and objectively justifiable): men must know clearly, and in advance of taking an action, what the law forbids them to do (and why), what constitutes a crime and what penalty they will incur if they commit it.

The source of the government's authority is "the consent of the governed." This means that the government is not the *ruler*, but the servant or *agent* of the citizens; it means that the government as such has no rights except the rights *delegated* to it by the citizens for a specific purpose. (Author's note: I no longer give them my consent.)

There is only one basic principle to which an individual must consent if he wishes to live in a free, civilized society: the principle

51

of renouncing the use of physical force and delegating to the government his right of physical self-defense, for the purpose of an orderly, objective, legally defined enforcement. Or, to put it another way, he must accept *the separation of force and whim* (any whim, including his own)."

So coerced charity is not charity; it is robbery. On a related topic, consider the following: Any civilized and great society, to be a civilized and great society, should embrace, support and nurture the arts. The visual and performing arts are at the core of our history and culture. Who could disagree? The question is, to use an Ayn Rand phrase, "At whose expense?" To be a patron of the arts is an individual decision. It is an infringement of individual rights for our government to take our property to pay for the arts.

The Makers and the Takers

Originally written in 2011

Ayn Rand's 1957 novel, "Atlas Shrugged" is a product of her background and her times. She was born in St. Petersburg, Russia, on February 2, 1905. In late 1925 she obtained permission to leave Soviet Russia for a visit to relatives in the United States. Although she told Soviet authorities that her visit would be short, she was determined never to return to Russia. She arrived in New York City in February 1926.

When she wrote "Atlas Shrugged" in the 1950's she was concerned with the problems of collectivism and government central planning. Her novel is about the time of the industrialists in the United States who built the railroads, mined the iron ore and copper, drilled the oil, produced the steel and invented and produced the machinery. In her fictional story, the government at that time formed central planning agencies that regulated the industries and labor. The government, in collaboration with labor unions, managed and controlled the industrialist owners' profits, prices, wages, competition and even production levels, who they buy from and who they sell to.

The meaning of the title comes from the metaphor of Atlas holding up the weight of the world. As his burden increases and increases to an unbearable level, what can he do? All he can do is shrug. In her story, the industrialists and their workers with ability decide to go on strike. Understand, this is not the union workers, but it's the owners and workers that have pride in their ability and work ethic that strike. What they do is walk away leaving the government with the mess they created. The economy and the country falls apart.

Ayn Rand refers to the central planners as the looters since they steal the owners' property and wealth for their collectivist purposes. Today we libertarians refer to the makers and the takers. Her view is that one should be entitled to keep what one earns but that no one is entitled to anything they have not earned.

The philosophy she describes is the evilness of collectivism- the idea that those with ability to work and produce must take care of those with need. As the "need" grows, those with the ability to work and produce become enslaved.

Her novel demonstrates her philosophy through a fictional story. The words "communism" or "socialism" are never used. They don't need to be. While her story and the circumstances of her time were not exactly as they are today, her philosophy certainly resonates with current events.

In our modern real world, after nearly 100 years of progressivism, we have arrived at a highly developed "nanny state". Our government says just give us your property and we will take care of you. The central planners and social scientists have shaped our culture and altered our lives. Our individuality and independent spirit has been traded for protection and safety from cradle to grave. Our sense of entitlement spans across all classes- from the wealthy corporate CEOs and financial Masters of the Universe to the union card carrying public and private middle class workers to the welfare mothers. We are all entitled. We have rights. We don't have obligations. We have traded away our freedoms for our false sense of comfort. Mostly, this is our own fault.

Point of View

Originally written in 2013

In the process of actually studying history, I was initially obsessed with the concern about point of view. This undoubtedly came from my attempts to understand diverse political views in modern politics and my developing cynicism in that regard. I have begun to understand from those wiser than myself, that in the study of history, point of view is not the prevailing aspect. I will never ignore point of view but I will never let it stand in the way of my quest for my "truth."

Most people I talk to have fully formed views on every topic, are completely satisfied in the comfort of their beliefs and in their understanding of what our history has meant to confirm them. I can never feel that way. My beliefs will forever be self-tested and I will never stop seeking more understanding and evidence of truth.

My liberal people dislike my views that guns rights, and the empowerment that affords me, is anarchistic, recklessly dangerous and inappropriate. It scares them. I am part of the problem in their view. They believe my understanding of the "Tea Party" movement somehow makes me a racist and an advocate for the destruction of our government. While they view government as good and corporations as bad, they are perfectly comfortable with the government dallying in joint partnerships to control more of the economy. As a Libertarian I have been called a closet, dope smoking Republican. This is good. This is right where I want them to be- ignorant.

My conservative people dislike my views that persons own their own bodies and can love and marry whomever they choose. That belief makes me a secular, immoral Liberal. To believe these things is to violate the first principles of our founding and its piety. Our first principles were questioned starting the day after the ratification of the Constitution, and every day since, and rightly so.

Milton Friedman established his Chicago School of Economics based on the principle of unfettered, free market capitalism. Yet, his disciples went out into the world and practiced corporatism. This is the collusion of governments and corporations (not laissez faire) to seize profit from disasters using predatory practices. My conservative people would not have any problem with this since corporations are good and government is bad. Neither do they rail against government subsidies to large agribusiness. I disagree with these hypocrisies. This is good. This is right where I want them to be- ignorant.

Both groups of my peoples passionately hold their positions of morality and immorality. If both groups of my people believe I believe in nothing and hold no principles, this is good. This is right where I want them to be- ignorant.

If I can always have the presence of mind to remember the best lesson I have learned from Ayn Rand, to always question the initial premise of any argument presented to me, I will be well served. This consideration is for me, not for them. They don't want to have a discussion not based on their premise.

I will hold the high ground with a superior weapon - an open mind. Do I sound like I feel superior to everyone? Maybe. Show me one other person, anyone, with an open mind willing to hold discourse and I promise to embrace humility.

If I can strike the balance in the beliefs I require, no political party could be satisfactory. I have already achieved this position. Neither party stands for all the liberties I require. If I were to declare myself an Independent, that wouldn't get me enough mileage either.

If I can strike a balance in my beliefs, based on a continuous learning process from every direction, and can reach a point such that both my groups of peoples despise my views equally, I will be where I want to be. Is this smug? Maybe. I don't care.

This position sounds to me like a personal Declaration of Independence, a nullification, and a retraction of consent. The freedom from the tyranny of point of view is liberating. A huge burden has been lifted from my shoulders. Tupac Shakur said it best when he said FYA, FAYA. If you don't know what his reference means, I will not tell you since some of you might view the language as politically incorrect.

Are We Politically Correct Enough?

Originally written in 2011

This topic is one of the cornerstones of my blog. I have wanted to write this article for a long time and have been collecting my thoughts on it for months.

A recent study rated the 10 best and 10 worst universities for free speech. In the list of the 10 worst universities were the University of Binghamton, Syracuse University and the University of Massachusetts. I don't have the source of the research but I don't think it matters in this case since the names of the universities are not important.

There is most likely a strong correlation between the fact that many universities are of a liberal mindset and therefore have almost a fascistic passion for politically correct thinking, attitude, speech and behavior. If the motivation is to prevent confrontation or hurting the feelings of various groups in order to be kind, that might have some merit. However, it does not seem that the motivation is that benign. It is too controlling.

In any case, it is cowardice and stifling to free speech. This form of collective-think stifles our ability to have an open give-and-take dialog. We can no longer look someone in the eye and have an honest conversation. It is an affront to free speech.

What we call political correctness seems more like social correctness. I can't see it having originated in the political realm. It is more societal than political. Socially correct became politically correct.

One theory is that political correctness originated in liberal academia; its banner was picked up and then voraciously foisted upon us by the liberal media; absorbed by the political realm and finally obediently followed by the populace at large. Out of fear, no one dares to confront it so it has become ubiquitous and domineering; even among non-liberal folk. Some may hate it but few dare to ignore its rules.

Decades ago we used to use euphemisms. This was the beginning of what today we call politically correct. Political correctness today is an enforced public discourse, the real purposes of which are to render disapproved thoughts literally unspeakable and to cower ordinary people into silence about the things that matter.

The acceptable practice is to avoid uncomfortable discussion by using a polite or elegant term as a substitute for an impolite or cruder term. But now we have gone so far in sanitizing our expression that we skew and distort meaning. More than that, certain topics are taboo.

As our children are taught in our politically correct schools, we have persons who are mentally challenged and others who are handicapable. No one is stupid, blind, mute, deaf or crippled. We have culturally diverse peoples and inner city dwellers. Sadly, and much to our loss, the melting pot has been replaced by the salad bowl.

George Carlin was brilliant at helping us to understand political correctness. He described a news reporter telling of a crazed, maniac shooter who came into a church and shot several people as a "disgruntled worshipper". George really understood irony and hypocrisy.

Maybe one of the best definitions ever of political correctness came from an annual contest at Texas A&M University calling for the most appropriate definition of a contemporary term. This year's term was: "Political Correctness". The winner wrote:

"Political correctness is a doctrine, fostered by a delusional, illogical minority, and rabidly promoted by an unscrupulous mainstream media, which holds forth the proposition that it is entirely possible to pick up a piece of shit by the clean end."

God bless the Texans for their ability to speak plainly.

Here are some examples of perfectly rational and reasonable viewpoints that are an anathema to the politically correct police who guard our lives in all matters of our health, diet, environment and treatment of our fellow beings:

1. Politically incorrect assertion- Affirmative action is racist.

Politically correct response- The students at a university recently held an affirmative action bake sale to stimulate discussion on the campus. Their sign for pricing on muffins read: "Asians- $1.50, Whites- $1.00, Hispanics- $0.75, Blacks- $0.50." University officials immediately shut it down.

2. Politically incorrect assertion- Al Sharpton and Jesse Jackson are racist and have profited immensely from racial strife. It is not in their interest to end racism. If racism were to go away tomorrow, they would be out of a job.

Politically correct response- Al Sharpton and Jesse Jackson have been champions for the cause of racial equality for decades.

3. Politically incorrect assertion- I speak my mind, and I stand up for what I believe. I vote, and I pay my taxes. I am a member of a free society, and I choose to smoke.

Politically correct response- Recently, a major airline banned the use of electronic cigarettes aboard flights. The thinking was that other passengers would perceive the activity as smoking and that would upset them. Did you get that- **perceived** smoking? You will recall that electronic cigarettes do not use tobacco and only output water vapor as the effluence. Apparently just the sight of this is disgusting to behold in our modern world.

4. Politically incorrect assertion- I am a law abiding citizen and I follow the rules. I choose to own firearms. I am not interested in handguns and do not hunt animals but collect powerful rifles and use them for target shooting. My collection has been legally acquired in compliance with all federal and state laws. Should I choose to purchase a grenade launcher for home protection and can lawfully acquire one, that is my right.

Politically correct response- Guns are dangerous and kill people. No one should be allowed to possess a gun except the military and police.

5. Politically incorrect assertion- John Stossel did a program recently on politically correct food. He analyzed and compared traditional standard agriculture versus organically grown crops. Crop chemophobia is the fear of fertilizers and pesticides. The current thinking is that these chemicals are bad whereas natural, organically grown crops are good. John Stossel's program debunked this conventional wisdom. No known deaths have ever been caused by the use of these chemicals.

Organically grown crops, in addition to being much more costly, use more land and time resources. Experts say these are no better and might be less safe. What really matters is bacteria. Natural manure is fecal matter and if not handled correctly, poses bacteria hazards.

Also, the raising of animals as free range and grass fed was compared to standard methods. It proved to be not measurably better or safer and was more expensive.

The conclusion was that standard agriculture is more environmentally sound since it uses less space and resources.

Politically correct response- Organically grown crops are better for you than traditional standard agriculture that uses fertilizers and pesticides. Also, free range, grass fed animals are better for you.

6. Politically incorrect assertion- Dick says to Jane at the office water cooler "Jane that's a particularly nice sweater you are wearing today. It fits you perfectly."

Politically correct response- Dick is perp walked to the HR department office where he is threatened with the loss of his job and put on probationary status.

7. Politically incorrect assertion- Merry Christmas

Politically correct response- Happy Holidays

Politically correct control is everywhere now; even in San Francisco, once the bastion of free thinking, but now a bastion of controlled thinking. So where does all this politically correct dogma come from? Maybe somewhere in the liberal north east, within short commuting distance for Michael Bloomberg, there is a loosely organized complex of buildings housing the Ministry of Social Engineering. Its mission is to work closely with the media and academia and insure that our free speech is censored and controlled by telling us what to believe, think, say and eat.

The Department of Political Correctness Police is in the same building as the Department of Food Police. PETA and the Sierra Club have offices in the adjacent building. Another building houses the Departments of Health Police, Ecological Police and Safety Police.

As a result of their diligent work, some topics are defined as so delicate, touchy or onerous we can't even talk about them. These censored speech topics include:

✓ illegal immigrant prosecution

- ✓ pornography
- ✓ racial profiling
- ✓ ethnic profiling
- ✓ affirmative action
- ✓ sharia law
- ✓ religious tolerance
- ✓ Islamic radicalism
- ✓ property rights
- ✓ cigar smoking
- ✓ firearm collection and use
- ✓ eating red meat
- ✓ using salt
- ✓ enjoying fat in food

Offensive Language

Originally written in 2012

When I attended my last trade show as an exhibitor in 2000 at McCormick Place in Chicago, I was introduced to the term "signage". Apparently "age" refers to the amount or quantity of something; in this case signs in a group or arrangement for display. So, a group of signs is signage. While the term struck me as poor use of the English language, I have subsequently seen it used on a sign in front of a store selling signs. I'm told it is also in newer dictionaries. This still doesn't, and never will, make it right with me.

For over 75 years automobile manufacturers have marketed cars with model names invented to create a feel and make you want to buy their car. Most often real words are used. Sometimes, however they invent made-up words that have no meaning but sound something like real words. We have all seen this. But when Korean car manufacturer, Kia came out with the "sportage", I was offended by their language. Does the Korean language quantify the amount of "sport" or are they just mimicking the American auto marketing tradition? In any case, we now see sportage signage on the SUVage. Good grief.

George Carlin, bless his soul, would have had so much fun with this. William Safire, ever the meticulous wordsmith, would be rolling in his grave.

I sure hope this article gets a lot of readage.

Third-hand Smoke

Originally written in 2010

Ref: Article titled "New Smoke Alarm" in Time magazine, November 8, 2010 issue on page 66 by Dr. Jonathan Winickoff, Harvard Medical School

"New Smoke Alarm" warns that third-hand smoke poses a danger according to a number of experts. Harmful compounds in tobacco residue get embedded in clothing, hair, furniture, etc. For the families of the more than 22 million children in the U.S. who are exposed to smoke in the home: it's not enough to have smokers stand outside on the porch – unless they're planning to take a shower and change their clothes before they rejoin the party in the living room.

I understand that smoking cigarettes and tobacco products injects many chemicals into your respiratory system that are carcinogens from the ingredients inherent in the tobacco plus the additives provided by the cigarette manufacturers. These will inevitably lead to respiratory problems, severe damage to lung tissue and death by COPD or, in some cases, death by lung or throat cancer. But I also understand that nicotine is not particularly harmful itself. It is just that smoking is the most efficient delivery system for getting nicotine into our bloodstream.

The only harmful tobacco residue specifically mentioned in the article is cotinine – a remnant of metabolized nicotine. Nicotine is a stimulant that increases the heart rate just like caffeine and naturally occurring adrenaline (epinephrine) from fear. If so, some risk is posed from all the above in that the increased heart rate may cause heart problems or a heart attack.

Since this great risk exists, caffeine and fear, as well as nicotine, should also be avoided. What about secondhand and third-hand coffee drinking or fear? What if you touch clothing from someone who has spilled coffee on their shirt? What if you get sweat on you from someone who has been scared?

What about fourth-hand smoke? That would be where you wash your clothes in the same laundry comingling with someone else's clothing that has third-hand smoke on it.

When our daughter and son were small, we took road trips in the car with two adults smoking in the front and two kids in the back seat with the windows up. This was fairly typical of the 1960's and 1970's. We all camped in a confined popup trailer full of smoke. Why didn't we kill our kids right there on the spot? Somehow they grew up past these formative years and turned out fairly healthy. My daughter may have some athletic, aerobic capacity limitations. She is a dance educator. My son outgrew food, animal dander, and grass allergies by the time he finished undergrad. Then the damn fool started smoking in grad school in his mid-twenties.

While this is a serious medical issue, it reminds me of a co-worker a decade ago with an extraordinary olfactory sense attuned to tobacco smoke. She claimed that from her desk, with the office window open, she could smell offensive cigarette smoke from a passing car a hundred yards away on the highway. Visualize the length of a football field. Presumably, the car window was also open. Since the car was moving at highway speed, the duration of the whiff of smoke would have been less than two seconds and that whiff would have to travel a 100 yards over several minutes without dissipating its concentration. Now, I am understanding of the concerns of non-smokers and respectful of the new rules, but as an engineer, I know this is absolute horses#@t.

I know I am a dinosaur, and I know what became of the dinosaurs, but this "politically correct" nonsense has gone way too far. Hasn't anyone a lick of common sense anymore? The more I read stuff like this, the more I push back.

Just leave me alone to smoke my cigar on my patio.

Footnotes:

1)   I'd send this to the editor of Time Magazine, but I know it would not fit their ideology, they would fail to see the mocking humor or irony. There can be no potentially meaningful dialog, and they wouldn't print it.

2)   This article, written by a medical doctor, is indisputably about a health issue. However, it has a social issue component also. Think about how much our social mores on smoking have changed in the last 30 years; and rightly so. But, progressives like Michael Bloomberg, have made this issue part of their social engineering agenda which defines what is politically correct for us. More to follow on "politically correct".

Liberty versus Equality

Originally written in 2014

For many years, I have been casting around in my mind, searching for a true understanding of the essence of Americanism. Furthermore, I have tried to understand the changes that have taken place in our national consensus, in our beliefs as a people, and for what reasons. Now, after studying 1000 pages of Western civilization text, 1000 pages of American history text, countless primary sources and American historiography, and after learning to think and write more critically and publishing nearly 60 of my own essays on the subject, and reflecting on the matter, it's meaning has come to me.

Americanism is based on its own unique idea of democracy. It is a balance of liberty and equality. Both of these are positive goods that Jefferson and Lincoln placed side-by-side in their declarations. But certainly, liberty and equality are rival siblings. The former values our differences and individuality, while the latter stresses our commonness and fair-mindedness. Even in the best of worlds, governed by the best of men, compatibility between these ideals is difficult.

In our country, the order in which these goods were adopted made all the difference. Liberty had to come first before equality could be possible. Our first war was fought against outside dominant forces for our liberty. The people did not undertake a social revolution, nor did the colonies revert to a lawless state of nature. Our second war was fought internally amongst ourselves for many reasons, but predominantly for our equality. That this happened in this way was necessary.

We have learned well the ugly lessons of cruelty and inhumanity in our history - the indentured servitude of Colonial whites, the enslavement of Africans, the displacement and slaughter of Native peoples, the abuse and exploitation of Chinese immigrants, the internment of Japanese citizens. But if we have that narrative here, we cannot have this narrative.

The first French revolution was fought for *Liberte*, *Egalite* and *Fraternite*. In reality, the bourgeois masses rose up to fight for equality. With this the first, if not the foremost concern, it failed miserably. Metaphorically, the country was reduced to a pile of ashes in a revolt that ended with no plan going forward.

In America, westward expansion began even while the War for Independence was being fought and continued to the end of the 19th century when the end of the continent was reached and the west coast was settled. This 200-year process continually renewed the spirit of independence and self-reliance with frontiersmen, traders, farmers and settlers at each new edge of the frontier as it incrementally moved from Ohio to the Pacific. Liberty was kept alive in American minds for a period greater than two centuries.

Frederick Jackson Turner captured the spirit of American individualism brilliantly in his essay and speech delivered in 1893 - *The Significance of the Frontier in American History*. Turner based his thesis of American exceptionalism on our geography. America had no established territories or boundaries of its own beyond the original colonies. Settlement consisted of Native peoples, French, Spanish and British but was sparse relative to Europe. Vast areas of land were open and unclaimed. Our continent was unique and the basis for our unique history as a nation.

Later, 20th century "revisionist" historians condemned the work as that of a romantic national consensus historian. This was understandable since it was necessary to first destroy the vision of individuality and then undermine the American belief system and national pride before the case for community could be made.

The idea of collectivism would be embraced and equality accomplished once individual liberty was eliminated. This process continues today. In most of the country, the argument is settled. While there are pockets of the frontier spirit still flourishing in the west, it has become a small minority. Even the term "frontier spirit" has become disparaged as a pejorative for lawlessness and wanton lack of concern for others. The debate has been craftily waged and skillfully won.

Today the remnants of American rugged individualism live on in the efforts of visionary entrepreneurs. Despite the lip service to the contrary, this too is under attack as a threat to an ever growing socialized society.

Understandably, liberty had to make way for equality. Still, it leaves some of us melancholy for the loss of the American spirit. It had to end with the last frontier and is lost forever.

Themes of Democracy: freedom, liberty, equality

Originally written in 2014

Introduction

History study is about the presentation and evaluation of evidence - people, events, causes, outcomes. With reason applied and past motives understood, it becomes the study of ideas. All this must occur before judgment is offered. In one sense, this might be considered half of history study. In this case, the other half would be what the spectrum of historians have written about it and the sense they brought to it - historiography.

It would be problematic to teach American history (or any history) and its experience with democracy, using a theme of liberty, if it were to confuse, intermingle, or use the words "freedom", "liberty", and "equality" interchangeably. These words do not mean the same thing. If that were the case, there would be no need for three words. The meaning of words is important and should be given thoughtful consideration.

I'm suggesting, in agreement with Alexis de Tocqueville, that American democracy is a unique definition based on a balance of liberty and equality. These ideals are certainly different and can be in conflict. This becomes apparent if we understand liberty to be about individualism and self-reliance and equality to be about commonness and fair-mindedness. And balance is essential - just liberty, without license (law), is anarchy; just equality is totalitarian tyranny.

Therefore, if a text is driven by a theme of freedom (portrayed as liberty), it must deal with that aspect in each and every historical event presented. While this might be generally workable, with this perspective, the depiction of the meaning of events may become confused. Within the broad context of democracy and for each instance of history, which freedom - liberty or equality - is being discussed?

Evidence

I'll offer two examples and hopefully, insights into our study of American history.

Example 1 – Spanish conquistadors

Concurrent with our understanding of Western civilization history, we have learned about the first European adventures in North America. Starting in the late 15th century, the Spanish conquistadors arrived in Central and South America in search of gold and treasure. Their approach was to conquer and subjugate indigenous native peoples in the most cruel and inhumane manner imaginable. While they professed the good of saving the "uncivilized" peoples with conversion to Christianity, they slaughtered and enslaved them. Their rationale was that in this way, they liberated them – gave them liberty. The irony in this is unmistakable and obvious. But, if liberty is about individualism and self-reliance, and equality is about commonness and fair-mindedness, wasn't the issue here about equality – fair and equal treatment of a cohabiting, pre-existing, vibrant and already free civilization?

Example 2 – African slavery and American democracy

A century after Spanish presence in North America, other Europeans came and forcibly brought Africans to America as enslaved labor – free labor for them. Slaves were imported to colonial Virginia in 1619 for the Anglican English settlement there and also to New Amsterdam in 1625 for Dutch settlers by the Dutch West India Company. Certainly this historical era, and subsequent history, was about the forced denial of freedom to a large group of human beings. But was the theme centered more on liberty or equality? At this point, for the enslaved, the issue of liberty v. equality was unsettled since neither were yet accomplished.

Since the history is well known to most of us, it will be briefly summarized as follows:

A century and a half after early English colonization, and with slavery firmly established in colonial society, the War for Independence from British dominance commenced in 1776, and brought a "freedom" to the new Americans. Liberty became available to white, male property owners to conduct their lives independently and within newly established law – the U.S. Constitution. The issue of slavery was largely deferred for political and economically selfish reasons. But more change would be necessary before either liberty or equality would be available to enslaved Africans.

The first French revolution was fought for three principles all at once – *Liberte*, *Egalite* and *Fraternite*. It failed miserably. As an aside, *Fraternite* – collectivism – was never part of our original established goals for American democracy and the whole of our society. However, it has bounded into our national conscience in the 20th century.

Another 90 years later, the Civil War was fought for numerous reasons but abolished slavery and provided liberty for African-Americans in 1865. They were free but not equal. Liberty absolutely had to be established first as a necessary precondition to provide an environment and basis for equality to follow.

One hundred years later, by 1968, African Americans were afforded equal treatment before the law. Equality was guaranteed but racism has persisted in diminishing degrees to this day. It has effectively ended but what remains must be resolved in the human heart.

Argument

Why was this discussion of semantics necessary? Eric Foner, in his American history textbook - *Give Me Liberty*, because of its theme of liberty, purposefully constraints himself to make the point throughout all American history, everything was about liberty. In most instances, he is successful operating under his self-imposed thematic approach and uses the descriptors "liberty" and "equality" as we would generally understand them. There are some biases however, that warrant mentioning. <u>Refer to Appendix A.</u>

He uses irony effectively to cast a dark view of America wherein liberty is always afforded to some but always denied to others. In his pessimistic thesis, he seems to suggest that liberty is a zero-sum game where there is not enough to go around. For some to acquire it, it must be taken away from others. This is interesting and may be true of the nature of humankind. Certainly the study of Western civilization provides countless examples of this over centuries of European history. While this is very often true, but not always, it is incomplete. Dr. Foner's "unforgiving" view of America for its racist past has earned him labels of "anti-American" and "Profs who hate America". In a balanced analysis, it is uncertain if this could be considered fair. History is subjective and historians have perspective. However, Eric Foner must understand that if he were "thinking historically" and he were a successful planter in the 1700's, he would have owned slaves. That is the point of honest historicity. Illuminate the past.

Historian and biographer, David McCullough has been criticized for giving our founders a pass on their actions regarding slavery. McCullough has said that he has no regard for that certain kind of historian who doesn't just paint the founders as having feet of clay, but paints them as wholly made of clay. Note: This quotation from David McCullough is paraphrased here without quote marks. It is a recollection from a television interview on either 60 minutes or with Charlie Rose on PBS.

Eric Foner's *Give Me Liberty* is a <u>social history</u> account. As its subtitle suggests, it is <u>An</u> *American History*. It does include enough political history, economic history, and military history to thread together it social history. It's all about emphasis, content and context. In this skillful and carefully crafted presentation, it becomes sensible to overlook or discredit the "great men" approach to history used in the past. Further, by reducing the study of individuals and events and focusing on social history and culture, Dr. Foner, like many contemporary historians, presents history in a gender-neutral, race-neutral, and inoffensive, politically-correct acceptable manner. Social structure becomes the theme of history and individual agency is kept to a minimum. In the most academic sense, this can be dishonest history and not objective if it attempts to condemn the past, not illuminate it. Without narrating the context of the past, some modern historians present history filtered and emphasized with their present-day morality and sensibility. Voltaire did just that in his "modern" time. See *The Significance of Historiography* in the bibliography.

With the shift toward social history, the interest in teaching about "dead white men" has become disparaged and avoided. The concern with this thematic choice is that so much American history is overlooked. Let's parse that phrase. All history is about dead men (and women). To assert otherwise is ludicrous. Rosa Parks, Harriet Tubman, Dred Scott, Medgar Evers, Frederick Douglas, W.E.B. DuBois, Martin Luther King, Jr. - all dead and gone, aren't they? To suggest that our history is not about white men (and women) is to deny our formation and genesis as an American society.

Historiography - Evaluation and Comparison

This study does not intend to examine a broad selection of history texts written at various periods of American history in order to provide a comprehensive survey. Rather, this is a case study intended to compare two modern progressive history text authors and evaluate their respective approaches to the subject. For reference and additional perspective, an older text as well as a current unconventional approach, using only primary source text, are included.

Alan Brinkley's text, *American History - Connecting with the Past* provides a neutral, thorough, traditional presentation of people and events and causes and outcomes. It also includes content with the modern approach of thematic passages illuminating cultural and societal issues. These are sufficient for a general American history text, but not so extensive as to attempt the specialty studies of race, ethnicity, and gender within one volume. Several inserts are included to provide topical historiography so that the reader can learn how various historians have given sharp perspectives on the topic. In my case, I completed the text with a satisfied feeling one gets from a good meal. I came away learning about the good, the bad, and the ugly, but still left with pride in my country. To roughly paraphrase Socrates, finding the good after all is what makes life worth living.

Eric Foner's text, *Give Me Liberty, An American History* seems to provide less detail in the presentation of people and events and causes and outcomes. At least it feels that way. The narrative is so smoothly written that some lack of detail might go unnoticed. It stresses societal and cultural change and reads more like a narrative with a mission in the tradition of a great novel. If a survey level American history text were to be presented as a social history (in the historiographical sense), this would be most appropriate. The text does provide some unusual aspects and deep insights into context that are quite unexpected. These perspectives are valuable and rare in standard texts for survey history courses. For example, he writes that the colonists, in their protests to the British parliament about unfair taxation and lack of representation, refer to themselves as being "enslaved" for these atrocities. They use this term in the context of their time in history while not recognizing enslaved Africans all about them and throughout their society.

The writing level and academic level of the text is higher than Alan Brinkley's. The American history is illuminated, but critically evaluated at each step. It left me with the feeling I would get coming out of church after a harsh sermon – filled with guilt and little hope. There was very little there offered for me to feel any pride in my country.

Both texts were valuable to my learning experience as a student and amateur historian. As non-elite, non-rich, but a white man, I do wish to learn American history with nuance and depth, but not be blamed for my history at every turn or stripped of all vestige of pride in my country. Without Dr. Brinkley's text and older texts from the past, this expectation might not have been met. But without Dr. Foner's text, my insights into my country's history would have been less complete.

George Brown Tindall and David E. Shi's text, *America, A Narrative History* was used as a college history text in the early 1990's. The volume I examined began with two chapters of post-Civil War reconstruction. As a textbook over 20 years old, this will be used for comparison with the two modern texts above for the reconstruction period. The authors provide a narrative of political history for a period where the history was contentious and open to a social history. The presidency of Andrew Johnson, successor to Lincoln after his assassination, is detailed in terms of his political motives and actions. Like Lincoln, Johnson wanted a moderate reconstruction but was too petty and contentious to be successful. He vetoed bills proposed by his Radical Republican opponents. Eventually, he was discredited, his vetoes were overridden, and he was impeached. He narrowly escaped being removed from office in the congressional impeachment trial. The programs that were enacted or defeated, failed or had limited success, were detailed.

As students of American history know, in the end, failed reconstruction did little to help the devastated South, or ultimately gave any significant opportunity or rights to the newly freed African Americans, or gave assistance to poor white citizens who became more impoverished. The South was embittered and responded with Jim Crow laws of segregation and violent hostility toward blacks brought by the Ku Klux Klan. Racism rose to unprecedented heights and impeded the economic development of the South and resolution of civil rights despite the passage of the 13th, 14th and 15th Amendments. President Grant inherited the legacy of Radical reconstruction and attempted to deal with its violent consequence during his scandal ridden administration. Economic crisis followed and reconstruction ended with the Hayes presidency. Certainly this period was complex and would require extensive study to understand the nuances that drove our history forward. To be sure, the efforts of the federal government, controlled by northern politicians, were characterized with "curfuffle"[1] and "schadenfreude."[2]

Another perspective, and rather unique approach, to American history education is taken by Hillsdale College. Hillsdale was founded in 1853 in the free state of Michigan. Some 400 Hillsdale men fought for the Union in the Civil War. Frederick Douglas spoke there twice during that time. They make no attempt at disguising their motive and do not use a standard textbook as secondary text, but rather supplement lecture with an extensive volume of primary source texts - *The U.S. Constitution: A Reader*. The book is poorly named since its reach and span far exceeds the U.S. Constitution.

In a pamphlet introducing their Politics 101 course, which is centered on the U.S. Constitution, they write about some aspects of liberty as follows:

The mission of Hillsdale College, as set forth in its original Articles of Association, is to provide the "sound learning" needed to perpetuate the "inestimable blessings" of "civil and religious liberty and intelligent piety." In keeping with this mission, Hillsdale is one of very few colleges and universities outside America's service academies where all students, regardless of major, take a course on the U.S. Constitution as part of their core requirements.

In addition to a careful and detailed examination of the Declaration of Independence, the Constitution, and other primary source documents of the founding era, the course covers the great challenge to constitutionalism in the secession crisis of the 1850s, culminating in the Civil War, as well as the departures from constitutional principles and practices during the Progressive era and Progressivism's modern heirs.

Students in Hillsdale's U.S. Constitution course will develop appreciation of the Founder's understanding of human nature, the rule of law, the separation of powers, federalism, justice, and property rights. They learn to distinguish liberty from license and legitimate from tyrannical government, and to recognize the connection between rights and duties.

In short, the course aims to teach students the conditions of liberty, the extent to which these conditions had been undermined, and how they might be recovered and preserved.

With its highly focused perspective and content, this would be another way to study American history. My experience with this, and other Hillsdale College courses, informs me that they are valuable for a clear and honest understanding of the meaning of liberty in the American experience. However, historical detail and equality are given scant attention. The "great men" and "dead white men" theorems are emphasized. This is fitting and essential as far as it goes.

Four founding documents are offered as the basis of Hillsdale's American history presentation. In addition to the expected two, the Mayflower Compact and Northwest Ordinance of 1787 are included. The former is included to inform students of the piety and moral purpose of the early English Puritan settlers. The latter is key to illustrate the intent of the founders to eventually abolish slavery; starting the effort immediately. It stresses the founder's plan to forbid slavery in all new territories that would become new states.

The attack from progressives of the 20th century and in modern times has been that the Ordinance was of little consequence since the territory was not suitable for the kind of agriculture conducive to slave labor. Therefore, the founders had not given any benefit to the cause of abolition and this was a political defense for their hypocrisy. The defenders of the founder's argue that the Ordinance was a legal model for all future states and therefore proved their intent. This ideological argument has not been resolved. While none of us can ever know what was in the heads and hearts of our founders, perhaps we modern Americans should give the founders, who lived in their time and context, more credit for their efforts to end the long established practice of slavery that had begun in early colonial times more than 150 years before them.

Late 19th century, romantic nationalist historians, like George Bancroft and Frederick Jackson Turner, would be very pleased with Hillsdale's American history presentation. Historians from the modern progressive school, like Arthur M. Schlesinger and Richard Hofstadter, would not be satisfied at all.

Dr. Larry Arnn, Hillsdale College's president, is one of the most gifted lecturers I have ever heard. His spoken and written language fairly soars with the sense of kindness and truth, and is poetic and often spiritual. Our early colonists and founders would have understood him clearly and would have been proud of him as an American descendent. He communicates with an elegance reminiscent of them in language lost to us today.

The Hillsdale College history course provides a sense of slavery in our early history and its dramatic shift before the Civil War. This harsh shift is very important to understand with regard to how much blame we might assign to the founders for slavery in America. It has to do with the demise of tobacco farming in the upper South, the invention of the cotton gin, and the rise of short staple cotton farming in the deep South. The large migration of the slaves to the deep South disrupted families and working conditions became horrific. The more benign "task system" was replaced by the much harsher "gang system". The southern Democrats began justifying the "positive good" of slavery and promoting popular sovereignty in the new western states. As Dr. Arnn explains, this led to the blowup in 1850, which he describes as a threat to Federalism and the Constitution, and the inevitability of the Civil War.

Conclusion

The purpose of history textbooks as secondary sources - and the requisite skill and honesty of their authors - is to present the historical evidence with sufficient evaluation for illumination, but not so much as to make excuse for or condemnation of the past. A textbook with a thesis may become a narrative of propaganda in support of an ideology. A theme-less approach might be best.

Eric Foner's *Give Me Liberty, An American History, volume 1: to 1877*, as a social history, would be a most suitable and valuable reference text for the many specialty studies of race, gender and ethnicity abundant in college study today. As a social history, the text is unsuitable for a college survey level American history course. It lacks the necessary detailed content to sufficiently present political history, economic history, and military history and give the college student a fair and complete understanding of our history. With its obsession of racism, it misrepresents the narrative of those periods and historical figures where racism was not the focus.

But to be sure, the themes of democracy (freedom, liberty, equality) have dominated our American history and its national conversation since the beginning. That, by itself, speaks volumes about the greatness of our country. Thomas Paine wrote in *Common Sense* in 1776, speaking of the quest for freedom all over the world, that America would "receive the fugitive, and prepare in time an asylum for mankind" [3]. Eric Foner wrote in *Give Me Liberty* - "From the beginning, the idea of 'American exceptionalism' - the belief that the United States has a special mission to serve as a refuge from tyranny, a symbol of freedom, and a model for the rest of the world - has occupied a central place in American nationalism".[4]

We were great, and even exceptional, as a country once because we were informed by great men. And these men were great. It is fitting and acceptable to say that. They were human beings, with frailties and faults who made mistakes, but without them and their sacrifice, courage, intelligence and service, we would have nothing to discuss here.

Notes

1. "curfuffle." *Dictionary.com's 21st Century Lexicon*. Dictionary.com, LLC. 03 Sep. 2014.
http://dictionary.reference.com/browse/curfuffle.

2. "schadenfreude." *Dictionary.com Unabridged*. Random House, Inc. 03 Sep. 2014.
http://dictionary.reference.com/browse/schadenfreude.

3. Thomas Paine, *Common Sense* (a pamphlet published and distributed to the American colonies in 1776).

4. Eric Foner *Give Me Liberty, An American History*, volume 1: to 1877, Seagull 3rd Edition, Custom Edition Columbia College (New York - London: W.W. Norton & Company, 2012), 199

Bibliography

Brinkley, Alan *American History - Connecting with the Past*, New York: McGraw-Hill, 2012.

As used at Columbia College of Missouri, Hancock Campus up to 2014.

Chernow, Ron *Washington: A Life*, New York: The Penguin Press, 2010.

Foner, Eric *Give Me Liberty, An American History*, volume 1: to 1877, Seagull 3rd Edition, Custom Edition Columbia College, New York - London: W.W. Norton & Company, 2012.

As used at Columbia College of Missouri, Hancock Campus in 2014.

Foner, Eric *Voices of Freedom- A Documentary History*, 3rd edition, volume 1, New York- London: W.W. Norton & Company, 2011.

Gilderhus, Mark T. *History and Historians - A Historiographical Introduction*, Upper Saddle River, New Jersey: Pearson Prentice Hall, 2010.

Hoefferle, Caroline *The Essential Historiography Reader*, Upper Saddle River, New Jersey: Pearson Prentice Hall, 2011.

Jennings, David *The Significance of Historiography*, August 27, 2014. http://awlos.wordpress.com/2014/07/30/the-significance-of-historiography/.

Jennings, *David Liberty versus Equality*, August 27, 2014. http://awlos.wordpress.com/2014/07/20/liberty-versus-equality/.

Johnson, Michael P. *Reading the American Past - Selected Historical Documents*, Volume 1: To 1877, Boston: Bedford/St.Martin's, 2012.

Paine, Thomas *Common Sense*, a pamphlet published and distributed to the American colonies in 1776.

Tindall, George Brown and David E. Shi, *America, A Narrative History*, Third Edition, Volume Two, New York: W.W. Norton and Co., 1992. As used at Potsdam College in the early 1990's. George Brown Tindall and David E. Shi are associated with universities in North Carolina.

Edited by the Hillsdale College Politics Faculty, *The U.S. Constitution: A Reader*, Hillsdale, MI: Hillsdale College Press, 2012. A compilation of primary source documents from U.S. history, historical figures, politicians and writers.

Author's footnote-

My interest in historiography and Americanism has lead me to study and compare historians, writers and educators Alan Brinkley and Eric Foner. Both are highly regarded and have numerous lifetime awards and accolades.

Dr. Brinkley is a progressive historian who writes with a balanced perspective and in an even-handed manner. His history text blends traditional, sequential, event-driven narrative with thematic, cultural and societal emphasized narrative. During his longtime affiliation at Columbia University, he has been Provost and Department of History chairman.

Dr. Foner has also had a longtime affiliation with Columbia University. His doctoral advisor was Richard Hofstadter. Dr. Foner is considered the leading authority on post Civil War reconstruction. His book, *Reconstruction 1863 – 1877: America's Unfinished Revolution*, copyright 1988, Harper and Rowe, is a masterwork on reconstruction. Hofstadter, while a left radicalist and former communist, rejected the New Left perspectives of some of his students, including Eric Foner, while giving them cursory attention due to scant interest in their work.

Through the Department of Education, and using instruments like Common Core, there seems to be a profound paradigm shift occurring in the way American history is being taught. Among mature citizens, some will agree and some will not. Unless there are future historians, authors, and teachers willing to present our heritage in its full, honest, rich and vibrant context, younger students will never know the difference.

Appendix A. - Examples from *Give Me Liberty*

1. Page 66 references "city set upon a hill" descriptive of early colonial Puritan society under a heading of Moral Liberty. This refers to John Winthrop's sermon on the deck of the Arabella in 1630 ("We will be as a city upon a hill. The eyes of all people are upon us, so that if we deal falsely with our God in this work we have undertaken and so cause Him to withdraw His present help from us, we shall be made a story and a byword throughout the world. ...") and the biblical passage of Matthew 5:14-16 quoting Jesus's famous Sermon on the Mount ("You are the light of the world. A city set on a hill cannot be hid. Nor do men light a lamp and put it under a bushel, but on a stand ......"). President Reagan in 1974 invoked it as a powerful visual image to instill patriotic love of American values as an example to ourselves and the world. At first I thought Dr. Foner was including this for its irony regarding the religious intolerance of Puritan society. But I'm not so sure. It could also be a condemnation of American patriotism and conservative ideology.

2. Page 66 and 71 refers to the early colonial Puritan society in Massachusetts as the "Bible Commonwealth". Since nothing in this textbook is cited, I must conclude that this label is the author's own invention for his purpose - a pejorative with his religious intolerance.

3. Page 123 under the heading The Colonial Elite mentions that "The days when self-made men could rise into the Virginia gentry were long gone; by 1770, nearly all upper-class Virginians had inherited their wealth." and "George Washington's father, grandfather, and great-grandfather had been justices of the peace" who used influence to gain possession of

large tracts of land. It has been noted elsewhere that 18th century historians have deified Washington while 20th century historians have crucified him. My readings of his biographies from Ron Chernow and David McCullough inform me that he inherited a modest amount of land from his moderately prosperous family of Virginia's middling class. He was self-taught and self-made. He amassed great wealth due to his own efforts. Over the many years that he served our country in the Continental Congress, as commander of the Continental Army in the Revolutionary War and as President, his wealth diminished greatly. Much of his landholdings were sold, and he left office in debt. Part of this was his love of fine things and pride as a former Englishman. Part of it was his dedication to his country, sacrifice, courage and service. Read his Farewell Address to understand his love of his country and countrymen. Eric Foner has included this in his text of primary sources – *Voices of Freedom*. It would have been noticeably irresponsible had he left it out.

4. Page 279 under the heading of Principles of Freedom states that "Race, one among many kinds of legal and social inequality in colonial America, now emerged as a convenient justification for the existence of slavery in a land that claimed to be committed to freedom." Is this an opinion Dr. Foner? or were you there?

5. Page 294 under the heading The Adams Presidency states that "In his Farewell Address (mostly drafted by Hamilton and published in newspapers rather than delivered orally; see the Appendix for excerpts from the speech), Washington defended his administration against criticism, warned against the party spirit, and advised his countrymen to steer clear of international politics by avoiding 'permanent alliances with any

portion of the foreign world'." This was presented as a byword in passing while introducing the Adams Presidency. Based on my familiarity with the document of this well-known speech, this characterization seemed incomplete. I checked the appendix of this text and found no excerpts of the speech there.

However, Washington's Farewell Address is printed in Eric Foner's *Voices of Freedom* as a primary source on page 144 . This "primary source" text is an <u>abbreviated</u> version of George Washington's farewell address. I compared the Foner version to the <u>abbreviated</u> version in Michael P. Johnson's *Reading the American Past* and to the full, unedited version published by Hillsdale College - *The U.S. Constitution: A Reader*. I noted that both the Foner and the Johnson "versions" omitted the section where Washington spoke of any mistakes he may have made in office. The Hillsdale unedited version presents all of his words and clearly conveys the humility and honesty of his character. Foner's remark "Washington defended his administration against criticism" mischaracterizes Washington while excluding any evidence to the contrary. While Johnson leaves it out also, he does not assail Washington's character in his introductory summary.

Neither the Foner nor the Johnson version include Washington's words expressing love for his fellow countrymen and his country as found in the full version. When a writer uses someone else's words as their own, without proper citation and accreditation, it is called plagiarism. What is it called when a writer reprints a primary document and leaves out selected portions in order to mischaracterize the document? Is it omission by intent? Is it dishonest? Is it fraud? It is shameful.

If a history text is written as a social history, it would be important to explain why Washington distributed a Farewell Address to the American people. It was because there was an outpouring of affection for him and he wished to give his countrymen fatherly advice and return his affection to them. He wanted to express to them that they should love one another, bind together as a nation, and love their country just as he did by example. This may be an opinion but it is just as valid as any Eric Foner may offer. Neither of us were there at the time.

6. Chapter 14 - *A New Birth of Freedom: The Civil War 1861-1865* would have been the opportunity for the author to concentrate on a military history, perhaps more than any chapter of his text. The opportunity was squandered however, as the presentation is dominated with social history. Refer to segment headings like *The Public and the War*, *The Second American Revolution* (perfecting the ideals of the founding for disenfranchised slaves, not the south's struggle for its independence from a dominating federal government), *The War and American Religion*, *Liberty in Wartime*, *The War and Native Americans*, *Women and the War*, *Women and the Confederacy*, *Black Soldiers for the Confederacy*, *The Sea Island Experiment*, *Wartime Reconstruction in the West*, *The Politics of Wartime Reconstruction*, and *The War and the World*.

There is absolutely nothing wrong with these topics and they bring many rich perspectives to the history of the Civil War. But the author displays his interest in these areas while paying only obligatory attention to the actual events of the war. It is as though the military history is not of interest to him but he is required to include it. A student in our class must have noticed something was awry in this chapter and tried to inquire about it in class discussion. He tried to understand what appeared odd to him about the text. He was not familiar with history orientations like social, political, military, economic, etc. This is my greatest concern. The uniformed student will not know enough to know what is happening and may not know the difference. His learning will be in concert with the biases of his text authors and teachers.

In those segments of this chapter that actually describe the war, the author breaks up the coverage very appropriately into its phases and geographical campaigns. The obligatory maps of the battles are included. Presumably the author did not draw them, but acquired them from public domain sources with any appropriate copyright compliances. In his text however, his descriptions of the war are in passing and appear as a byword.

7. In the insert - *Voices of Freedom, From the Lincoln - Douglas Debates (1858)* following page 491 - Eric Foner quotes from Lincoln: "I say when this government was first established it was the policy of the founders to prohibit the spread of slavery into the new territories of the United States, where it had not existed." Here Lincoln is referring to the Northwest Ordinance of 1787 - a key document in conveying the founders' intent toward the future of slavery. It was a cornerstone in their effort to immediately begin the process for slavery's demise. Throughout his writing, Dr. Foner conveys a respect, perhaps an admiration, for Lincoln. If this was good enough for Lincoln, and Eric Foner respects him, why isn't it good enough for him? In his writing of the Federalist period and the founding era, he paints the "dead white men" as racist consistent with

his theme of American racism in his text ironically titled, *Give Me Liberty, An American History*.

For those readers unfamiliar with the historiographical trend, many modern revisionist historians have used the terms "dead white men" and "great men" as snarky, sarcastic pejoratives to demean the founders and control the narrative to sell their agendas. Consistent with this train of thought, the term "elites" has been created in recent decades to further this purpose also, as though wealth, prominence, intelligence and education are somehow disqualifiers for political leadership. To me, it is just as offensive as the term "niggers" and serves the same purpose to control thought and meaning. Am I predisposed toward a positive view of the founders and blinded to their shortcomings? I try to keep an open mind and, to the best of my ability, stubbornly refuse to let an ideology blindly slam my mind tightly shut.

Camp Life

Originally written in 2015

Sometimes memory knows but without our remembering. Eyes, hands, and even muscles know, while the active mind has no recollection, doesn't know source or reason. It is skill and feeling without conscious knowing. As Bill Faulkner wrote - "Memory believes before knowing remembers. Believes longer than recollects, longer than knowing even wonders". Uniquely and perfectly partitioned from the rest of it, some experiences lasting only a few fleeting months or years influence the remainder of our lives without our even knowing or remembering you see.

Over 50 years ago in 1955, when I was 12 years old, my father bought a large wood lot located off the Mountain Road between Mayfield and Northville, New York. This quiet country minor road ran parallel to the more major touristy lakeside road running northward along the west shore of the manmade Great Sacandaga Lake in the region known as Cranberry Creek.

His lot was 200 acres facing westward toward the foot of a mountain in the eastern Adirondacks. On the property, the slope was gradual at first but grew steeper the farther the elevation reached toward the distant cascade of peaks.

Dad had been doing some carpentry renovations for a farmer named Ted Roosevelt whose farmhouse lie across the Mountain Road adjacent to his wooded property. Ted claimed to be a grandson of the late President with the same name. We weren't certain if Ted was correct. He and dad settled on a modest price and dad bought his land.

Ted's farmhouse was surrounded on all sides with fallow fields, now in his old age, except for the small vegetable garden his wife kept behind it. They kept a few chickens in the backyard also but the days of active farming had passed. Directly across the Mountain Road, Ted's large barn was empty except for his old Belgian workhorse, Dick and two milk cows. The animals they had had the run of the fenced-in field around the barn and facing the wood lot.

In Ted's kitchen there were many conversations between him and my father about the land, the past in their region before it was flooded to create the lake, the country life and its required skills. I sat impatiently in the house with them squandering the opportunity to pay attention and learn, except for what I absorbed without knowing. The house reeked of garlic and I couldn't wait to escape there for the fresh air outdoors. Ted ate whole cloves of it every day as a home medicine to help with his chronic heart condition.

My father was 42 and in his prime. That is, his physical prowess may have begun to decline, but his skills were at their peak. It is impossible to understand that time without understanding my father- his view of life, his dreams, his motivations, his abilities and talents, his vulnerabilities, his demons and his melancholy sadness.

I was a very young man with everything to learn. What I had learned from books and other children to that point had no bearing on the lessons I would unconsciously learn there from him and that place and time.

It was just a few years there growing up before I left for tech school in Troy and Syracuse in central New York. After that, there were visits with my wife and children and lastly with my new fiancé after my divorce. But that was later and things were not the same.

My father's land was densely forested with mainly maple, hemlock and pine trees. His first task was to make an entrance road to the property. He bought a homemade farm vehicle, he affectionately called a doodlebug, to help him carry away rocks and move dirt.

It was custom fabricated from a Model A Ford frame and engine but had an International Harvester rear end with large tractor wheels and two transmissions bolted together in tandem. It was geared for low speed but provided extreme torque to climb hills, pull stumps or whatever was needed. There was a small wooden truck bed in the back for hauling things. The gas tank was the firewall immediately in front of the driver's face and the gas was drip-fed by gravity through a thin metal tube to the carburetor of the small old engine in front of the tank.

I learned to drive with that vehicle and helped my father by bringing him sand and rocks for various needs that he had. It did catch fire once but we quickly doused it out before it exploded or otherwise spread harm.

With the entrance road completed, we needed to build a temporary bridge over the creek running along the foot of a hill and parallel to the forest. Then we had to clear trees along 200 feet up the hill to a plateau about 100 feet elevated above the creek. No matter how many times we rebuilt that road up the hill, and widened it, and covered it with stone, it continued to wash out every year. It took a running start across the bridge to get a car to the top of the hill without getting stuck in the mud.

The bridge washed out too, from the fast running water during the spring melt-off, and had to be replaced with more substantial construction using steel beams, concrete sidewalls and sluiceway construction. Standing in the freezing mountain water of the creek, we did that work too.

City folk, who are nature lovers and occasionally visit parks and forested areas, have no understanding what man has had to do to tame the land, make it livable and enjoyable by converting it from its rough pristine state to its unnatural state of refined groomed beauty. This process has occurred across our whole continent throughout our American history.

The elevated plateau above the creek was selected as an ideal location to build a camp. It was secluded by enough trees to hide its view from the Mountain Road, but not too deep into the woods to make it difficult to access. We cleared the trees throughout that natural flat area. To get lumber to build the camp, dad decided to harvest his own from the indigenous maple throughout a few nearby acres.

He contracted with Ted to borrow Dick to help skid and drag the felled logs out of the forest. He was the biggest horse I had ever seen in action. Dick was old but very strong and used to hard work. Up above the future campsite, dad felled trees with a chainsaw, trimmed their branches with a limb axe, and cut them into manageable length logs. He hitched Dick up to one or two logs at a time with a harness and heavy chains. The haul was steep and followed downhill along a creek bed or nearby rough paths.

I remember that once Dick had broken the inertia and got the weight moving, he was smart enough to not want to be stopped and have to exert himself all over again. Dick moved fast and dad ran along behind him holding the leather reins attached to Dick's harness. With his short legs, dad had all he could do to keep control and keep up as he hollered, "Whoa Dick, whoa". Dick ignored him and raced to the bottom of the hill as fast as he could. During all these harrowing runs, neither beast nor man broke a limb.

The logs were stacked on the entrance road across the bridge in what would later become a parking area for visitors who feared driving their cars up the hill. A lumber mill in Northville picked them up and milled them into useable lumber for dad to build his camp. They kept some to pay for their work so the lumber was free, if you don't count dad's labor.

He built the camp, starting in the late winter. My grandfather Ed Tallman, his father-in-law, helped him put up the roof timbers and I helped in whatever ways I could. I learned a little about basic carpentry and sawed and nailed where I was instructed. He finished the whole interior of the camp with knotty pine boards bought from a local lumber mill.

There was a full width enclosed porch along the front of the camp with permanent screen panels. It had a view of the creek at the bottom of the hill, the parking area across from it and across the field at eye level to Ted's farmhouse on the Mountain Road. We could see people arriving and greet them from our perch on the hill.

After that we built a massive stone fireplace at the living room end of the building. I ran the doodlebug and brought loads of field stone and sand from locations around the property. I mixed concrete by hand in a wooden box on the ground and passed it and rocks up to him in buckets as the chimney slowly rose up over a summer. Dad built temporary scaffolds to work from as he worked his way 25 feet to the top.

He drank a lot of beer in quart bottles throughout this project. He called them 3-fers since they cost a dollar for three bottles at the country store down the road. Many of the empty bottles were built into the chimney. Dad said the air pockets were necessary for expansion. That didn't make sense to me.

Dad came up with an ingenious way to bring water to the camp for the kitchen sink and the indoor toilet. He constructed a quarter-mile long galvanized pipe from a freshwater spring way up the hill and gravity fed the water with good pressure to the camp. As carefully as he drained them late each fall, they often froze and burst each winter at a few points along the way. Eventually he replaced most of it with more freeze-tolerant plastic pipe.

There is danger working alone and self-sufficiently as we did. On one occasion, dad was felling trees in a location well above the campsite. Despite his skill, a falling tree can get hung up in the canopy and nested at an angle, with its trunk stuck in the ground next to the stump, without falling to the ground.

The thing to do to resolve this is to undercut the tree a few feet above the ground to give it another chance to break free of the canopy and fall all the way to the ground. You cut underneath most of the way through, and then make a small touch of a cut on top, watchful for the moment it breaks apart and falls.

This time it jammed and would not fall. Dad ran the chainsaw underneath a second time. It broke free abruptly, caught him by surprise and he had no time to react before the falling tree drove the running chainsaw into his thigh.

He was bleeding profusely and I was scared he would die right there. I helped him walk out with his arm on my shoulder. We made it the half mile to Ted's farm house. Dad was very weak and faint from shock and loss of blood. Ted temporarily staunched the bleeding and drove us up to the closest doctor in Northville. The doctor stitched him up and in a few days he was good as new with a huge permanent scar on his leg. He was a tough old bastard.

We moved in some old comfortable furniture and began enjoying our weekends at our secluded retreat. It was just a 17 mile commute from our home on Market Hill in Amsterdam.

Mom began coming up for weekends and my folks passed their time drinking and playing cards. Dad drank too much. The work was endless and never done. There was always brush to clear out around the grounds. When he wasn't working, he was drinking.

Eventually, electricity was brought in from the Mountain Road and service was connected to the camp which was all prewired with outlets and lighting fixtures. We put aside the oil lamps and the

Coleman white gas lantern. We had a small black and white television with local coverage from an antenna.

The whole upstairs of the camp was one bedroom with a row of four beds. There was a staircase to it from the back of the living room. One night mom had one of her recurring nightmares about getting trapped in a fire. She screamed and dad and I woke up. The camp was full of smoke and there really was a fire about ready to break out.

The fireplace had been stoked for a cold night and had overheated adjoining timbers to its walls under the camp. The timbers were glowing and about to ignite. We put out the incipient fire with buckets of water. The next day dad re-constructed the wood structure with more concrete for separation and insulation from the hot fire box. It never caused any further problems after that.

We developed another flat area for recreation about 100 feet away from the camp. There was an old dilapidated sap house there from an earlier time when sap was harvested from the maple trees and boiled down in the evaporators in the small building to make maple syrup. We demolished it and carted the remains away. We planted a nice green lawn and played horseshoes and Jarts.

Dad showed me how to take a bail of hay and fashion it into a long thick rope bound with string. Then he rolled it into a coil and bound it together as an archery target. He put it on an easel and covered it with canvas painted as a target. I practiced with my 40-lb pull long bow and once in a while with his 60-pound bow.

Dad bought me a used .22 rifle made by Sears for thirteen dollars. It was a simple bolt action single-shot with a manually cocked hammer. I hunted birds and squirrels and learned to make a kill shot with the single bullet. Dad had a Mossberg tubular-fed semi-automatic .22 rifle that always jammed and frustrated him no end.

I always regretted the small animals I had killed for no good reason. I must have carried guilt about that since, as an adult, I only shoot at paper targets at a private rifle range, but never would be a hunter or kill animals again. I am grateful for the knowledge dad gave me about the use and safety of firearms. It is better to know about them than not and fear them.

He built a huge outdoor stone fireplace in back of the camp and built a fence around the defined yard and cultivated a nice lawn. He built a free-standing tool shed in the yard and a service bar, with running water of course, along the fence and an open-faced woodshed next to it.

He bought a 1940's old Ford flathead eight pickup truck to replace the old doodlebug. It was always parked on his service road behind the shed and fence. I really enjoyed running that truck through our service roads up into the woods.

They had many adult couple friends up to camp for cookouts, card playing and all-weekend drinking binges. He would burn half a cord of wood in the outdoor fireplace to get a deep bed of red coals to cook his steaks the way he wanted them. Always inebriated, he loved to party.

In high school, as fraternity president, I hosted some clandestine parties at camp when my folks were away. There was drinking and girls involved.

I brought my young boys and wife to camp from Syracuse on weekends. They enjoyed filling jars with dozens of bright orange newts after a heavy rain just as I had as a boy.

Over the years, mom grew bored sitting weekends in isolation at camp. I went off to college and then moved away. A few years after I was gone, they sold the camp and land to someone from New York City who planned to use it as a retreat. My folks used the money to buy a mobile home in Florida and spent the next ten winters there.

Those were the days.

The South

Originally written in 2015

It is a difficult task to attempt to encapsulate the American South, historically and today, its land and its people - their beliefs and their conduct. It might be more difficult to describe its mood and its feel. The essayist would need to be a poet and a philosopher with a thousand eyes.

For due consideration of the South, I draw upon my coastal travels, personal experiences, our history, the books of our American southern writers, and of course my dear Alabama muse, Joan Austin.

There is a South in ages past – the Old South – and the modern contemporary one – the New South - although that has become old now since the completion of the 20th century, with its settled industrialization and cosmopolitan cities populated heterogeneously with people from everywhere.

And there are at least five geographical Souths – maybe more.

There is the South I have seen along the Atlantic coast arguably extending from Annapolis, Maryland to Key West, Florida. All along this coast there are diverse geographies. In the Upper South, it is the Chesapeake Bay, the Potomac River and the Shenandoah Valley. Along the coast there are the ocean ports of Norfolk, Virginia and Charleston, South Carolina and the river access ports at Savannah, Georgia and Saint Augustine, Florida. Along South Carolina and Georgia there is the low country with its sentimental tidewaters and its mysterious sea islands.

There is the Creole South and the Gulf South of Louisiana and the southern shores of Alabama and Mississippi, the panhandle of Florida and even the Gulf coast of Texas.

There is the Mississippi River South, the line where the river waterway bisects the continent from north to south and extends from the heartland to join with the Missouri in St. Louis, continues through Tennessee, passes along the border of Arkansas, to its delta in Louisiana where it terminates in the Gulf of Mexico.

There is the Appalachian Mountain South, with the Blue Ridge, the Ozark and the Allegheny in North Carolina, West Virginia and Arkansas.

There is the rural South in the remote and desolate inland backroads of southwest Georgia, Alabama and Mississippi.

All of these are bound together with a similar, if regionally unique, culture spread over a vast region of America.

There are the literary Souths that are intellectual and poetic enrichment for our lives. Many of the great southern writers have described the landscape, including the seascape, and the sky with the eye of the artist - just as Van Gogh and Rembrandt would have considered them. It is so often about the light – the sunrises, sunsets and vast panorama of stars in the night.

There are the modern contemporary writers like Pat Conroy and the earlier 20th century writers like William Faulkner and Mark Twain before them in the 19th. So many American writers have been southern writers. Why is that?

They write about the southern angst of guilt and inferiority – apology for lack of refinement and the deep sins past. They write about glory, chivalry, gentility and courtliness, maybe sewn from an older European past. They write about the human condition and the old verities of good and evil, love and hate, cruelty, kindness and faith.

There is an arrogance about northerners that view them from their puritan, liberal and superior pedestal. There is a hatred imbued in southerness from the devastation wrought upon them from the North.

From the beginning, while America continually looked to the West, the South was fully half of our country. With all this, there is a fascination about the people and places of the South that is timeless and endless - of a unique vast portion of Americana.

Section 2 – Bureaucracy

Bureaucracy's Finest Hour

Originally written in 2010

This is a little story but a gem. Perhaps you will enjoy it if your humor runs toward snarky.

My son recently hit a deer with his car at night on a dark country road. Not quite sure if his car was drivable and what to do next, he took the common sense approach and called 911 to summon the police. The officer who arrived at the scene was very nice, supportive and sympathetic. He checked the car and judged that it was drivable. He asked my son where the deer was. My son pointed to the fields and said that he ran away after he smashed the car's hood, left headlight, left fender and then skidded along the driver's side door.

The officer said that it was unnecessary to call him for hitting a deer but it was not a problem. He filled out his police report, gave my son a copy and left. Here is where the story gets good.

A few days later, my son gets a letter from the NYS Dept. of Motor Vehicles with an accident report form for him to fill out. As is standard practice, there was a stern warning that the report must be returned within 10 days of the accident. Of course, by the time the letter came, there was only 1-2 days left to meet the deadline.

You may be familiar with these forms. You describe the accident as a narrative, make diagrams showing location and position of the vehicles, report the extent of damage, etc. So, my son filled out the report where, as always your car is vehicle #1 and, in this case, the deer was vehicle #2. He reported that the damage to vehicle #2 was at least a severely damaged hoof. Of course, vehicle #2 left the scene of the accident. That is illegal.

So, where judgment cannot override procedure, bureaucracy fulfills its mission and this report will be filed for posterity. Have they not a lick of sense?

Mikey What's Next?

Originally written in 2012

Michael Bloomberg, the Mayor of New York City, has a long record of over-reaching, social engineering achievement for the perceived benefit to humanity; starting with the masses in his fiefdom.

The dictator of New York has successfully banned transfat, handguns, smoking in public places (which is almost everywhere) and now large sugary soft drinks within the walls of his kingdom.

I pick on him incessantly since his antics are so visible. There's no sneaking around behind the curtains for this guy. There is no constitution standing in his way. He just does whatever the hell he wants. And then he travels around to other cities, other states and to the federal government in DC to sell his benefits to society (health, safety and the environment) to anyone who will listen.

In all fairness, Mike Bloomberg is a likable and very generous man. As a billionaire, he has donated a lot of his personal fortune in support of his causes. I believe he sincerely cares about those less fortunate than himself - which is just about everybody. He is obviously intelligent; although not highly intelligent. More about that later.

I have also heard him make sensible statements from time to time. He once offered to come to Arizona to help them with improvement of their gun control laws. While I think this offer was very arrogant, I do give him kudos for recently saying (to paraphrase him) "There are lots of gun control laws. We have enough gun control laws. We need to enforce the laws we have and that will require that we fund the enforcement." Amen; the only liberal I know who gets it.

Arrogance is bred in his DNA. He can't help but know better than anyone else what is true, right and best for them. The development and realization of intelligence in arrogant people is limited to semi-intelligence. That is the most they can attain because their minds are handicapped with the inability to visualize or understand anything outside of themselves.

But I digress. So Mike; what's next. Here is an idea for your next project. Think mandatory bathing and hygiene regulation. Some people smell bad. This is true in both urban and rural areas. But in high population density metropolitan areas like your kingdom, the odor is intensified.

The huddled masses need to bathe as a government mandate. It would be fitting and appropriate for a guy in your position to require it. If some of your poorest do not have facilities and cannot afford your shiny new public facilities, you could subsidize them with taxpayer funding on an as-needed basis. The important thing is that you will obtain compliance and verifiable certification on a frequent basis. I leave the final details of the rules of this socially beneficial plan to you. This is what you live for. This is how you roll. Your city will smell better.

Note: My inspiration is Jonathan Swift's "A Modest Proposal" written in pre-Victorian 1729 for the benefit of Dublin and eventually London. Try as I might, I will never achieve Swift's level of cynicism. The link is:
http://emotionalliteracy.com/classic_books_online/mdprp10.htm

Finally Mike, my advice for your political future. Remain serving at the municipal level. You can pretty much dictate whatever you want and not be frustrated by the checks and balances of power from a bipartisan (ie. two-party) legislature. There is no constitution to harness your ability to take away individual liberties. There is no division between executive and legislative function. It won't be difficult for you to overpower a city council or equivalent ineffective body and insure that your will is done.

Love and Best Wishes.

P.S. Before this blog got posted, Mike found his next socially invasive project. He is coercing hospitals to promote breastfeeding for new mothers. The use of baby formula will be strongly discouraged. Way to go with what you know best Mike.

Section 3 – History

A Brief History of North America and Its People

Originally written in 2016

INTRODUCTION

In the course of American history study at the senior high school or freshman college level, a survey overview textbook is used to provide a general detailed coverage of the subject as an edited secondary source, occasionally including some primary source documents. Often it is written without unnecessary perspective but offers most of the salient facts of the political, military, economic and social histories.

These tomes are often published in glossy large format, heavy, hard cover, 800-900 page volumes and are used over two semesters. I have read several of these for my comparative purposes and for the value they afforded me.

My purpose with this essay is to provide a brief thumbnail sketch of a summary of those massive summaries. It is a good place to start.

EARLY HISTORY

Most historians agree that the first peoples to inhabit North America were from Siberia and had crossed the temporary ice bridge across the Bering Strait about 13,000 years ago. They were of Mongolian DNA and traveled as family groups south toward warmer climate to settle near what is now Clovis, New Mexico. They are called the Clovis people. Eventually they spread south through Central America and into northwest South America. They were the early native people who were hunters, gatherers and eventually farmers.

A few historians believe the very earliest immigrants crossed broad oceans by boat to settle the continent during those very early times. Other historians, without broad consensus, believe there is evidence that Scandinavian people from northern Europe traveled by boat and came to the northeast coast of North America some centuries later. Some believe they may have moved south and west into inland America.

How pristine that land must have looked to those first people. Whether they had any concept of gods, heavens or the cosmos, the sheer primal raw beauty of the forests, the mountains, the lakes, the deserts must have filled their eyes with wonder even while they struggled to survive and settle this new world.

They developed great civilizations – the Aztecs and the Maya from Mexico and Central America and the Incas from Peru – with growing knowledge of astronomy, mathematics and architecture that must have come from inspiration of this world and their love of life upon it.

The centuries passed and we learn from the study of western civilization that the ancient Egyptian, Greek, Roman and Arabic peoples passed a civilizing development onto Europe. The continents of Asia and Africa influenced and informed the mighty Monarchies and nation states that grew there during the Renaissance following the regressive times of the dark ages. The ancient knowledge and wisdom pre-dating those black sorry centuries was partially preserved for newly rekindled advancement. Christianity moved through the dark age – early medieval ages - but added little benefit to the woeful existence of the European people of that time.

The old world developed in a more structured way as tribalism yielded to feudalism. Eventually the ages of nobility and monarchy led to a scientific revolution and ultimately to an age of enlightenment. Enlightenment was a secular view looking ahead from the crude, dark-age that preceded it. It rejected religion, and Christianity in particular, as the way forward for mans' advancement and instead looked to the power of the human mind for wisdom and guidance. But Christianity survived, became less corrupted in its human leadership, and was reformed.

EXPLORATION

The great age of exploration across the oceans began first with the Portuguese and the Spaniards. These men launched fearful voyages to seek more knowledge of the world and most importantly, riches. The study of western civilization begins to include the Americas at this point.

In the late 15th century, the Spanish came to the Caribbean and explored Florida, Mexico and Central America. The Portuguese came to northwest South America. They scorned the indigenousness peoples they found there and forced Christianity upon them even while subjugating their culture and stealing their riches.

By the early 16th century, the French, Dutch and English began to come to North America, arriving on the north Atlantic coast.

The French established footholds in North America beginning in 1524. Early settlements were established in Canada and the frontier far west of the Atlantic coast by French hunters and fur traders. They established good working relationships with the Indians out there in the wilderness.

The Dutch began arriving at the beginning of the 1600's. They explored the Hudson River into northern areas up to the confluence with the Mohawk River near Albany. They established a territory they named New Netherlands. Later, on the tip of Manhattan Island, they established a settlement they named New Amsterdam in 1625. They were a small presence on the continent.

BRITISH COLONIZATION

The English came also in the early 1600's, in two small groups. The first were Royal Cavalier adventurers arriving in Jamestown, Virginia in 1607-1612. The second were Puritan religious refugees arriving in Plymouth, Massachusetts in 1620. Each established a small tenuous foothold. These became permanent and grew to become more successful. They were the seeds from which would grow the rivalry and contention between the American North and the American South.

The American colonies developed with its British citizens throughout the Colonial period. The British Americans became embroiled in the French and Indian War in 1763 on their western frontier along the Allegheny mountain spine while England and France were simultaneously at war in Europe - the Seven Years' War. The young George Washington fought as a British officer in that conflict on this continent. The resolution of that conflict diminished France's foothold and established British dominance on the North American continent.

A larger wave of immigrants - the Ulster Scots – arrived in Colonial America after the first English between 1717 and 1775 with some a few decades earlier. They settled in Maine and backwoods areas of the frontier up and down the spine of the Appalachian Mountains and down into the South.

AMERICA DEFINED

After years of interference and taxation from the mother country throughout much of the 1760's, the disgruntled British American colonists declared their thirteen colonies independent of England in July of 1776, having already begun to fight for their independence in June of 1775 close by Boston, Massachusetts. They fought and barely won a Revolutionary War with their former Monarchy culminating with the surrender of Lord Cornwallis's in Yorktown, Virginia. France had come to George Washington's aid at that crucial moment in October of 1781. The Treaty of Paris in

1783 concluded the break from British control of these new United States of America.

After the War of Independence the new Americans replaced their meager Articles of Confederation with a more thoughtful and structured U.S. Constitution ratified in 1788.

President George Washington took office in March 1789. The Bill of Rights concluded the matter with ratification in 1791. The Northwest Ordinance of 1787, written for the frontier territory of the Ohio River valley, established a plan with intent to prohibit slavery in future territories and states.

A representative form of government called a Republic was established in the 1787 Constitutional Convention. Representation for the states in the House of Representatives (half of the bi-cameral legislative branch) would be based on the population of each state with slaves counting as three-fifths of a person for that purpose. Voting rights were given to white, male property owners. Democracy was therefore indirect and limited to a select group of citizens. Inalienable rights were guaranteed for citizens. Citizenship was not yet defined.

The American 19th century began with the acquisition of the Louisiana Purchase from France in 1803. This doubled its size to include all lands east of the Mississippi with the exception of British and later Spanish influence remaining in Florida. Finally the Spanish vacated at the time when Andrew Jackson raided Seminole Indian peoples in 1818.

Again in 1812, the new America fought a small war with the British over contentions on the high seas and dispute over control of Canada. The new American capital city was sacked, its White House and Capital buildings burned, and it ended with a peace treaty while the British were resoundingly beaten in New Orleans after the peace agreement was signed. Not much changed. England still held Canada and abused American shipping.

The Mexican-American war of 1846-1848 was fought in the wake of U.S. annexation of Texas in 1845. Ultimately the U.S. acquired southwestern and pacific coast regions in New Mexico and California as well as the Texas Republic. New borders were established and more Spanish influence was displaced, while at the same time absorbed into American culture, under the philosophy of Manifest Destiny.

Immigrants continued to pour into the United States from many European countries including Ireland and Germany.

THE SECOND AMERICAN REVOLUTION

After decades of disagreement and conflict over the issues of slavery, states' rights, taxation and tariffs, economic and societal differences during the first half of the 19th century, the Civil War between the North and South begun in 1861 and concluded in 1865. It resolved the issue of slavery, diminished the power of the individual states and firmly and finally established the power and central authority of a strong Federal government at a cost of 620,000 American lives. Subsequent, reconstruction in the South failed to accomplish rebuilding it or secure rights for the newly freed African Americans.

Prior to that the expression "the United States are … " referred to a confederation of individual states with individual rights. After that the expression "the United States is …" referred to a country united as one thing, under one central authority of government. From then on, one size would fit all.

COMPLETION OF THE AMERICAN CONTINENT CONQUEST AND DEVELOPMENT

After the Civil War, the United States continued to make agreements, treaties and purchases, like the Gadsden Purchase and Seward's purchase of Alaska from Russia, until all vestiges of holdings of Spain and England were removed. England continued a relationship with Canada as part of the British Empire and Mexico was an independent country.

The United States continued to commission territories as new states until there was the "lower 48" plus Alaska and Hawaii to complete the 50 states we have today. The Spanish-American war ceded Quam and Puerto Rico and the Philippines (for a time) to the U.S. as protectorates.

EMERGENCE AS A WORLD POWER

The United States emerged as the major industrial power throughout the world and supported its allies late at the end of World War I. Again it supplied and supported its allies in World War II and fought with them to defeat the axis powers, including Germany and Japan, throughout the European continent and Pacific campaigns.

As the Soviet Union was formed and its power arose after World War II, America fought wars in Asia, in Korea and Viet Nam, to reduce the spread of communism. Ultimately the Soviet Union collapsed for economic and failed ideological reasons, leaving the U.S. as the sole military super power.

What is History? – An Introduction

Southern Heart Publishing, 2017

INTRODUCTION

When I say "prejudice" or "bias", it is immediately offensive. If I say "opinion", it raises the small hairs on your arms and you are suspicious. But if I say "perspective" or "viewpoint", that is bland and acceptable. Yet all these words mean the same thing.

Historians, ordinary citizens, the media and political leaders – human beings – use perspective and either advertently or inadvertently commit errors of commission or omission. In this way their bias is revealed for ill or good.

HISTORY DEFINED

In my first freshman American history course my professor stated that we were to turn in an extra paper at the end of the semester entitled *What is History?*[1]. He asked that we think about the meaning of that and turn in the paper. And so I did.

At the end of the semester, the professor changed his mind and said the assignment was cancelled. But I had written it, so he accepted it to read for no credit. That was fine by me since I needed to contemplate it and write on the subject.

At the beginning of the second semester, the professor made the same request. This time he meant it. I had more thoughts on the subject and was happy to write a second paper on this subject. And so I did. This one I titled *What is History? – revisited* [2] and turned it in for extra credit, even though he knew it was a second unrequired effort in my case.

By then I couldn't stop obsessing about this topic and so I wrote two more unsolicited essay papers – *An American Historiography* [3] and *The Significance of Historiography* [4]. He graciously accepted them and promised to read them one day when he had time which was at a premium. He must have begun to wonder about me at that point.

Why was I compelled to keep thinking and writing about this subject?

When I learned that the college was changing the author for its American history 2-semester course text (secondary source overview for survey level history), I grew concerned that the new author held a reputed bias for his approach – that he held certain personal views and had an agenda. It was disconcerting since the text I first used seemed even-handed and objective, honest historiography with intellectual integrity.

With special permission from the college director and the professor, I was permitted to audit the first course again with the same professor facing this new text for the first time. I did a six-month independent study of comparing these two history texts on my own for no credit. It made my professor a little uncomfortable but by then we had built a friendship based on mutual respect.

What did I learn from all this unrequired effort? When I started to compare just these two modern history-text authors, I knew both were renowned men from Columbia University coming out with their PhDs at about the same time under their graduate advisor Robert Hofstadter in the 60's.

The first had written an honest one balancing the traditional political, military and economic histories with the newer social histories about common people. He further proved his sincerity by unselfishly including inserts of historiographies contrasting what other historians had thought about the subject at hand in the past.

The second one presented a biased history in my opinion. He glossed over, and treated superficially, much of the tradition information and emphasized the social history including his own insights and perspectives. He left out the historiographies, seeming to not care what other historians currently or before him thought. This is appropriate in some specific, narrowly focused history books but inappropriate for a survey course overview.

My professor reluctantly agreed. He was a bit disappointed in the new text selection, not of his choice, but wanted to stay out of trouble. He was an incredible inspirational history instructor.

Before this extra semester and my six-month special study was over, I had expanded the goals, delved into and read survey level complete history texts from the 1970's, 1980's and 2000. I noticed a trend away from traditional views of political, military and economic histories toward specialty studies of social issues with increasing agendas for social justice and equality for minorities and diminishment of the greatness of our founders – the dead white men.

I wrote a summarizing essay – *Themes of Democracy: freedom, liberty, equality* [5] and turned it in to my professor to read over when he found time for this unessential effort. He was gracious and did that after some time.

CONCLUSION

The presentation of history texts has become darker and more negative of our country's founders' goodness and greatness. No good could be found in our American history, in its major figures and great men of the past. No forgiveness is offered for their human frailties. No credit is given for their lofty ideals that necessitated time for fulfillment. The academic intelligentsia had shifted to a negative view of our greatness and refuted our exceptionalism.

Globalism became a focus as Western Civilization courses became optional and World History courses became mandatory.

This was not subtle if you took time to look at the whole sweep of it over several decades, starting in the 1970's. It began, I believe with the tumultuous times of the 1960's and history would never be taught the same way ever again. It would go the way of unbiased, honest journalism. It is a frightful concern for the succeeding generations of Americans.

This concern has proven to be genuine in our 21st century. I don't see any way or likelihood this nearly 50-year trend will reverse.

Notes

1. David Claire Jennings, *Collected Essays on Americanism* (Liverpool: Southern Heart Publishing, second edition 2017), 125.
2. Ibid, 129
3. Ibid, 133
4. Ibid, 139
5. Ibid, 75

What is History?

Originally written in 2013

Three views:

1) History is a collection of facts concerning people and events and is not subject to interpretation.

2) There is no "truth". Everything is subject to interpretation and reinterpretation at every age.

3) Interpretation, to be of any value, must be based on a solid foundation of observable facts.

The Socratic method uses questions as a means of inquiry and discussion to stimulate critical thinking and illuminate ideas. Using the Socratic method, one must ask "What is interpretation?" Perhaps it must inevitably fall short of proving truth since it inherently must contain unavoidable bias with two main aspects:

1) Content- What information about a person or event is included versus omitted.

2) Emphasis- What information about a person or event is given a large amount of copy versus a little.

So, for example, here are two brief accounts of George Washington's life:

George Washington was born in 1732 in Westmoreland County, Virginia. His ancestors came to Virginia in North America from England. His religious roots came from his Anglican faith. He was home schooled and studied with the local church sexton and later a schoolmaster in practical math, geography, Latin and the English classics. More importantly, much of the knowledge he would use the rest of his life was through his acquaintance with backwoodsmen and the plantation foreman. By his early teens, he had mastered growing tobacco, stock raising and surveying.

As a Virginia planter, George acquired and operated many properties scattered across the colony and did farming, milling and winemaking. He was a slave owner but was troubled about the practice and emancipated them upon his death.

He served as a general and commander-in-chief of the colonial armies during the American Revolution, and later became the first president of the United States, serving from 1789 to 1797. Over the course of his forty years of service to our country, much of his personal wealth was diminished. He was a very humble man and his abiding faith in God governed all aspects of his life. This became especially apparent in his writings and speeches over his career. He died on December 14, 1799, in Mount Vernon, Virginia.

George Washington was born in 1732 in Westmoreland County, Virginia. His ancestors came to Virginia in North America from England. He was home schooled and studied with the local church sexton and later a schoolmaster in practical math, geography, Latin and the English classics. More importantly, much of the knowledge he would use the rest of his life was through his acquaintance with backwoodsmen and the plantation foreman. By his early teens, he had mastered growing tobacco, stock raising and surveying.

As a Virginia planter and part of the landed gentry, George acquired and operated many properties scattered across the colony and did farming, milling and winemaking to become very wealthy. While he professed to be against slavery, he had many slaves considered part of his property as much as his landholdings.

He served as a general and commander-in-chief of the colonial armies during the American Revolution, and later became the first president of the United States, serving from 1789 to 1797. He died on December 14, 1799, in Mount Vernon, Virginia.

Both accounts are factual but differ in content and emphasis. Notice the somewhat subtle differences regarding his faith, his humility, his wealth and his response to slavery.

We cannot enter into a discussion about what history is without discussing how it should be taught and learned.

For an American citizen, or an immigrant with aspirations of American citizenship, American history should be taught and learned with a balance of the good and bad aspects of our history. It is likely impossible to learn our history without the bias of a point of view.

However, it does not serve us well to emphasize the atrocities of our past without teaching of the people and events that produced our greatness. It also does not serve us well to emphasize the lofty designs of our founders and praise our unique system of government while overlooking the sins of the fathers.

Therein lies the challenge and the responsibility of the teacher and the student. Perhaps the best solution to the challenge of understanding history is to study many diverse accounts, not just relying on any one, to obtain the fullest understanding and to form our own conclusions.

An American Historiography

Originally written in 2013

The neophyte student of American history, or any history, will likely first encounter point of view as a most natural concern, both challenging and impeding his critical thinking. He will be wary of the interpretation of history, and its bias, as a negative encumbrance to his personal search for truth. Worse than that, he may apply his own bias, so that history confirms his ideology.

Moving beyond that, he will become aware of what all historians know. The path away from this is in the study of historiography. This is an approach where the goal is not to merely collect facts about the past, although that is an essential requirement, but to gain further insight into the ideas and realities that shaped the lives of men and woman of earlier societies. To do this, the historian applies multiple points of view intelligently, intentionally, and for good purpose. This approach will challenge our assumptions, and rightly so.

A potent example of this would be the study of the brief Federalist period in our American history. To some, this is the only period of American history worth studying. As is commonly known, it was a turbulent period in which much happened. The diligent student will know the details. If we consider the period from the First Continental Congress in Philadelphia in 1774 to the culmination of George Washington's Presidency in 1797, the period spans roughly twenty years.

The study of the Federalist period must involve the study of the many great people of that time and the important founding documents that emerged. The men were the best we could muster. They arose to the occasion, bravely confronted the challenges, and brought with them the greatest minds of their time. They were both intelligent and well educated (arguably better educated than their 21st century counterparts are), and perhaps because of these attributes, were often the wealthiest and most successful of their colonial society.

They drew upon their classical study of governance and politics from the earliest documented theses of the Greeks and Romans, from their forbearers' understanding of the rights of Englishmen, from their experience in town government, and from their early experiments with legislative governmental design. They understood that pure, direct democracy works in small local government but cannot work for a large nation with diverse factional interests. Given this reality, direct democracy would produce a "tyranny of the majority". They brilliantly synthesized these ideas to create the best possible, albeit imperfect, governmental system that they could conceive of and agree to.

Madison understood that no system of government could function properly without men of good faith willing to set aside self-interest when he said, "If laws are required by the fact that men are not angels, controls on the government are required by the fact that angels do not govern men."

The system of checks and balances would falter without good faith and unintended consequences would occur from inadequate or devious deliberation.

The two most significant of the founding documents were the Declaration of Independence, which stated our fundamental, eternal and natural human rights, and the U.S. Constitution, which defined the structure and mechanics of our governmental design.

Most often, we have considered these documents separately. It is rare that the inter-relationship between them has been articulated. Lincoln however, did just that in an eloquent metaphor. In a fragment of a speech he wrote, but never delivered, he drew from Proverbs 25:11 - "A word fitly spoken is like apples of gold in pictures of silver" - to describe the relationship between the principles of the Declaration of Independence (the Apple of Gold) and the Constitution (the Picture Frame of Silver).

Federalism's plan did not produce a design to create a small, limited government, as some would like to believe today. It was a plan to replace an impotent government under the Articles of Confederation with a powerful central government based on the concept of indirect democracy through representation - a Republic. The Articles of Confederation, drafted at the Continental Congress in 1776 and approved for states' ratification in 1777, created a unicameral legislature, with representation based on population, a presiding moderator called a President (George Washington), but with no executive or judicial branches. It had no power to tax or raise an army and was dependent on the powerful states for those necessities. This is the model for a small, limited federal government.

The Constitution's design attempted to cover future contingency but, for pragmatic reasons, deferred the enumeration of individual rights and the resolution of slavery. The former would be resolved three years later with the passage of the Bill of Rights amendments. The latter would be resolved 77 years later with the passage of the 13th Amendment.

Other contingencies were just simply overlooked until the issues arose that required solutions. Jefferson had to consummate the Louisiana Purchase with no guidance from the Constitution or legislation in place from Congress. Lincoln had to take actions, based on executive authority, to respond to the outbreak of the Civil War since no modern war powers act existed at that time. The Andrew Johnson administration, that followed the death of Lincoln, passed the 14th Amendment to provide a definition for citizenship that did not exist in the Constitution.

While some future problems were foreseen, contingency plans were not contrived. George Washington, in his farewell address to the nation, advised that we stick together - North, South, East and West - as one nation. In his wisdom, he must have known that one day sectionalism would drive us to Civil War. He advised that we avoid party faction and foreign entanglements. We did not heed that advice either.

In conclusion, the Federalist period did not produce much democracy. That would come later during the Jeffersonian and Jacksonian eras, with the impetus of westward expansion, and the shift from federalism to nationalism. The idea that the Federalist period produced a Constitution cast in granite, that was later treated as clay during the progressive 20th century, is simplistic and ignorant of (meaning it ignores) the full context of American history. Arguably, the greatest challenges to the Constitution came from 19th century sectionalism, not 20th century progressivism.

What is History? - revisited

Originally written in 2014

The attempt to answer the question "What is History?" leads to a discussion of the many perspectives and aspects of historical study which, in turn, leads to further fascinating questions, and eventually to the study of historiography. Firstly, the issue of interpretation or bias must be at least settled, if not resolved, in the minds of both the teacher and the student. Secondly, the approach to, and purpose of, the learning experience will determine the choice of the source information and the organizational method of its presentation. Finally, the importance and value of the study of history to the student and teacher must be determined in both personal context and in the frame of the present time. If fitly done, it can be one of the most rewarding of academic endeavors.

Interpretation may also be referred to politely as point-of-view. Likely, due to intentional or unintentional bias, interpretation of historical "truth" is based on the content and emphasis of historical evidence presented. Content is about what is included or omitted. Emphasis is about how much copy is presented for one aspect or how little for another. This can be of minor consequence if the teacher and student are mindful of the pitfalls.

Ideology has no appropriate place in the honest and neutral study of history. To consider that point in another way, there is no useful purpose in studying history if the motive is to selectively pick and choose historical evidence just to confirm an ideology. The benefit of historical study is therefore to discover new ideas and views based on the past. It can be most rewarding to dispel a long-held view or understanding based on a new "discovery" or insight.

Alan Brinkley is a respected historian and author of *American History - Connecting with the Past,* the textbook used for the Columbia College HIST 121 and HIST 122 American history courses. With regard to the interpretation of history, Brinkley included in his text a *Debating the Past* insert sidebar titled *Why Do Historians So Often Differ?* In that article, he wrote:

Early in the twentieth century, when the professional study of history was still relatively new, many historians believed that questions about the past could be answered with the same certainty and precision that questions in other, more scientific fields could be answered. By sifting through available records, using precise methods of research and analysis, and producing careful, closely argued accounts of the past, they believed they could create definitive histories that would survive without controversy. Scholars who adhered to this view and believed that real knowledge can be derived only from direct, scientific observation of clear "facts" were known as "positivists".

Many areas of scholarship in recent decades are embroiled in a profound debate over whether there is such a thing as "truth". The world, some scholars argue, is simply a series of "narratives" constructed by people who view life in very different and often highly personal ways. "Truth" does not really exist. Everything is a product of interpretation. Not many historians embrace such radical ideas; most would agree that interpretations, to be of any value, must rest on a solid foundation of observable facts. [1]

With regard to sources of historical information, primary sources provide firsthand accounts of people and events and can be most beneficial if the source is truthful and knowledgeable. Secondary sources are a step removed from people and events but can provide a more accurate "bigger picture" of history. The best approach to the understanding of history would likely be obtained by employing as many sources of each type as possible.

With regard to the approaches to the study of history, there appear to be two. The traditional approach has been to present a date-sequenced stream of evidence describing people, events, acts, causes and outcomes. This is still very valuable for understanding the linkage between facts based on their order. The modern approach is more thematic and is based on cultural considerations and societal change. Having grown up with the traditional approach, the more thematic approach was at first confusing to me. The information is organized differently. However, the value of its different perspective became readily apparent.

The discussion above leads to the study of historiography. This is an approach to the study of history where comparison is made between diverse sources of evidence in order to not merely collect facts about the past, although that is an essential requirement, but to gain further insight into the ideas and realities that shaped the lives of men and woman of earlier societies. To do this, the historian applies multiple points of view intelligently, intentionally, and for good purpose. I believe, and this is the most important point, historiography's purpose is to accomplish the difficult balance of minimizing bias and interpretation while still finding some reliable truth. This approach will challenge our assumptions, and rightly so.

In my view, history is what it means to the individual in his time. To learn and understand history well is a different matter. Therefore, we can benefit from placing our personal context and the frame of the present time in abeyance until we have reflected upon what we have learned.

Ben Franklin, as a young man of 20, wrote out a plan for himself to achieve a list of the 13 virtues he believed important for his development, self-improvement, and perfection as a person. Among these were order, frugality, sincerity, and humility. He worked on one item per week and reprocessed every 13 weeks. He worked on them every day until his death at age 79. History tells us he died a happy man.

While I do not possess Ben's discipline, I respect his ordered approach. My personal approach to the study of history, and to learning it well, would be the following objective, 8-point plan:

- As a general principle, listen to all the current, diverse, and divisive political viewpoints, but defer your judgments into the future. Wait for the historical perspective.
- Collect from your study a solid body of evidence based on observable facts by studying multiple secondary texts and attending lectures.
- Gain personal perspectives by reading diverse primary sources such as historical speeches, personal accounts of events, articles, essays, and other texts of a similar nature.
- Avoid the pitfalls of accounts filtered with point-of-view, interpretation, and bias. Learn to recognize these aspects while reading multiple texts, biographies, primary and secondary sources.
- Avoid the pitfalls of personal point-of-view, interpretation, and bias by setting aside pre-conceived notions.
- Read the traditional timeline approach texts to obtain the understanding of the date-sequenced linkage among the causes of events, the events themselves, and the outcomes of events.
- Read the thematic approach texts to gain understanding of broad cultural and societal changes and development.
- Reinforce your understanding by writing about what you have learned. This forces reflection and hopefully better objectivity.

If you wish to study history on its own merits, don't be partisan or bipartisan. Be non-partisan.

Notes

1. Alan Brinkley, *American History - Connecting with the Past* (New York: McGraw-Hill, 2012), 8- 9.

Bibliography

Brinkley, Alan *American History - Connecting with the Past*, New York: McGraw-Hill, 2012.

Author's comment -
This is my third effort to write about this subject. If this is a subject of special interest to the reader, additional perspective is available from the online article titled *An American Historiography* on the blog - *Americans With a Lick of Sense* at:
http://awlos.wordpress.com/2013/10/05/an-american-historiography/

The Significance of Historiography

Originally written in 2014

The study of history study is called historiography. More simply stated, it is the study of historians and their writings. It is a review of various histories that have been written on a subject. It is also a critical examination of philosophies, theories, and methods used by historians in the past.

History, as we are defining it, began when mankind became literate. His written records became the basis for recorded history. Prior to that, man's life on earth is the subject of anthropology and archaeology. Throughout recorded time, historians from all ages have made direct observations of their current history, listened to oral accounts, or examined written documents left by writers from their past as evidence to write their histories. There have been several "schools" of history based on philosophies governing the histories. Examples of these would be the Empiricist, Progressive, Marxist, Consensus, Annales, New Left, and Post-structuralist schools.

Over the past three centuries history philosophy has taken three directions: cyclical, providential, and progressive. The cyclical approach, originating from ancient Eastern cultures, proposes that history revolves in circles and repeats endlessly. The providential approach, proposed by St. Augustine, follows a linear process led by divine providence, ultimately leading to an end of time and history. The progressive approach is also linear and suggests that natural metaphysical forces drive history without consideration to an end. Western civilization history has emphasized the thinking of a linear past.

History is subjective and arguably not a hard science. In an effort to find some "truth", empirical methods have been used to examine evidence and, through reason and logic, come to some conclusions. To complicate matters, the subjects of philosophy and sociology are often intertwined with history study. There are religious, political, economic, and military histories.

Philosophers and poets from antiquity, like Clio and Homer, are not considered authentic historians since their histories were mythopoetic narrative stories not based on evidence. The earliest Greek historians include Herodotus and Thucydides. As the first genuine historians, these writers used eyewitness accounts and other evidence as a basis for their histories. Early Roman historians include Polybius and Tacitus.

Following the ancient Greek and Roman era, the next group of historians in Western civilization included the early Christian writers who focused on the life and teachings of Jesus Christ and his followers. These were followed by later medieval religious historians like Eusebius, Augustine, and Bede. Bede has been considered one of the most learned men of the early Middle-Ages. Much of the Middle-Ages followed the tradition of religious history. It included the rise of the papacy and monarchies as well as religious, political and military conflict.

The Renaissance brought the scientific revolution and secular enlightenment thinking into history writing. Much of the written history during the Enlightenment was flawed in that it did not comprehend historical behavior on its own terms; a lack of context in the past. Arrogantly blinded by the beliefs of their time, scholars viewed their own values and aspirations as absolute and the best humankind could achieve. Consequently, they regarded disagreement in other times as false or distorted.

Voltaire was a noted philosopher from this period. However, in some academic circles, he was considered a dishonest historian. He blatantly and overtly broke the cardinal rule of objectivity. He was so sublimely smitten with the enlightenment thinking of his time that he impressed it on the earlier history he wrote about and refused to report it in its own context. His contemporary, Vico asserted that fellow scholars failed at the primary task of historians - to illuminate the past rather than to condemn it. He believed that contemporary scholars failed at their obligation and lacked the intellectual integrity to honestly observe the mindset of the people in previous times in order to account for their actions. It is interesting and surprising to me to learn that Enlightenment giants, like Voltaire, were so arrogant and narrow-minded. Ignorance so often follows arrogance. The Greeks understood hubris as the self-destructive pride of mortals. Most historians believe that different people of different times have viewed the world differently. They caution that the pursuit of grandiose purposes can often run amuck.

Years ago, Rush Limbaugh, upset with progressive "relativistic" history, said that history is what happened. Post-modern academic historians were aghast at the simplicity of his definition. His statement was accurate but incomplete. Traditional empiricist school American history and much of Western civilization history writing, well into the 20th century, was viewed as a sequence of events controlled by the powerful, elite game changers. Thus, history for the most part was written about influential and educated white rich men. These figures were thought to be the most important subjects since it was believed they alone exerted influence on historical outcome. Monarchs, aristocrats, nobles, patricians, and the intelligentsia were the figures depicted in the mainstream of historical accounts.

Without affixing any moral attributes to this, it is actually a sensible approach since these figures were indeed the game changers. There have been numerous notable exceptions where groups of non-elites have made great impact on history. These would include the masses revolting in the French Revolution, the settlers moving into the American west and their impact on Native peoples, and the multifaceted youth protests in the 1960's. These were certainly game changers too. None of this was overlooked by the traditional empiricist historians.

It was later in the 20th century that historians came to realize that direct consideration had not been given to non-elite, non-white, non-males. Doing so would provide a better understanding of cultural and societal changes. This introduced a thematic approach to history study leading to the specialty studies of race, ethnicity, and gender that are popular today. Modern historians and philosophers, such as Marx, had also become concerned with the underclass - masses of the common man - as subjects for social, economic, and political consideration.

David McCullough is a well-respected modern day American historian and author. He has discussed his views of history on numerous TV interviews with Charlie Rose of PBS. McCullough believes that writing is hard work but that the excitement of history is to research and learn about a historical figure and the events surrounding his or her life. As a footnote here, I strongly prefer the term "historical figure" to "historical character" or worse, in modern political parlance, "historical actor" since these persons are neither fictional nor participating in a play or movie. In any case, McCullough is a traditional historian and biographer. He feels that, in his way, he has gotten inside the subject's skin and he comes to "know" them. When he writes about them, he enjoys sharing his well-researched and profound knowledge with his readers by telling them what he has learned. While I greatly lack his talent and ability, this is exactly how I feel about history study and writing. The most enjoyable writing for an author and a reader is written with the intimate touch of humanity.

Modern 20th and 21st century American historians, by general consensus, have ranked our presidents as Abraham Lincoln #1, Franklin D. Roosevelt #2, and George Washington #3. Without equivocation, David McCullough disagrees and ranks George Washington as our best President. He stated very simply that without George Washington, there would be no United States of America. He makes a strong point. In fairness, he may not be separating Washington's military career from his political career. All the same, his lifetime of dedicated public service and sacrifice is less appreciated by today's progressive relativistic writers than it was in the past. American historians first deified him; then crucified him. Possibly now his life can be presented in realistic balance.

In the final analysis, history is about what happened - all of what happened to everyone and by everyone over the span of mankind's time on Earth. However, without historians to write it, there is no history to know. But before it can be written, a test of reason must take place. Historiography - the history of history writing - still holds this idea in high esteem.

The difficulties come from the vast amount of conflicting information available and the paradoxical lack of information, the accuracy and reliability of the information, and the intentional or unintentional bias of the writers based on their value system and the dominant value system of their time and contemporaries. Despite these challenges, through recorded time, there have been thousands of historians willing to dedicate their efforts to bring history to us.

Bibliography

Gilderhus, T. *History and Historians - A Historiographical Introduction*, Upper Saddle River, New Jersey: Pearson Prentice Hall, 2010

Hoefferle, Caroline *The Essential Historiography Reader*, Upper Saddle River, New Jersey: Pearson Prentice Hall, 2011

Author's comment -
The texts listed above as Bibliography were used as reference information for this article.

This article may be viewed online on the blog - *Americans With a Lick of Sense*:

http://awlos.wordpress.com/2014/07/30/the-significance-of-historiography/

Additional perspective on this subject is also available from the articles titled: *An American Historiography-* http://awlos.wordpress.com/2013/10/05/an-american-historiography/ and *What is History?* and *What is History? - revisited* from the book, *Collected Essays on Americanism.*

_____

Words from the Founding Fathers

Originally written in 2010

Ref: "John Adams", David McCullough

Both Jefferson and Adams had spent many years in France as diplomats working with Franklin before and after the conclusion of the war. Years later Jefferson was very enthusiastic about the French Revolution which followed shortly after our own and the founding of our democracy.

But Adams had reservations and concerns about the devastation occurring in France. He could not accept the idea of enshrining reason as a religion, as desired by the philosophies. He said "I know not what to make of a republic of thirty million atheists." From experience he knew the kinds of men such upheavals could give rise to, Adams told another correspondent. In revolutions, he warned, "the most fiery spirits and flighty geniuses frequently obtained more influence than men of sense and judgment; and the weakest man may carry foolish measures in opposition to wise ones proposed by the ablest." France was "in great danger." Ahead of anyone in the government, and more clearly than any, Adams foresaw the French Revolution leading to chaos, horror, and ultimate tyranny.

Jefferson wrote in The Gazette of the United States responding to a welcome he had received by his Virginia neighbors. He declared his faith in reason and democracy. He wrote:

"It rests now with ourselves to enjoy the peace and concord the blessing of self-government so long denied to mankind: to show by example the sufficiency of human reason for the care of human affairs and that the will of the majority, the natural law of every society, is the only sure guardian of the rights of man. Perhaps even this may sometimes err, but its errors are honest, solitary and short-lived. Let us then, my dear friends, forever bow down to the general reason of society."

But to Adams the "sufficiency" of reason alone for the care of human affairs was by no means clear, and it was exactly the will of the majority, particularly as being exercised in France, that so gravely concerned him.

After Washington and Adams were re-elected for their second term as President and Vice President, Abigail saw it as proof not only of the wisdom of the people, but their faith in the administration. The "newspaper warfare" had only strengthened support for the government, she felt certain. "There may be, however," Adams responded, "more employment for the press in favor of the government than there has been, or the sour, angry, peevish, fretful, lying paragraphs which assail it on every side will make an impression on many weak and ignorant people."

Like Washington, Adams could not bring himself to say anything publicly. But to a correspondent in England, he warned, "Mankind will in time discover that unbridled majorities are as tyrannical and cruel as unlimited despots," and he lamented that so much more blood would have to flow before the lesson was learned.

Washington had warned that parties (political partisanship) would cause great harm to the development of our country. But by 1798, political party wrangling had already taken hold in our government. Jefferson was a Republican who believed in small government, States rights, and individual liberty and freedom. He was romantically disposed to the French Revolution and all things French.

Hamilton was a High Federalist who favored the creation of a standing army and imperialist intervention into Florida and

Louisiana held by the Spanish who were allies with the French. He was a very ambitious and devious political operator.

Adams was a Federalist who favored a larger federal government involvement in world affairs and the creation of a Navy for national defense ("a wall of wood") but above all fought to obtain lasting peace with France and England. He also foresaw the anarchy that would follow the French Revolution, its horrors, and resultant despotism. Further, Adams was always chastened by Washington's warnings and worried about the problems of governing through political parties.

In early 1805, after four years at Quincy (Adams post-Presidency retirement in Massachusetts), during which he had made little effort to contact others, Adams decided to send a letter of greetings to his old friend Benjamin Rush.

"Dear Sir," Adams began on February 6, "It seemed to me that you and I ought not to die without saying goodbye, or bidding each other adieu. Pray how do you do? How does that excellent lady, Mrs. R?

Is the present state of the national republic enough? Is virtue the principle of our government? Is honor? Or is ambition and avarice, adulation, baseness, covetousness, the thirst for riches, indifference concerning the means of rising and enriching, the contempt of principle, the spirit of party and of faction the motive and principle that governs?

Footnotes:

1) Note the founders' concerns above about the rule of the majority. Washington warned that the rule of the majority could potentially prove to be as oppressive as the rule of one (King). Since the founders viewed the form of government they were creating as a Republic, not a

Democracy, some of them were worried about too much democracy.

2) In my estimation, Jefferson was strong on freedom (liberty) and democracy and did not seem to make much distinction between the two terms. They are different. Today, many of us use the terms interchangeably without really thinking about it.

George Washington Fairly Judged

Originally written in 2014

Introduction

In our early history, George Washington was revered by the American people and early American historians. He was thought of as the "father of our country". For a number of reasons in historical context, he was essentially deified. Eventually some of the myths about him, like the story of chopping down the cherry tree, were dispelled.

Later, modern historians, obsessed with racism and social history, crucified his character, and that of other founding fathers, as a necessary part of their mission. Most of the criticism toward Washington was based on his supposed hypocrisy as a Virginia plantation owner and a slaveholder. While he was undoubtedly a slaveholder, he was not hypocritical about it as the "positive good" southern leadership would be a century later.

Today we need to take another assessment of George Washington, make a fair judgment of his life, and present him in an honest way as a legacy for future American generations.

Evidence

At the end of the Civil War in 1865, the Italian artist Constantino Brumidi painted the fresco inside the dome of the U.S. Capital building. It is called "The Apotheosis of Washington" and is visible from the rotunda floor through the oculus. The magnificent scene is complex and glorifies Washington, portraying him as ascendant and sitting in the heavens alongside figures of classical mythology. Apotheosis refers to ascending and becoming a God.

Later, near the end of the 19th century, Washington would be depicted in much this same way by romantic nationalist historians like George Bancroft and Jackson Frederick Turner. Gradually the mythology was dispelled, became dissipated, and was replaced with merely a warm, affectionate and positive portrayal. This trend continued well into the 20th century.

This account is from a history text in 1968 and might have been one of the last to portray him in a flattering and positive light. In *History of a Free People*, George Washington's Presidency is characterized as follows:

Washington accepted the presidency unwillingly. On the day he set off for his inauguration, he confided in his diary: "At about 10 o'clock I bade adieu Mount Vernon, to private life, and to domestic felicity, and with a mind oppressed with more anxious and painful sensations than I care to express, set out for New York."

Washington's practical training had been in agriculture and military service. Because of his lack of experience in government and limited knowledge of political science and history, he felt himself unfitted to be chief magistrate.

Although Washington doubted his own capacities, his countrymen regarded him with admiration bordering on awe. No sooner had he won his first victories at Trenton and Princeton than a Philadelphia newspaper wrote of him: "If there are any spots in his character, they are like the spots on the sun, only discernible through a telescope. Had he lived in the days of idolatry he would have been worshiped as a god." This hero worship continued, and it had its uses for the new government. As a visible symbol of the unity and power of the new government, Washington provided a focus for loyalty to the new nation. It is not far-fetched to say that he filled a psychological void that had been left when the concept of George III was suddenly altered from that of the beloved father of his people to that of the detested tyrant.

As president, he was far more than a symbolic figurehead. He knew the United States as well as any man alive, having traveled to every state except Georgia and having met or exchanged letters with most of the prominent men of the country. From the time he took over the army in 1775, he had worked, as he said, to "discourage all local attachments" and to substitute "the greater name of American." Washington's mind moved with deliberation; he studied public questions with great care and reached decisions only after consulting men with differing points of view. After making a decision, he often turned over the job of expressing his ideas to men with abler pens than his own, such as Madison or Hamilton. But no one dictated his conclusions, and one of his greatest personal qualities was good judgment, both of men and of courses of action.

Although Washington's reputation is that of a man of action, he was surely not a political philosopher, he was devoted to the principles of the American Revolution. In the course of the Revolution, for instance, he had changed his opinion of slavery. Whereas in his early life he had accepted the institution unthinkingly, he now believed that it was a terrible evil. He saw its continuance as leading to a national disaster. "Not only," he wrote a British friend, "do I pray for it {the abolition of slavery} on the score of human dignity, but I can clearly foresee that nothing but the routing out of slavery can perpetuate the existence of our union, by consolidating it in a common bond of principle." In his will, Washington freed all the Negroes he owned and provided that they should be educated at the expense of his estate. As the excerpt from his inaugural address at the head of this chapter reveals, Washington was one of those who thought that the American experiment in trying to found a government based on popular will was of vital importance for the whole world.

At almost every town and village on the way to New York, where he was to be inaugurated, Washington was met by cheering crowds, troops of cavalry, and addresses of welcome. When he reached the capital on April 22, he was rowed across the Hudson River on a barge built especially for the occasion, manned by thirteen harbor pilots in white uniforms. Practically the whole population of New York lined the wharves and cheered as he neared the shore. On April 30, 1789, he took the oath of office and gave the first inaugural address, an event celebrated by the ringing of church bells in the firing of cannon. Public rejoicing over Washington's taking office was fully justified. He was perhaps the only indispensable man in the history of the United States. [1]

It was later, in the late 20th century and to the present that modern revisionist historians, driven by their philosophical school of social history, began to take a harsher view toward him. It became necessary to bear down on his owning of slaves as a means to tear down the beloved view of him, and the other "great men", in order to put forth their agenda. Little more would be said about Washington's character, superior leadership, sound judgment, or mutual affection with the American people.

We must remember that as our first President, everything was new and unprecedented for Washington. He governed with a balance of authority and humility. In that circumstance, he conducted himself with grace in much the same way as modern-day Nelson Mandela. As an early Federalist, he was most concerned about the danger of tyrannical government and did not want to act as, or be viewed as, a king. Washington's parting advice was both visionary and prophetic, although we did not take heed.

Conclusion

The modern thinking, oriented toward social history, is important and valuable. It helps us to think more, and deeply, about perspectives that are too easy to overlook. Understanding must be gained from learning, but must be tempered and fair-minded.

Washington's life is now presented as a byword in what appears to be a neutral manner. But it is really not. Omitting his greatness of character and love of his country and countrymen is not a neutral portrayal.

The general consensus from polls of many historians taken over the last 30-40 years is that Washington ranks as the 3rd best president after Lincoln and Franklin D. Roosevelt. Depending on the criteria used, this may be fair. Our view of George Washington, perhaps more than our view of Lincoln and FDR, reflects our traditional positive view of ourselves as American people and ourselves as a nation. Perhaps it is romantic, or simplistic, but his life is inspirational and gives us hope for greater accomplishment and perfection.

Notes

1. Henry W. Bragdon and Samuel P. McCutchen, *History of a Free People* (Toronto, Canada: The Macmillan Company Collier-Macmillan Limited, 1969), 156-158

Bibliography

Bragdon, Henry W. and Samuel P. McCutchen, *History of a Free People*, Toronto, Canada: The Macmillan Company Collier-Macmillan Limited, 1969.

Author's comment -

The text listed above as Bibliography was used as explicitly quoted and reference information for this article.

Additional perspective on this subject is also available from the articles titled:

The Significance of Historiography -
http://awlos.wordpress.com/2014/07/16/the-significance-of-historiography/

An American Historiography -
http://awlos.wordpress.com/2013/10/05/an-american-historiography/ and *What is History* and *What is History - revisited* from the book, *Collected Essays on*

Two Views of America

Originally written in 2013

Embarking on an interesting comparative educational experiment in the study of American history, I am concurrently taking essentially the same history course from two colleges - college A and college B. My goals are to dramatically increase my knowledge of American history while learning to become a more effective, and hopefully more relevant, writer.

College A is a small, mid-western, private, non-profit, coeducational institution founded in 1851 as a women's college.

The course duration is 8 weeks and provides 3-credit hours toward a BA degree. There are in-class lectures and videos requiring attendance, in-class discussion, required textbook and primary source text readings, written response to discussion questions, required student papers, and mid-term and final examinations.

The course covers the period from the earliest known settlement of the North and South American continents by native peoples at about 11,000 B.C. to the post-Civil War reconstruction in 1877.

The course textbook is a massive volume from which a portion (approximately the first half) is used for the course. There is a supplemental text of 79 primary source documents containing letters, essays, diary accounts, speeches, etc.

College B is a small, mid-western, private, independent, coeducational, liberal arts institution founded in 1844 with a mission of academic excellence and institutional independence. The college does not accept federal or state taxpayer subsidies for any of its operations.

163

The course duration is 10 weeks and is online and not for credit. There are online video lectures by the college's various professors, readings of lecture summaries, primary source readings, online discussions, and chapter quizzes; but no examinations or student papers required.

The course covers the period from the earliest English settlements of the North American Atlantic coast to the Ronald Reagan Presidential administration.

There is no course textbook. There is a primary source text that contains 113 letters, speeches, essays, etc.

Both colleges have a viewpoint. College A, by its selection and presentation of information, emphasis and content conveys its ideology. College B declares its ideology at the outset and uses its selection and presentation of information to fulfill its educational goals.

While I believe that both colleges present truthful evidence, the key to understanding each college's educational motivations is in the specific content of their respective primary source texts.

College A conveys its view of America in the writings of its chosen textbook and in its primary source text selection. Through its selections, it leaves the student with a clear-eyed, honest and accurate view of our country without conveying much of its greatness or uniqueness. Its truthful, forthright and comprehensive passages vividly and convincingly illustrate what bastards the white European settlers were. While all historical events are economically driven, one is left with the honest feeling that history reflects our insufficiency in avoiding the inhumane treatment of native peoples and the institution of slavery. In doing so, our belief in the truth of America's greatness is necessarily de-emphasized. There is a minimum of textual content documenting the thinking of the founders that led to our Declaration of Independence, war for independence and our unique, constitutionally based Republic.

College B, through its primary source selections, largely overlooks the sins of the fathers. The necessary content is included, but no more. Its view proudly focuses instead on the incredible intelligence and foresight of our founders and the unique system they created. The course content centers on the brief Federalism period during the critical years of the last quarter of the 18th century. It continues with the subsequent history pertinent to demonstrate the destruction of the founding ideals. It omits nearly all of the historical development of our culture and society. Without this, we lack the insights to understand ourselves as a civilization.

Undoubtedly the emphasis on the founders' idealism, wisdom, bravery, and optimism are truly inspirational to us even today. Their thoughts and actions were a product of their own unique moment in time. Their view of America's potential, and our own of its realized greatness, do have validity.

It is true that many chapters of our American history are shameful, unforgivable and fell prey to human self-interest despite our self-view of piety and morality during its incubation. It is also true that much good has been done by our society, through its government, throughout our history subsequent to our founding that has provided restitution for our original sins, be they of circumstance or intent.

In either case, the result of our democratic experiment is now essentially complete. Much has changed, for good or for bad, since the brief generation of the Federalists. Our Republic, as originally intended, is over. There will always be a United States, but it is no longer, and never will be again, great or unique. It has evolved into a socialistic democracy that places it alongside the many societies of that kind in Europe. We are no longer a unique example to the world. We are not the "city upon the hill" we once wanted to be and thought that we were.

Any proof of this assertion cannot be found in current events or in the current leadership of Congress or in the current makeup of the Supreme Court or in the current administration within the executive branch. Nor can it be found in the previous administration or the six administrations before that. If any proof can be found, it lies in the macroscopic view of the sweep of our American history throughout the 17th, 18th, 19th and 20th centuries as viewed from our 21st century vantage point. If our original idea has failed, if it was valid or not, where we went wrong and how we went wrong are subject to the views of the observer. For those that wished for this outcome, there is reason to take solace. For those that did not, there is justification for honest feelings of sadness and loss.

During our history we have had many emergent and diverse visions of who we should be and who we are as Americans. Our early views of Federalism yielded to ideas of increased democracy. Our abiding greatness is, and always has been, in our people.

Footnote:
In writing this article, I have made my best effort at honesty and academic integrity. It offers no decisive conclusion. The reader can draw his own.

American Exceptionalism

Originally written in 2014

The debate about American exceptionalism has come to the fore again in our modern time, likely due to our deeply troubling economic and geopolitical problems. The aftermath of 9/11 has changed us forever as we have strived to confront the threat of global Islam, deal with the self-imposed damage to our own economy, and struggle to find a balance between liberty and security.

The idea of American exceptionalism is the proposition that the United States while not better than other countries, is qualitatively different and distinct. It was first postulated after our revolution and with the observation that we were the first new nation. It is a unique American ideology based on the concepts of liberty, egalitarianism, individualism, republicanism, populism, and laissez-faire. It has been viewed from different historical perspectives, starting with Alexis de Tocqueville.

Tocqueville was the first writer to describe the United States as exceptional. He visited from France, his home country, and traveled here to observe our prison systems, but became interested in our political and societal system. He wrote about us extensively in two volumes titled *Democracy in America* in 1835 and 1840. At that time, America was experiencing a market revolution, westward expansion, and Jacksonian democracy – all of which were radically transforming the fabric of American life. With the decline of the aristocratic order and the emergence of the democratic order, he observed that democracy was an equation that balanced liberty and equality and was concerned with the individual as well as the community. He postulated that the human heart has a depraved taste for equality which compels the weak to want to bring the strong down to their level. This, he speculated, reduces men to

167

preferring equality in servitude over inequality in freedom. He believed in liberty and the need for individuals to be able to act freely while respecting others' rights. Thus, centralized government excels in preventing, not doing. Inequality, he proposed, is incentive for poor to become rich. For Tocqueville, as for Hegel and Marx, civil society was a sphere of private entrepreneurship and civilian affairs regulated by civil code.

Following Tocqueville, in the 1920s, Joseph Stalin supported the idea of American exceptionalism from his view that America was independent of the Marxist laws of history due to its natural resources, industrial capacity, and absence of rigid class distinctions. American Communists began using the term.

Modern neoconservative American writers have evoked a powerful, visual image of America inspired by the biblical "City upon a Hill" idea of our greatness and its model of inspiration to aspiring democracies around the world.

The idea of American exceptionalism is closely coupled with our belief, and the belief of some others, that we are the greatest country in the world. Many modern Americans despair that we are no longer the greatest country in the world – economically, politically, or scientifically. China is emerging as an economic threat even as our economy is declining in the world marketplace. Our inability to obtain energy independence has placed us vulnerable, dependent, and unnecessarily involved in matters of the middle-east. We are perceived as weak by our allies and enemies alike. In the aftermath of the demise of the Cold War, we became the worlds' only remaining superpower. However, even with our military might, we have not been able to prevail over Islam. Even hegemonic power is insufficient to combat this threat to worldwide democracy. Others cynically believe that we never were the greatest country in the world and that our belief in exceptionalism is flawed. This essay will attempt to distinguish between the goodness of our ideas (ideals) and the realities of our history.

Larry Arnn, the current president of Hillsdale College, is a gifted lecturer who focuses on the founding of our country's government and its principles. He speaks in a manner that is pleasant and kind, often poetic, and sometimes spiritual. He makes a powerful case for the idea, if not the reality, of America. Using an idea from Lincoln's writing, in a speech he never delivered, Dr. Arnn presents imagery from the biblical passage about the apple of gold within the picture frame of silver to describe the intimate relationship between the Declaration of Independence and the U.S. Constitution. He speaks of these things as positive goods. Describing them that way, he has two meanings – the goodness of these treasures and also that they are beautiful and tangible commodities.

When Jefferson wrote: "We hold these truths to be self-evident, that all men are created equal, that they are endowed by their Creator with certain unalienable rights, that among these are life, liberty and the pursuit of happiness" and Lincoln affirmed at Gettysburg: "Four score and seven years ago our fathers brought forth, on this continent, a new nation, conceived in liberty, and dedicated to the proposition that all men are created equal", they evoked and confirmed unassailable truths about our American ideals.

The reality of America has been different than the idea of America. We have always believed that we are a nation of immigrants who came to America with honest intent and through proper means to escape war, poverty, and religious persecution. This is only part of our story. Many of us were brought here forcibly from Africa and enslaved. Others of us were already here as native peoples and were killed and displaced by whites during westward expansion. Others of us came here under the arrangement of indentured servitude and were treated shamefully – whites during very early colonial times and Chinese who came to the West Coast to work in mines and on railroads during the 19th century. Others of us were citizens of Japanese heritage who were taken from our homes, along with our families, and interred in camps during World War II. We must never forget. We must acknowledge these uncomfortable shameful truths and condemn them as the offenses to God that they are.

In our unique American ideology - based on the concepts of liberty, egalitarianism, individualism, republicanism, populism, and laissez-faire - let us discuss further two of them - egalitarianism and laissez-faire.

egalitarianism – The meaning of this term is a trend of thought that favors equality for all people. Some sources define this point of view as a quality reflecting the natural state of humanity. It maintains that all humans are equal in fundamental worth or social status. It is defined either as a political doctrine that all people should be treated as equals and have the same political, economic, social, and civil rights or as a social philosophy advocating the removal of economic inequalities among people. These are two distinctly different views.

In terms of economic egalitarianism, there are two conflicting potential meanings. There is the belief in the equality of opportunity and the view that the society ought not to discriminate against citizens or hinder opportunities for them to prosper. There is also the belief in the equality of outcome in which the government promotes equal prosperity for all of its citizens. Economists like Milton Friedman supported the egality of equal opportunity, whereas economists like John Maynard Keynes supported more equal outcomes.

Certainly our founding principles, as ideals, were based on equal opportunity. The belief was that humans are inherently unequal in their abilities, talents, intelligence, and other attributes given to them by birth. Hence, while most aspire, some will rise to success and wealth while others will not. Given equal opportunity, all will become what they are willing to and capable of becoming.

In the former group, and remaining in the economic realm, writers like Ludwig von Mises, F.A. Hayek, Alan Greenspan, and Ayn Rand have written extensively on the merit of unfettered individual achievement. Of these, I am most familiar with Ayn Rand. I have read virtually everything she has written – three significant fictional works, a few academic theses, and the writing of her protégé, Nathaniel Branden who founded the Ayn Rand Institute based on objectivism. Of these, the most insightful of her views, concerning the rebuke of egalitarianism, were her masterworks of capitalism, *Atlas Shrugged* and individualism, *The Fountainhead*.

Atlas Shrugged is her fictional story of a dystopian American society that is cynical, dark and desperate. There is no nuance and the message is clear and simplistic. The ills of society are inverted in that it is the rich and accomplished who are oppressed. Undoubtedly, she was influenced by her deep hatred for the communism and collectivism of her childhood in Bolshevik Russia and her observation of Franklin Roosevelt's response to the Great Depression. FDR, during the first 100 days of his first term, confidently passed more legislation than any other president. His goals were relief, recovery and reform. Much of his experimentation proved helpful to the country. Some did not and was later abandoned. Of these, the National Recovery Act and National Recovery Administration of 1933 sought to establish codes for fair practices to eliminate cutthroat competition. It attempted to help workers by setting minimum wages and maximum weekly hours. To do so, it tried to establish minimum prices and even management of production output. In 1935, the US Supreme Court declared the law unconstitutional and thereafter, the NRA quickly stopped its operations.

In the end, FDR's legacy is that he accomplished some of his goals while it was the onset of World War II that ended the Great

Depression. He has left us with a permanent and much more powerful federal government than the one he inherited. Even though Richard Nixon applied wage and price controls to deal with his troublesome economy, FDR's NRA program was unique in American history. Certainly Ayn Rand had this in mind when she wrote *Atlas Shrugged*.

Rand has left me two valuable thoughts. The first is to reject the premise of an opponent's argument rather than let it lead you to their conclusion. The second is my disagreement with her idealistic concept of force. She believed that the citizenry should be disarmed because force is the sole prerogative of the government and it will always act with restraint and fairness since its sovereignty comes from the citizenry.

laissez-faire – This is a theory of economics, based on free-market capitalism, that is also an ideal but not a reality. It has never existed. In the history of our American economy, there have been two impediments.

The first one is that our government has never left our commercial business enterprise to its own devices. It has always attempted to regulate American capitalism in order to improve its outcome and fairness. This has led believers of this view to the conclusion that capitalism has been corrupted by Keynesian economic theory at a time when America is in decline and threatened by the rise of Chinese economic power.

The second one is that American corporations have always colluded with government to obtain advantage over their competition. The government has been a willing partner in this corporatism or crony capitalism, and has been grateful for the arrangement of contributions given in return for favors granted. American corporations have always touted the goodness of competition, but have always acted in self-interest to destroy it.

America is an exceptional nation based on our ideas (ideals) and our frequent generosity offered to other nations, without the motivation of imperialism and sometimes, without self-interest. We were unique, relative to European society at the time of our founding, in that white individuals could rise above and out of the social class they were born to. Over time, we have made much progress so that non-whites can now do the same. Lastly, as a good teacher has taught me, our accomplishments in improving our society are proof of America's greatness – evidence that we are not perfect but perfectible, and our reality has moved closer to our ideals.

I agree with Tocqueville that democracy is a balance of liberty and equality. Both of these are positive goods that form the essence of Americanism. Jefferson and Lincoln placed them side-by-side in their declarations. But certainly liberty and equality are rival siblings. The former values our differences and individuality, while the latter stresses our commonness and fair-mindedness. If we examine our history, setting aside politics and economics, and concentrating on our society, some of us regret the losses of our liberty, while some of us are heartened by the gains in our equality. For some of us, liberty and equality are just words that merely evoke emotions of patriotism but are not examined for their significance in our exceptionalism. Our American story is not yet complete.

Newtonian Design for Democracy

Originally written in 2014

The European Enlightenment, that followed the scientific revolution, fostered many new ideas about how to conceptualize politics and government. Along with other sources of thought, this intellectual movement shaped the ideas of the founders of our country. The Enlightenment ideas crossed the Atlantic and took root in the Framers' minds. Provisions in the Declaration of Independence and U.S. Constitution are the physical manifestation of these thoughts.

Examples of these influences would include Beccaria's ideas about the rights of people accused of crimes (no cruel or unusual punishment), Locke's ideas about people's consent to have government authority over them (life, liberty and property), Montesquieu's ideas about separation of powers (checks and balances), and Voltaire's ideas about free speech and religious tolerance (the Bill of Rights). Certainly, Thomas Jefferson was influenced by these philosophers in his writing of the Declaration of Independence.

However, it was Isaac Newton's scientific concepts about equilibrium and the balance of forces that formed the overarching theme that dominated the thinking of Federalists, like John Adams and James Madison, in their design of government for the new nation – the U.S. Constitution.

It is well documented and understood that later in American history, in the early 20th century and during Woodrow Wilson's presidency, the new Darwinian concept of evolution took hold in political thinking about the role of government and the meaning of the U.S. Constitution. The traditional view was supplanted and was replaced with an evolutionary view – progressivism. With this new view, the U.S. Constitution was considered less absolute, eternal, and sacrosanct. This view was actually a contradiction in terms since the founders understood their design for government to be imperfect and provided for perfectibility through provision for change by amendment (article V.). What is not documented or understood however, is the role that Newtonian thought played in the creation of our new government, and the U.S. Constitution, at the end of the 18th century.

The intellectual inspiration for the Enlightenment came primarily from two Englishmen, Isaac Newton and John Locke, acknowledged by the philosophes as great minds. Newton was frequently singled out for praise as the "greatest and rarest genius that ever rose for the ornaments and instruction of the species".
[1]

Sir Isaac Newton's (1642 – 1727) accomplishments and contributions to both the Scientific Revolution and the Enlightenment were numerous and included:

- His chairmanship of the department of mathematics at Cambridge University
- The Principia (1684 – 1686) - His masterwork on the mathematical principles of natural philosophy
- His formulation of the three laws of motion and the theory of gravitation
- His development of the Calculus which he used for mathematical proofs of his work in planetary and terrestrial physics

Newton viewed the world in mechanistic terms. He believed in God and that religion and science were inseparable. He united Bacon's empiricism and Descartes's rationalism. His interests and pursuits were diverse and included the physics of motion, optics, and alchemy to further the understanding of chemistry and materials.

During Newton's later years, freemasonry became prevalent in England, as well as in the American colonies, as 18th century Enlightenment and the societies of the philosophes arose. It is not known with certainty whether Newton was a Freemason. However, he had many friends and acquaintances who were, usually in the Royal Society.

Secret societies also developed. The most famous was the Freemasons, established in London in 1717, France and Italy in 1726, and Prussia in 1744. It was no secret that the Freemasons were sympathetic to the ideas of the philosophes. [2]

In Bruno Gazzo's review of Alan Bauer's book *Isaac Newton's Freemasonry – The Alchemy of Science and Mysticism,* he referred to chapter 3 and wrote:

Loup Verlet writes of the conditions of the "miraculous" discovery of Newton's unpublished manuscripts. Several are put in a stack in 1696 when Verlet was leaving the directorship of the mint in London. These personal documents of Newton's had escaped from being burned just after his death. John Maynard Keynes won the manuscripts and   revealed that Newton was not only the "first physicist" but the "last magician". [3]

In his review, Gazzo states that the author, Alan Bauer, "presents a swirl of historical, sociological, and religious influences that sparked the spiritual ferment and transformation of that time. His research shows that freemasonry represented a crossroads between science and spirituality and became the vehicle for promoting spiritual and intellectual egalitarianism".[4]

René Descartes (1596 – 1650) has been called the father of rationalism. He led a movement toward a new thinking of deductive reasoning and rational thought during the European scientific revolution. The scientific revolution greatly influenced the age of Enlightenment that followed in the 18th century. The deductive method is an approach to reasoning that leads from the general to the specific. Using his deductive reasoning, the following is a circumstantial proof:

The Enlightenment was a major influence on the thinking of the 18th century American founders in their creation of our system of government. Locke and Newton were major contributors to the thinking of the Enlightenment.

The emergence of freemasonry concurrently in Europe and North America was a connective factor for the intellectual thinkers during the Enlightenment. George Washington (1732 – 1799) in Virginia, Benjamin Franklin (1706 – 1790) in Pennsylvania, Mozart (1756 – 1791) in Austria, and Voltaire (1694 – 1778) in France were early members. Freemasonry followed many of the Enlightenment ideas such as the movement toward secularism which was in opposition to the Catholic Church. This view was not atheistic but was a view of Deism. It followed the idea of the laws of nature and nature's God, and by extension man's natural rights, where God was viewed as the creator and architect of the universe. Isaac Newton, as well as the founders of American government, were in concurrence with this view. This was a departure from early colonial Puritan and Anglican belief.

The U.S. Constitution is based on English Law (Magna Carta, English Parliament, English Bill of Rights), our own historical documents (Mayflower Compact, Articles of Confederation), and our own 170-year experience with legislation (The House of Burgesses in Virginia and town councils in Massachusetts and throughout New England). Finally, it was devised by the framers after discussions and deliberations before and during the Constitutional Convention in Philadelphia in 1786. It was ratified and became the law of the land in 1788.

The founders, having won independence from England, looked to several sources for inspiration and guidance in the design of their new government. While they drew on the experiences detailed above and the ancient classics, perhaps the greatest inspiration was the movement of European Enlightenment. They were most concerned with designing a government system that would prohibit tyranny to the greatest degree possible. To accomplish this they devised a system based on the separation of power and checks and balances. There is a high degree of likelihood that Newton's physics of motion and gravity, with its balance of forces and equilibrium, influenced their thinking.

There is a definitive reference to Newtonian thought dominating the design of the U.S. Constitution, but it is a retrospective from the 20th century. It is Woodrow Wilson's 1913 paper entitled: *What is Progress?*. The paper was a campaign speech he delivered in 1912 as part of a collection of speeches called the New Freedom. In that speech, he proposed the view that the Constitution was a cumbersome instrument unfit for the government of a large and vibrant nation. Wilson said in his speech:

I had been casting around in my mind for something by which to draw several parts of my political thought together when it was my good fortune to entertain a very interesting Scotsman who had been devoting himself to the philosophical thought of the seventeenth century. His talk was so engaging that it was delightful to hear him speak of anything, and presently there came out of the unexpected region of his thought the thing I had been waiting for. He called my attention to the fact that in every generation all sorts of speculation and thinking tend to fall under the formula of the dominant thought of the age. For example, after the Newtonian Theory of the universe had been developed, almost all thinking tended to express itself in the analogies of the Newtonian Theory, and since the Darwinian Theory has reigned amongst us, everybody is likely to express whatever he wishes to expound in terms of development and accommodation to environment.

179

Now, it came to me, as this interesting man talked, that the Constitution of the United States had been made under the dominion of the Newtonian Theory. You have only to read the papers of The Federalist to see that fact written on every page. They speak of the "checks and balances" of the Constitution, and used to express their idea the simile of the organization of the universe, and particularly of the solar system, – how by the attraction of gravitation the various parts are held in their orbits; and then they proceed to represent Congress, the Judiciary, and the President as a sort of imitation of the solar system. [5]

Regarding Wilson's smug rebuke of the Newtonian influence, and following his insight about the power of the dominant thought of an age, perhaps some future 21st century political candidate will look back upon the influence of Darwinian Theory during Wilson's time. With the dominant thought of Stephen Hawking's Quantum Mechanics Theory prevalent at that time, he will muse about Professor Wilson's Darwinian notion, based on mutating cells, squishy organs, and feathered reptiles becoming furry mammals, as a simile and justification for an "organic", "evolutionary" government with a "living" Constitution. Hopefully, at that time the Constitution will no longer be regarded as an impediment to executive authority, but will again be valued for its well-crafted benefits and protections to American citizens.

Other than Wilson's 20th century retrospective, no conclusive evidence was found to prove the hypothesis that Isaac Newton was responsible for the design of our governmental system. Nor was any specific linkage found that James Madison was directly influenced by Isaac Newton when Madison wrote the Virginia Plan for the U.S. Constitution. However, there is an abundance of circumstantial evidence connecting the Enlightenment views of the philosophes and the awareness and concurrence that the founding fathers held for the views.

Using René Descartes approach to deductive reason, it is most logical that Newton's science of balanced forces and equilibrium equates closely with Madison's views of separation of powers and checks and balances in our government's design. An alternative thesis, and the subject for another research paper, would be that Professor Wilson's notion was entirely wrong and that it was Montesquieu's thought that was the key to Madison's inspiration.

Notes

1. Jackson J. Spielvogel, Western Civilization, Eighth Edition (Boston: Wadsworth-Cengage Learning, 2012), 516

2. Ibid., 526

3. Alan Bauer, *Isaac Newton's Freemasonry – The Alchemy of Science and Mysticism* (city of publication unknown: Inner Traditions, 2007), page number unknown - excerpt from Chapter 3 as found from the link:
http://www.freemasons-freemasonry.com/book_bauer.html

4. Reference the review of *Isaac Newton's Freemasonry – The Alchemy of Science and Mysticism* by Bruno Gazzo (editor, PS Review of Freemasonry) as found from the link:
http://www.freemasons-freemasonry.com/book_bauer.html

5. Woodrow Wilson, *What is Progress?* in *The New Freedom* (New York: Doubleday, Page, and Company, 1913), 33 – 54.

Bibliography

Spielvogel, Jackson J., *Western Civilization, Eighth Edition,* Boston: Wadswoth-Cengage Learning, 2012.

Bauer, Alan, *Isaac Newton's Freemasonry – The Alchemy of Science and Mysticism,* city of publication unknown: Inner Traditions, 2007.

Reference the review of this book from an excerpt of Chapter 3 by Bruno Gazzo (editor, PS Review of Freemasonry) as found from the link:
http://www.freemasons-freemasonry.com/book_bauer.html

PBS - Nova, *Newton's Dark Secrets*, viewed March 25, 2014
http://www.pbs.org/wgbh/nova/physics/newton-dark-secrets.html

Wilson, Woodrow, *What is Progress?* in *The New Freedom*, New York: Doubleday, Page, and Company, 1913.

Author's comments-

The 8th edition of *Western Civilization* by Jackson J. Spielvogel, as used in the Columbia College HIST 102 Western Civilization course, has been referred to as secondary source context for this research paper. Additionally, I have considered the instructor's lecture notes, the video *Newton's Dark Secrets* viewed in class, and other sources for relevant ideas.

In the instances where the research paper's detailed language is not cited, citation is not required since the content uses common historical knowledge, has been published numerously, and is in the public domain.

John and Abigail Adams: A Lifetime Partnership

Originally written in 2013

The relationship between John and Abigail Adams was one of the critical keys to John Adams' success. Their letters, as historically documented, provide us insight into their extraordinary relationship. Undoubtedly, they kept in constant communication when they were apart. According to the Massachusetts Historical Society, "John Adams (1735-1826) and Abigail Smith Adams (1744-1818) exchanged over 1,100 letters." [1]

In 18th century colonial America, the relationship between a husband and wife was typically characterized as one where the husband was the master and the wife followed and in the case of a prominent figure, stayed out of the limelight. John and Abigail Adam's marriage did not fit this paradigm and theirs was one of the great American love stories. Their letters best characterized their view that they were dearest friends. McCullough exemplified this when he wrote:

And to no one was he more devoted than his wife, Abigail. She was his "Dearest Friend," as he addressed her in letters - his "best, dearest, worthiest, wisest friend in the world" - while to her he was "the tenderest of husbands," her "good man." [2]

Abigail was John's muse and confidant. Recognizing his brilliance, she encouraged and motivated him. Referring to John's long absences from Braintree, MA, McCullough wrote:

She began signing herself "Portia," after the long-suffering, virtuous wife of the Roman statesman Brutus. If her "dearest friend" was to play the part of a Roman hero, so would she. [3]

They were equal partners. She understood her role as his guide to fulfill his destiny as a key leader in the movement for

183

independence from British domination and the establishment of the American government.

John, in his own right, was both brilliant and full of ambition; occasionally tempered with self-doubt. In 1760, after graduating from Harvard, and while apprenticing for law practice in Braintree, he kept in touch with his friends and colleagues. McCullough wrote about one of his friend's assessment of Adams:

Jonathan Sewell had already concluded that Adams was destined for greatness, telling him, only partly in jest, that "in future ages, when New England shall have risen to its intended grandeur, it shall be as carefully recorded among the registers of the literati that Adams flourished in the second century after the exode of the first settlers from Great Britain, as it is now that Cicero was born in the six-hundred-and-forty-seventh year after the building of Rome." [4]

Abigail's importance in John's life and career cannot be overstated. McCullough summarized this when he wrote:

His marriage to Abigail Smith was the most important decision of John Adams' life, as would become apparent with time. She was in all respects his equal and the part she was to play would be greater than he could possibly have imagined, for all his love for her and what appreciation he had for her beneficial, steadying influence. [5]

Abigail advised John often and he listened, as in these passages where she urged him to declare independence:

She followed at length, this time with thoughts on his concerns, writing that "a people may let a King fall, yet still remain a people, but if a King let his people slip from him, he is no longer a King. And as this is most certainly our case, why not proclaim to the world in decisive terms our own importance?"

"I think you shine as a stateswoman," he responded exuberantly, and in another letter wrote:

Your sentiments of the duties we owe to our country are such as become the best of women and the best of men. Among all the disappointments and perplexities which have fallen my share in life, nothing has contributed so much to support my mind as the choice blessing of a wife....

I want to take a walk with you in the garden--to go over to the common, the plain, the meadow. [6]

Note: Abigail's reference to a King is again cited below as part of her letter to John of May 7, 1776.

Abigail and John each bravely bore their share of the partnership and played their separate parts through the trying times leading up to the signing of the Declaration of Independence. One can readily consider them as two heroic figures from those times.

Of the 767 letters from John to Abigail and the 430 from Abigail to John as electronically archived by the Massachusetts Historical Society, perhaps Abigail's letters to John during the Continental Congress (1774-1776) are most illustrative of her continued devotion to John's efforts in their cause. Abigail's letters from Braintree of May 7th and 9th, 1776 are cited below in full and depict her efforts to manage the home front while inspiring John at the Congress in Philadelphia to not forget the rights of women in his considerations. The following reflect her punctuation, spelling and writing as befitting her time in history:

May 7

How many are the solitary hours I spend, ruminating upon the past, and anticipating the future, whilst you overwhelmd with the cares of State, have but few moments you can devote to any individual. All domestick pleasures and injoyments are absorbed in the great and important duty you owe your Country "for our Country is as it were a secondary God, and the First and greatest parent. It is to be preferred to Parents, Wives, Children, Friends and all things the Gods only excepted. For if our Country perishes it is as imposible to save an Individual, as to preserve one of the fingers of a Mortified Hand." Thus do I supress every wish, and silence every Murmer, acquiesceing in a painfull Seperation from the companion of my youth, and the Friend of my Heart.

I believe tis near ten days since I wrote you a line. I have not felt in a humour to entertain you. If I had taken up my pen perhaps some unbecomeing invective might have fallen from it; the Eyes of our Rulers have been closed and a Lethargy has seazd almost every Member. I fear a fatal Security has taken possession of them. Whilst the Building is on flame they tremble at the expence of water to quench it, in short two months has elapsed since the evacuation of Boston, and very little has been done in that time to secure it, or the Harbour from future invasion till the people are all in a flame; and no one among us that I have heard of even mentions expence, they think universally that there has been an amaizing neglect some where. Many have turnd out as volunteers to work upon Nodles Island, and many more would go upon Nantaskit if it was once set on foot. "Tis a Maxim of state That power and Liberty are like Heat and moisture; where they are well mixt every thing prospers, where they are single, they are destructive."

A Goverment of more Stability is much wanted in this colony, and they are ready to receive ~~them~~ it from the Hands of the Congress, and since I have begun with Maxims of State I will add an other viz. that a people may let a king fall, yet still remain a people, but if a king let his people slip from him, he is no longer a king. And as this is most certainly our case, why not proclaim to the World in decisive terms your own importance?

186

Shall we not be dispiced by foreign powers for hesitateing so long at a word?

I can not say that I think you very generous to the Ladies, for whilst you are proclaiming peace and good will to Men, Emancipating all Nations, you insist upon retaining an absolute power over Wives. But you must remember that Arbitary power is like most other things which are very hard, very liable to be broken -- and notwithstanding all your wise Laws and Maxims we have it in our power not only to free ourselves but to subdue our Masters, and without voilence throw both your natural and legal authority at our feet

"Charm by accepting, by submitting sway

Yet have our Humour most when we obey."

I thank you for several Letters which I have received since I wrote Last. They alleviate a   tedious absence, and I long earnestly for a Saturday Evening, and experience a similar pleasure to that which I used to ~~experience~~ find in the return of my Friend upon that day after a weeks absence. The Idea of a year dissolves all my Phylosophy.

Our Little ones whom you so often recommend to my care and instruction shall not be deficient in virtue or probity if the precepts of a Mother have their desired Effect, but they would be doubly inforced could they be indulged with the example of a Father constantly before them; I often point them to their Sire"engaged in a corrupted State Wrestling with vice and faction."

May 9

187

I designd to have finished the sheet, but an opportunity offering I close only just inform you that May the 7 our privateers took two prises in the Bay in fair sight of the Man of war, one a Brig from Irland the other from fyall loaded with wine Brandy and the other Beaf &c. The wind was East and a flood tide, so that the tenders could not get out tho they tried several times, the Light house fired Signal guns, but all would not do, they took them in triumph and carried them into Lyn.

Johnny and Charls have the Mumps, a bad disorder, but they are not very bad. Pray be kind enough to remember me at all times and write as often as you possibly can to your Portia [7]

Note that many of the prominent figures of those harrowing times in American history used pseudo names. They signed their papers and correspondence choosing Roman and Greek names. Hence James Madison was Publius, John Adams was Brutus and Abigail was Portia. This practice was likely for two reasons. To the degree that they could, they tried to disguise their identities since their very lives were in jeopardy. Also, as classicists who had studied Roman and Greek history, often in the original languages, they considered the names heroic and appealing.

In February of 1778, accompanied by young John Quincy, John sailed to France on his first diplomatic mission. During their long separation, he wrote to Abigail about his frightening passage across the North Atlantic, his observations of culture and society at the court of King Louis XVI, and the French countryside. This was the first of his four ocean crossings. Abigail accompanied him in 1784 on his mission to England.

In 1789, Abigail remained at home, and they were apart again, as John moved to New York to begin his service as the first Vice President. He was to serve two terms under George Washington.

Adams succeeded Washington as the nation's second President and served one term with his rival, Thomas Jefferson, as Vice President. He moved into the President's House in Philadelphia vacated by Washington. John later moved to the new Federal City by the Potomac as the first occupant of the new President's House. It was still under construction for a time until Abigail joined him on November 16, 1800. The Adams' held the first New Year's Day reception there in 1801.

After Jefferson defeated Adams in the Presidential election and took office March 4, 1801, the Adams' retired to their farm in Quincy to live out their retirement. Throughout their long adult lifetime together, John was away much of the time in Philadelphia, New York, France, England, Holland and finally the new Capital city. While they were apart, scarcely a day went by that they did not write to provide each other advice, consolation and loving concern.

The events of their time in history are well documented from many reliable sources. Their preserved letters however, are the body of direct evidence left to us that depicts their lives, their relationship, and the context of their time in history. While the letters only document those times when they were apart, they provide sufficient threads to define the fabric of John and Abigail's story.

In conclusion, the historical evidence is clear that while John Adams will always be regarded as one of our most exceptional and gifted founders, it was his wife Abigail who enhanced his successes. She was his beacon and his compass and will forever be remembered as his "dearest friend".

Notes

1. Massachusetts Historical Society, Adams Papers Editorial Project, *Adams Family Papers: An Electronic Archive*. Accessed July 31, 2013.
http://www.masshist.org/digitaladams/aea/letter/index.html

2. David G. McCullough, *John Adams* (New York: Simon & Schuster Paperbacks, 2001), 18.

3. Ibid., 26

4. Ibid., 48

5. Ibid., 57

6. Ibid., 107

7. Abigail Adams to John Adams, 7-9 May 1776, in *Adams Family Papers: An Electronic Archive*. Massachusetts Historical Society. Accessed July 31, 2013.
http://www.masshist.org/digitaladams/

Bibliography

Massachusetts Historical Society, Adams Papers Editorial Project, *Adams Family Papers: An Electronic Archive*, accessed July 31, 2013.
http://www.masshist.org/digitaladams/aea/letter/index.html

McCullough, David G. *John Adams*, New York: Simon & Schuster Paperbacks, 2001.

Adams, Abigail to John Adams, 7-9 May 1776. In Massachusetts Historical Society, *Adams Family Papers: An Electronic Archive*, accessed July 31, 2013.
http://www.masshist.org/digitaladams/

Further note that the original manuscript is: Adams, Abigail. Letter from Abigail Adams to John Adams, 7 - 9 May 1776. 3 pages. from the Adams Family Papers, Massachusetts Historical Society. The source of transcription is: Butterfield, L.H., ed. *Adams Family Correspondence*. Vol. 1. Cambridge, Mass.: Belknap Press of Harvard University Press, 1963.

Author's comments on source selection

The 5th edition of *Reading The American Past* by Michael P. Johnson, as used in the Columbia College HIST 121 course, provides primary source documentation of a few of John and Abigail Adams' letters. These were selected from L.H. Butterfield, ed., *Adams Family Correspondence*, vols.1 and 2 (Cambridge MA: Harvard University Press, 1963), 193-202. While these provide an insightful, first hand view of history through their eyes, this author did not consider these particular letters as best illustrative of the thesis for this paper.

The Massachusetts Historical Society provides essentially all of the Adams' letters and therefore the broadest selection of primary source material from which to retrieve material in support of this thesis. The individual documents therein also attribute the source as L.H. Butterfield, *Adams Family Correspondence*.

David G. McCullough's Pulitzer prize-winning biography, *John Adams*, was selected as the secondary source for this paper due to its author's exceptional skill and abilities as an historian to detail the pertinent history in context.

Letters of John and Abigail Adams

Originally written in 2013

The letters of John and Abigail Adams are important for two reasons- their interactive accounts of their critical time in our American history and insights into their incredible relationship. Theirs was a love story for the ages.

According to the Massachusetts Historical Society, "John Adams (1735-1826) and Abigail Smith Adams (1744-1818) exchanged over 1,100 letters ..." [1] In fact there are 767 letters from John to Abigail and 430 from Abigail to John electronically archived by the Massachusetts Historical Society. Their letters, as true of all primary source documents, give us contextual, personal, first-hand accounts of history.

The relationship between John and Abigail Adams was one of the critical keys to John Adams' success. Their letters, as historically documented, provide us insight into their extraordinary relationship. Undoubtedly, they kept in constant communication when they were apart.

The letters in *Reading the American Past* [2] were written in 1776 during the critical weeks and months leading up to the signing of the Declaration of Independence, while John was attending the Second Continental Congress in Philadelphia and Abigail remained at home in Braintree, Massachusetts. The selections illustrate "the determination tempered by anxiety that accompanied the fateful passage of the Declaration of Independence." [3] What follows are brief excerpts of the 12 selections in the text for the period leading up to July 4, 1776.

John Adams to Abigail Adams (from Philadelphia), February 18, 1776-

He wrote her that he had sent her a copy of *Common Sense*. He saw no possibility of reconciliation or prospect for peace with England. He wrote: "The events of war are uncertain: we cannot insure success, but we can deserve it." [4]

Abigail Adams to John Adams (from Braintree, Mass.), March 2 - March 10, 1776

Saturday Evening March 2-

She wrote him that every Tory (loyalist) should be deported, that she liked the sentiments of *Common Sense* and asked how it was being received in Congress. She was anxious about the cannon fire from our army while Boston was besieged by British ships. She wrote "... but hark! the house this instant shakes with the roar of cannon." [4]

Sunday Eve March 3-

She wrote him the cannon fire kept her awake last night. She wrote "... the cannon continued firing and my heart beat pace with them all night." [4]

Monday Evening-

She wrote him it was quiet today. She later wrote: "I have just returned from Penn's Hill" [4] and referred to new cannon fire: "Tis now an incessant Roar. But O the fatal ideas which are connected with the sound. How many of our dear countrymen must fall?" [4]

Tuesday Morning-

"I could no more sleep than I had been in the engagement. The rattling of the windows, the jar of the house and the continual roar of the 24 pounders .... I hear we got possession of Dorchester Hill last night. 4000 men upon it today-lost but one man. The ships are drawn round the town." [4]

Sunday Eve March 10-

"My hand and heart will tremble, at this domestic fury, and civil strife, which cumber all our parts. Tho, blood and destruction are so much in use and dreadful objects so familiar, ... I feel still more for my bleeding countrymen who are hazarding their limbs ...." [4]

John Adams to Abigail Adams (from Philadelphia), March 19, 1776-

He told her about everything that mattered to him when he wrote: "My ease, my domestic happiness, my rural pleasures, my little property, my personal liberty, my reputation, my life have little weight and ever had, in my own estimation, in comparison of the great object of my country .... " [4]

Of Thomas Paine's *Common Sense,* he wrote her: "This writer seems to have very inadequate ideas of what is proper and necessary to be done, in order to form Constitutions for single colonies, as well as a great model of union for the whole." [4]

Abigail Adams to John Adams (from Braintree, Mass.), March 31, 1776 -

"I wish you would ever write me a letter half as long as I write you, and tell me if you may where your fleet are gone?" [4] Referring to Virginia, she wrote: "I am willing to allow the colony great merit for having produced a Washington but they have been shamefully duped by a Dunmore." [4] Then she made her historically famous point: "I long to hear that you have declared an independency - and by the way in the new code of laws which I suppose it will be necessary for you to make I desire you to remember the ladies, and be more generous and favorable to them than your ancestors." [4]

John Adams to Abigail Adams (from Philadelphia), April 14, 1776-

While busy at work, he wrote: "You justly complain of my short letters, but the critical state of things and the multiplicity of avocations must plead my excuse. - ask what sort of defense Virginia can make. I believe they will make an able defense." [4]

"Depend upon it, we know better than to repeal our masculine systems. Although they are in full force, you know they are little more than theory. We dare not exert our power in full latitude. We are obliged to go fair, and softly, and in practice you know we are the subjects." [4]

John Adams to Abigail Adams (from Philadelphia), May 17, 1776-

"Great Britain has at last driven America, to the last step, a complete separation from her, a total absolute independence, not only of her parliament but of her crown, for such is the amount of the resolve of the 15th. I have reasons to believe that no colony, which shall assume a government under the people, will give it up. There is something very unnatural and odious in a government 1000 leagues off." [4]

John Adams to Abigail Adams (from Philadelphia), July 3, 1776-

"You will see in a few days a declaration setting forth the causes, which have impelled us to this mighty revolution, and the reasons which will justify it in the sight of God and man. A plan of confederation will be taken up in a few days." [4]

John Adams to Abigail Adams (from Philadelphia), July 3, 1776-

" ... The delay of this Declaration of Independence to this time, has many great advantages attending it..... But the day is past. The second day of July 1776, will be the most memorable epoca (Spanish for age), in the history of America. - .... I can see that the end is more than worth the means." [4]

Notes

1. Massachusetts Historical Society, Adams Papers Editorial Project, *Adams Family Papers: An Electronic Archive.* Accessed July 31, 2013.
http://www.masshist.org/digitaladams/aea/letter/index.html

2. Michael P. Johnson, *Reading the American Past, Selected Historical Documents* (New York: Bedford/St. Martin's, 2012), 123-130.

3. Ibid., 123

4. Ibid, 124-130 (some quotes use modern spelling for clarification)

Bibliography

Massachusetts Historical Society, Adams Papers Editorial Project, *Adams Family Papers: An Electronic Archive,* accessed July 31, 2013.
http://www.masshist.org/digitaladams/aea/letter/index.html

Johnson, Michael P. *Reading the American Past, Selected Historical Documents*, New York: Bedford/St. Martin's, 2012.

Author's comments

The 5th edition of *Reading The American Past* by Michael P. Johnson, as used in the Columbia College HIST 121 course, provides primary source documentation of a few of John and Abigail Adams' letters. These were selected from L.H. Butterfield, ed., *Adams Family Correspondence*, vols.1 and 2 (Cambridge MA: Harvard University Press, 1963), 193-202. They provide an insightful, first-hand view of history through the eyes of John and Abigail Adams at a critical moment in our American history. We were preparing to declare our independence from Great Britain and formally declare war while the fighting was already underway.

The Massachusetts Historical Society provides essentially all of the Adams' letters and therefore the broadest selection of primary source material from which to retrieve information in support of this topic. The individual documents therein also attribute the source as L.H. Butterfield, *Adams Family Correspondence*.

For additional context on this subject, David G. McCullough's Pulitzer prize winning biography, *John Adams*, is a valuable secondary source.

Another secondary source is David Jennings' article, *John and Abigail Adams: A Lifetime Partnership* available on http://awlos.wordpress.com/2013/08/16/john-and-abigail-adams-a-lifetime-partnership/

The Louisiana Purchase

Originally written in 2013

One of the major contributions of Thomas Jefferson's first term as U.S. President was the Louisiana Purchase in 1803. He was interested in expanding the United States in order to provide for growth and land expansion by pushing westward beyond the line along the Mississippi River.

Acquisition of the Louisiana Territory would double the area of land occupied by the new American country and open a vast new area for expansion. The circumstances of the purchase, however, were to become both fortunate and legally challenging. In 1803, during his first term as President, Thomas Jefferson was presented with a rare but troublesome opportunity.

The circumstances leading up to the eventuality of the Louisiana Purchase were complex and as follows: In the same year that Jefferson became President, Napoleon declared himself Emperor of France and wanted to regain the lands west of the Mississippi. He signed a secret agreement, The Treaty of San Ildefonso, with Spain in 1800. France regained title of the Mississippi Valley, including the port of New Orleans at its mouth. Napoleon hoped this would be the heart of his great French empire in America.

Napoleon was having difficulties regarding an African slave revolt in San Domingo of the West Indies, and had sent a military force there. Jefferson had appointed Robert Livingston minister to France and sent him there to work out the ratification of the Franco-American settlement of 1800. This was in support of a cooperative and friendly relationship with France regarding the slave revolt. Jefferson was unaware of Napoleon's imperial ambitions in America.

When Jefferson heard rumors of the secret transfer of Louisiana to France, he began to reconsider his position. He became more alarmed when he learned of the fall of New Orleans in 1802 from the Spanish to the French. With the Pinckney Treaty of 1795 with Spain now invalidated, he became concerned about American rights to deposit cargo in New Orleans for transfer to ocean going vessels. He learned of a disturbing new regulation where the port intendant was now forbidding the practice.

Jefferson saw a solution where he would offer to purchase New Orleans from France. He sent Robert Livingston and James Monroe as emissaries to France to negotiate for that purchase. Livingston decided to offer Napoleon a bid for the entire western portion of what was then Louisiana. Since Napoleon needed funds to conduct his war against the British and realized he lacked the resources to defend the territory, he entertained Livingston's offer. As a result, Napoleon accepted $15 million for the territory with exclusive trading rights in New Orleans and an agreement for the full rights of U.S. citizenship throughout the territory. Livingston, fearful that Napoleon might change his mind, signed the agreement immediately without Jefferson's instruction or approval on April 30, 1803.

When Jefferson learned of this, he became concerned about its legality since the Constitution made no provision for the federal government to purchase a territory. He considered recommending to Congress that an amendment be added to the Constitution He was warned that this would take too long, and Napoleon might change his mind. In the end, Jefferson moved forward under Presidential authority, and the Republican Congress promptly approved it.

The Louisiana Purchase had great significance for the United States. It became a tremendous resource for wealth, provided full control of the Mississippi, and established a precedence for future purchase of territories. Additionally and importantly, the

Republicans had moved toward a looser interpretation of the Constitution.

The impact for the native peoples would once again become tragic. Jefferson's hypocrisy surrounding this event was that he had stated publically in his meetings with native peoples that his treatment of them would be humane and brotherly. Privately, he schemed with William H. Harrison to finesse them out of more land as opportunity presented itself. As a result of the new territorial purchase, native peoples would be displaced and concentrated in areas not immediately needed for white westward expansion.

All governments act in self-interest and are economically motivated. Altruistic motives are historically rare. The continual land seizure and displacement of native peoples was immoral, reprehensible and illegal from one point of view. However, the Louisiana Purchase was beneficial for the growth of the United States, which ultimately expanded to the Pacific Ocean.

Bibliography

Brinkley, Alan *American History - Connecting with the Past*, New York: McGraw-Hill, 2012.

Johnson, Michael P. *Reading the American Past, Selected Historical Documents*, New York: Bedford/St. Martin's, 2012.

Author's comments

For this essay, I have referred to the instructor's lecture notes and the two texts used for the Columbia College HIST 121 American History to 1877 course.

The essay's detailed language does not require source note citation since it contains common historical knowledge, has been published numerously, and is in the public domain.

202

Federalism v. Democracy

Originally written in 2014

Introduction

The founding fathers of the Federalist period were motivated by their current events and were compelled to develop a system of government for the new American people. At first glance, the ideals of democracy would be conflated with the aspirations of the Federalists as among their goals. While some ideologists may disagree, scholarship demonstrates that democracy was not part of their deliberations or their results. The focus was directed elsewhere.

Evidence

Federalism refers to both the Federalist period in American history and the Federalists who were the designers of our government system. The Federalist period ranged from 1776 (Declaration of Independence) to 1800 (the election of Thomas Jefferson). This 24 year period was dominated by a single political party – the Federalists. These included Madison, Hamilton, Jay, Adams, and somewhat reluctantly Washington, who argued for a new system of government. Madison, Hamilton, and Jay wrote the Federalist papers to assert their case. Jefferson was an anti-Federalist but not the author of the anti-Federalist papers.

The Second Continental Congress in 1775 declared our independence from Britain and established a loose governmental framework as an alliance between the 13 colonies - the Articles of Confederation. The Constitutional Convention in 1787 met in Philadelphia to further define an American government. It was quickly decided to abandon the Articles of Confederation and design a new central government based on representation - a

Republic. The U.S. Constitution was crafted for that purpose. The Bill of Rights that followed enumerated specific rights of citizens.

Upon successful conclusion of the Revolutionary War with Britain, the founders were motivated to produce a government that would protect citizens from tyranny as witnessed under King George III and British Parliament. Upon consideration of man's natural rights, they devised a plan for protection of individual and property rights, proper representation in government by consent, and taxation only where agreed to and deemed necessary.

The result was a design for government called Federalism. It may be visualized in two planes. The horizontal plane would be the three co-equal branches of government – legislative, executive, judicial – with the balance of power regulated by checks and balances. This is easily understood and familiar. The vertical plane is actually the system called Federalism. This is somewhat more subtle to understand. At the top is the federal government. Below that are the many state governments. At the bottom is the citizenry. The idea is that consent of the governed (the citizenry) flows upward. The Constitution defines the role of the federal government and enumerates its powers. All powers not reserved to the federal government default to the states and local governments. Similarly, the powers not enumerated by the states and local governments default to the citizenry. Whatever is agreed upon as not forbidden by law citizens are free to do.

Argument

With federalism understood, democracy may be defined as the degree of participation in government by its citizens. Thus democracy is centered about suffrage and ability to hold public office. In the brief Federalist period, voting was limited to white male property owners. Adams and others believed that this was necessary and appropriate since this group was properly educated and stakeholders in government and its outcome.

While some believe the Constitution was a design for a small limited government, this is not true. The Articles of Confederation was designed for that purpose, provided essentially no power over the many colonies, and proved inadequate. The Constitution, envisioned by Adams and others, was a design for a powerful central government with representation by a select few.

If we may set aside the topics of slavery, women's rights, and the treatment of native peoples for now, we will be able to move forward with this narrative. If these topics must be considered immediately and concurrently, we may abandon this narrative and have that one.

It was later, beginning in Jefferson's time that consideration was given to democracy which fostered a feeling of nationalism. Jefferson's philosophy created a new political party – the Republicans. Soon after, with John Quincy Adams as the last Federalist, the Federalist Party dissolved. Their time in our history had ended.

With a view toward westward expansion, Jefferson envisioned an agrarian society of small farmers populating the North American continent. He wasn't aware of the inevitability of the rise of industrialization and capitalism.

Later, in the Jacksonian era, further consideration was given to populism, nationalism, and democracy. Jackson was widely popular and was considered a protagonist for the common man. He advocated for democracy, as we are defining it here, with more participation of the nations' citizens. With rugged individualism manifesting as entrepreneurship, industrialism and capitalism had begun taking root during his time.

Gradually suffrage was offered to a broader base of the citizenry - first to non-property owners, then to blacks, and finally to women. The vision of democracy, beyond Federalism, had become fulfilled.

Conclusion

Adams and Jefferson were lifelong rivals and held different visions. Adams envisioned a society of merchants. Jefferson envisioned a society of farmers. Neither foresaw an industrial society with capitalism at its core.

It is important to understand that the Federalist period was brief and did not define all of American history. Some consider only two eras in American history consequential – Federalism and its adversary, 20th century Progressivism and its modern heirs. This is an ideological position, not an historical one. To be sure, this overlooks most of our American history and heritage.

Antebellum Sectionalism

Originally written in 2013

Sectionalism was inherent in America since its inception. After the Revolutionary War, the founders of our nation formed a governmental system, based on compromise, to accommodate two essentially different societies. At that time, Massachusetts represented a northern urban-based society, grounded in commercial and industrial interests, that abhorred, and did not require, the practice of slavery. Virginia represented a southern rural-based society, grounded in agricultural interests, that was deeply vested in slavery. John Adams, and perhaps Virginian George Washington, epitomized the Federalists views of the northern society. Thomas Jefferson, and perhaps James Madison, epitomized the states' rights views of the southern society.

Pertinent to our historical roots in these two sectionalist views, Brodsky wrote about Benjamin Rush's February 17, 1812 letter to John Adams regarding the repair of the relationship between Adams and Jefferson:

I rejoice in the correspondence which has taken place between you and your old friend Mr. Jefferson. I consider you and him as the North and South Poles of the American Revolution. Some talked, some wrote, and some fought to promote and establish it, but you and Mr. Jefferson thought for us all. I never take a retrospect [sic] of the years 1775 and 1776 without associating your opinions and speeches and conversations with all the great political, moral, and intellectual achievements of the Congresses of those memorable years. [1]

Throughout our history, and our development, the North and South, along with the West, would move from sectionalism to nationalism and back to sectionalism again. Three of the driving issues were slavery, tariffs, and transportation development.

Slavery

Obviously slavery had always been a major sectional issue since the formation of our country. With westward development and the formation of territories and states, the many compromises drafted served to briefly pacify sectional factions, but ultimately failed to resolve this core issue. Events like the Sumner-Brooks Affair of 1856 on the floor of the Senate over the Kansas-Nebraska Act, the violent events of "Bleeding Kansas" in 1856, John Brown's militant activities in Kansas in 1856 and Harpers Ferry, Virginia in 1859, and the Taney court's Dred Scott decision in 1857, all fueled sectionalism and led to the Civil War.

Tariffs

Northern Republicans were generally in favor of high tariffs, while southern Democrats opposed them. In John Quincy Adams' Presidency, the issue of tariffs inflamed sectionalism. His 1828 "Tariff of Abominations" became a serious issue for the South. While intended to discourage importation of British textile goods to protect the northern economy, it was opposed in the South since their British customers would have difficulty paying for their exported cotton.

Later in 1841, John Tyler took office as President. He belonged to the Whig party but, as a longtime Democrat, he abandoned the Whig party. Tyler vetoed a tariff bill in 1842. When John Quincy Adams was elected President, he was a Democratic-Republican. His party eventually became the Republican party. Adams later served as a congressman in the House of Representatives and led a movement to impeach Tyler. Also, he initiated an amendment to change the two-thirds needed to override a Presidential veto to a simple majority. While both measures failed, this was an example of sectionalist party politics differing over the tariff issue.

Transportation Development

During the 1800's, the North developed a network of railroads to supplement or replace their developed system of canals. This fueled economic growth in that eastern manufacturers could effectively serve their western markets. This would become a strength for the North's military effectiveness in the Civil War.

The South was short-sighted and did not see a need for major investment in railroads and sufficed with their river systems and boats for transporting their major agricultural cash crops, like cotton from the lower south to their foreign markets. Their limited rail systems also lacked standard gages and could not easy connect the lines. This would become a limiting factor for the South's military effectiveness in the Civil War.

Our country's shift toward a view of nationalism did occur during the early 1800's before sectionalism became dominant during the later antebellum years leading to the Civil War. The political situation in the early decades of the 19th century was affected by occasions where there was a foreign threat or by other circumstance of common interest. In the aftermath of the War of 1812, and during the Presidency of James Monroe (1817 to 1829), there was an "Era of Good Feelings" when Monroe traveled the nation on a goodwill tour and was greeted with enthusiasm. Monroe had appointed a diverse cabinet which was appealing to all areas of the country. He announced the Monroe Doctrine in 1823, and the country was enthusiastic about our nation as a whole. The doctrine asserted that the Western Hemisphere was closed to further European colonization.

Nationalism prevailed until the election of John Quincy Adams in 1824 when the "Era of Good Feelings" fell to an increased number of sectional disputes. As the two party system revived, nationalism gave way to sectionalism.

For a time in the 1840s & 1850s, sentiments of nationalism rose again as Americans believed that Almighty God had "manifestly" destined the American people for a hemispheric career. This view of Manifest Destiny was fueled by land hungry Americans who eyed tracts of rich, sparsely settled lands, patriots who feared British land desires, Eastern merchants who desired Pacific ports for trade with Asia, democratic-minded people who equated expansion with spreading freedom, and nationalists who sought American greatness.

In conclusion, other than those times and circumstances that compelled us to nationalism, sectionalism necessarily prevailed and prohibited nationalism. In almost every decade of the antebellum period, the fundamental differences between the industrial North versus the agrarian South, and the Republican politics of central governance versus the Democratic politics of states' rights, compelled us to perpetuate sectionalism.

Notes

1. Alyn Brodsky, *Benjamin Rush, Patriot and Physician* (St. Martin's Press, New York, 2004), 18).

Bibliography

Brodsky, Alyn, *Benjamin Rush, Patriot and Physician,* New York: St. Martin's Press, 2004.

Brinkley, Alan *American History - Connecting with the Past*, New York: McGraw-Hill, 2012.

Johnson, Michael P. *Reading the American Past, Selected Historical Documents*, New York: Bedford/St. Martin's, 2012.

Author's comments

For this essay, I have referred to the instructor's lecture notes and the two texts used for the Columbia College HIST 121 American History to 1877 course.

The essay's detailed language does not require source note citation since it contains common historical knowledge, has been published numerously, and is in the public domain.

Jeffersonian Yeoman Freeholders

Originally written in 2013

Thomas Jefferson believed in individual rights and liberties. His political philosophy was at odds with the Federalists in that he ascribed to a small, limited central government with the sovereignty of the people at its core.

Brodsky wrote about Benjamin Rush's February 17, 1812 letter to John Adams regarding the repair of the relationship between Adams and Jefferson:

I rejoice in the correspondence which has taken place between you and your old friend Mr. Jefferson. I consider you and him as the North and South Poles of the American Revolution. Some talked, some wrote, and some fought to promote and establish it, but you and Mr. Jefferson thought for us all. I never take a retrospect [sic] of the years 1775 and 1776 without associating your opinions and speeches and conversations with all the great political, moral, and intellectual achievements of the Congresses of those memorable years. [1]

In the controversial election of 1800, Jefferson prevailed over John Adams and the Federalists. As a Republican (Democratic-Republican - don't ask), he expressed his personal view of the "common man" and his vision for an agrarian society based on small farmers and landowners.

The expression "Jeffersonian Yeoman Freeholders" captures his beliefs. It refers to dutiful working class or middle class people who are free men and own property. Some have said it is why we mow our lawns today. We take pride in our homes and properties. This may not apply to, or be as well understood by, city folk who live on concrete and take elevators too small and expensive rented apartments.

But Jefferson soon learned as President, one often has to act in conflict with ideals. Further he was hypocritical as a slave owner and in his treatment of native peoples. These two points would come together and pose challenges for Jefferson as the fortuitous opportunity for acquisition of the Louisiana territory was presented to him.

As problems developed with American access to the port of New Orleans, he sent Robert Livingston and James Monroe as emissaries to Napoleon to purchase New Orleans from France. When Livingston assessed Napoleon's position, he decided to bid for the entire o western portion of what was then Louisiana. Napoleon agreed and Livingston immediately signed the agreement, concerned that Napoleon might change his mind, and without instruction or approval from Jefferson.

When Jefferson learned of this, he was concerned that the Constitution made no provision for the federal government to purchase a territory. He decided to move forward under Presidential authority and the Republican Congress promptly approved it. Jefferson and the Republicans had moved toward a looser interpretation of the Constitution.

The acquisition of the Louisiana Territory in 1803, had roughly doubled the area of land occupied by the new American country and opened a vast new area for expansion. Now Jefferson had to deal with the native populations in the new lands.

Publically, he met with Indian peoples and offered to take their hand in friendship and brotherhood. He told them not to be fearful since the French, Spanish and British had all left. Americans would be their partners in settling and sharing this vast country together. Our government would protect them as a father would his children.

Privately, he corresponded with Governor William H. Harrison and asked him to keep their discussion private. He advised him to be friendly to the Indians and to consider two approaches toward them. As westward expansion of Americans would often place them around tribal settlements, he advised that our policy should be first to try to get them to assimilate. Failing that, we should remove them from those areas in the path of our movement and settlement. As a result, Indian peoples west of the Mississippi were displaced and relocated as they had been east of the Mississippi.

The Louisiana Territory was to become settled. With a future progression of conflict and acquisitions, America ultimately came to hold North American lands all the way to the Pacific. To a degree, looking westward, Jefferson's vision was realized. The lands across the middle and western portions of our country became settled by "freeholders" with pride in their properties and independent agrarian enterprises.

1. Alyn Brodsky, *Benjamin Rush, Patriot and Physician* (St. Martin's Press, New York, 2004), 18).

Author's comments

For this essay, I have referred to Michael P. Johnson's *Reading the American Past, Selected Historical Documents*, New York: Bedford/St. Martin's, 2012 and its article *10-1 - President Thomas Jefferson's Private and Public Indian Policy* containing two primary source letters - *Letter to Governor William H. Harrison*, February 27, 1803 and *Address to the Wolf and People of the Mandan Nation*, December 30, 1806.

I have paraphrased from this primary source and have therefore, not cited direct quotation.

Antebellum Compromises

Originally written in 2013

After the Revolutionary War, the founders of our nation formed a governmental system, based on compromise, to accommodate two essentially different societies. At that time, Massachusetts represented a northern urban-based society, grounded in commercial and industrial interests that abhorred, and did not require, the practice of slavery. Virginia represented a southern rural-based society, grounded in agricultural interests that was deeply vested in slavery. The framers of the U.S. Constitution, ratified in 1788, devised a system of government that did not advocate or explicitly permit slavery. However, the Constitution was written to temporarily accommodate slavery by deferring legislation to prohibit it, with regard to migration or importation, until 1808.

With continuing westward expansion, acquisition of new land brought new territories, which became new states. The issue of slavery required a succession of compromises in order to hold the nation together. For a time, during the first half of the 19th century, compromise was effective in accomplishing that goal. Ultimately, compromise became no longer possible, and the schism leading to the Civil War became inevitable.

Enacted under the Constitutional Convention of 1787 and with the leadership of George Washington, the Northwest Ordinance of 1787, while not a compromise, created a single territory out of the lands north of the Ohio River, the frontier at that time. It defined the requirements for sub-division and statehood. Importantly, it prohibited slavery in the territory, thereby establishing an early precedent for future expansion and development.

Enacted under James Monroe's Presidency, the **Missouri Compromise of 1820** prohibited slavery in the former Louisiana Territory north of the parallel 36, 30, while permitting it in Missouri, and prohibiting it in Maine. This was the first in a pattern of political and legislative compromises that attempted to satisfy the two aforementioned societies. It was based on the idea of admitting one free state and one slave state at a time, maintaining a balance of free and slave states. This theme was politically acceptable as a compromise solution. Enacted under Andrew Jackson's Presidency, the **Compromise Tariff of 1833** was introduced by Henry Clay, Senator from Kentucky, as a compromise to appease southerners, alleviate their concerns over tariff acts which negatively impacted their economy, and avoid armed conflict. This was on the same day that Jackson's force bill was passed which authorized the President to use the military if necessary to see that acts of Congress, the 1828 "tariff of abominations", were obeyed. At this time, South Carolina voted to nullify the tariffs of 1828 and 1832 and Jackson's force bill. Clay called for a gradual reduction in tariff rates over 10 years, and South Carolina withdrew its Ordinance of Nullification. This was another example of an effective compromise that temporarily averted a permanent rift with the South. The tariff issue was resolved, but the issues of states' rights and nullification continued.

Enacted under Millard Fillmore's Presidency, the **Compromise of 1850** again dealt with the consideration of the slavery issue as was necessary for admitting new states into the nation. Older Senators Henry Clay, John Calhoun and Daniel Webster had assembled one last time to try to save the Union from internal destruction. Their compromise proposals were defeated. New Senators Stephen Douglas, William Seward, and Jefferson Davis approached the issues by proposing separate bills to appease the North and the South. Their plan would not be a product of widespread agreement on common national ideals. It was a victory of bargaining and self-interest.

California would be admitted as a free state. The territory disputed by Texas and New Mexico would be surrendered to New Mexico. Abolition of the slave trade (but not slavery) would apply to the District of Columbia. The remainder of the Mexican Cession area would be formed into the territories of New Mexico and Utah, without restrictions on slavery and would be open to popular sovereignty. Texas would receive $10 million from the federal government as compensation for New Mexico lands. A more stringent Fugitive Slave Law, going beyond the stipulations of the 1793 Fugitive Slave Law, would be established. President Fillmore supported the bills and signed them into law.

In addition to the acts of compromise, further dramatic events occurred which would make future compromise difficult or not possible. The Dred Scott decision of March 6, 1857 by Chief Justice James Taney has been called the worst Supreme Court decision in our history. As a Missouri slave, Scott had lived in the free states of Illinois and Wisconsin. He brought suit in 1846-1847 at the circuit court in St. Louis, Missouri (*Scott v. Emerson*) to claim his freedom on that basis. The Missouri court declared he was free. But then his current owner, John Sanford, appealed and the court reversed its decision. Finally, Scott appealed to the United States Supreme Court (*Dred Scott v. Sandford*), where Justice Taney denied his right to petition the court on the basis that no person descended from Africans, whether free or slave, is a citizen. Taney's decision ruled that the Ordinance of 1787 could not confer freedom or citizenship in the Northwest Territory to non-whites. It further ruled that the Missouri Compromise of 1820 was voided as a legislative act, since the Congress had no authority to exclude slavery and declare freedom or citizenship to non-whites in the northern part of the Louisiana Purchase territory. This ruling incensed northern abolitionists and was viewed with satisfaction by southern slaveholders. It undoubtedly strengthened opinion that further compromise on the slavery issue would not be possible.

John Brown's extremist, abolitionist, military acts in "Bleeding Kansas" and the attack on the federal arsenal at Harpers Ferry, Virginia in 1859 further set the stage for cessation and the Civil War.

Under James Buchanan's Presidency, the **Crittenden Compromise of 1860** was proposed by Senator James Crittenden of Kentucky as an attempt for reconciliation with the South. He proposed Constitutional amendments aimed at appeasing the South. Under the proposal, these amendments would prohibit slavery in territories north of 36, 30. Slavery would be allowed in existing and future territories south of that line. Future states, north or south of the line, could come into the Union with or without slavery as they chose. This would be on a basis called popular sovereignty. The distinction here was about territories versus states. As long as a territory in the South remained a territory, slavery could exist. When Lincoln took office in 1861, he rejected the proposal.

In conclusion, the decades of compromise yielded limited, temporary success in maintaining a union between our two dissimilar societies. As events unfolded, passions increased, and compromise became no longer possible.

Our southern society, as represented by the Democrats, came to the belief that they were fundamentally different than our northern society, as represented by the Republicans. They viewed the federal government as increasingly intrusive of their states' rights. Tariffs, while beneficial to northern industry, were an impediment to the southern economy dependent on exportation of its cash crops.

Southerners became convinced that their fundamental differences were incompatible with northern society and the federal government. They concluded that their "peculiar institution" and way of life could not coexist with the North. They were compelled to secede.

The federal government under President Abraham Lincoln and its Republican Congress, was determined that the Union could not be broken apart and required the Civil War to force its preservation and ultimately abolish slavery.

Bibliography

Brinkley, Alan *American History - Connecting with the Past*, New York: McGraw-Hill, 2012.

Johnson, Michael P. *Reading the American Past, Selected Historical Documents*, New York: Bedford/St. Martin's, 2012.

Author's comments

For this essay, I have referred to the instructor's lecture notes and the two texts used for the Columbia College HIST 121 American History to 1877 course.

The essay's detailed language does not require source note citation since it contains common historical knowledge, has been published numerously, and is in the public domain.

Failed Reconstruction

Originally written in 2013

Lincoln rushed to get the 13th Amendment to the Constitution passed by the Congress before he entertained peace entreaties from representatives of the Confederacy. With Lee's surrender at Appomattox, the fighting was concluded and the Union had been preserved with slavery abolished. The Republican-led federal government had to determine how to deal with the aftermath of the Civil War.

First there was a paradox. In consideration of the law, which was the way Lincoln referred to the Constitution, he believed that there was no legitimate means for the southern states to have left the Union and form their own Confederate government. Given this, the war was not between two countries, but was a civil war between a government and rebellious citizens. With this belief, the southern states, and its citizens, had never left the Union.

At the conclusion of the war, federal forces remained in the south for years. Lincoln, and the federal government, searched for ways to re-admit the southern states that had technically never left the Union. That was the paradox in Lincoln's mind that may not have been understood by others.

The south was devastated. Its homes, businesses, land, manufacturing plants and infrastructure like railroads, were all destroyed and gone. So many lives were lost. It is estimated that 20% of the adult, male, white population had perished. Many widows and their children were impoverished to the point of starvation.

The former slaves were now freedmen who wandered looking to re-unite with their families. They were impoverished also. With some time, the freedmen worked as sharecroppers for their former white southern land owners. Some acquired land and became farmers in their own right. Many migrated to the north looking for employment and a new life in large cities like Detroit and Chicago.

The radical reconstruction factions of the federal government wished to punish the devastated south for the losses the north had suffered in blood and treasure in order to defeat the insurrection. They proposed to seize land from whites and parcel it out to freedmen as a means to help the freed slaves and accomplish retribution. Along with President Lincoln, the Republican Party held the majority in the legislative branch of the federal government. For political reasons, they were reluctant to allow southern Democrats re-entry to the Congress, thereby diluting their power.

All agreed that the southern states must re-write their constitutions and submit them to the federal government for approval. The earliest states that were re-admitted were also required to ratify the 13th amendment, agreeing to abolition. The later states were required to ratify the 14th amendment, agreeing on the definition of citizenship, and finally the 15th amendment, agreeing to voting rights for all men (not women).

Lincoln believed in a more moderate reconstruction plan. He was more sympathetic to southern white Americans and fervently wished to heal the nation. He was killed before he could implement his more heartfelt and humane approach. How different our country would have been had he had that opportunity.

In the end, after a decade, in the late 1870's, the federal government put aside its efforts for reconstruction in the south as the country once again looked westward for its expansion, growth and development.

The Missing Narrative

Originally written in 2014

We have learned about three narratives driving the post-Civil War failed reconstruction. The fourth is missing.

The first narrative describes the political situation in the federal government. It tells us that the Republican majority in the government was reluctant to readmit the Democrats from the South. This would have diminished their power.

The second narrative describes the concern and efforts of the federal government to assist the freedmen in making the difficult transition from slavery to full rights of citizenship and equal participation in American society.

The third narrative describes the wishes of factions in the North to punish the South after destroying its economy and society. This was likely motivated by resentment for the great cost of blood and treasure expended by the North to put down the rebellion.

The missing fourth narrative would have been about efforts by the federal government to assist the devastated South to rebuild its economy and society. After all, this is what we did for the Japanese and Germans after World War II.

Perhaps there were efforts to assist the South in rebuilding after the Civil War, but this narrative was omitted from our text. Most likely it is missing because it never happened.

Because of this, I will always have a sympathy for the forgotten southern Americans extending to this very day.

Truth about the Civil War

May 2017

Where is the truth, the real truth, the God's honest truth in what we hear and know and believe?

If I say bias or prejudice, those are bad words that are unacceptable. But if I say perspective or viewpoint, those words are fine, Yet all four of those words really mean the same thing. The viewport is in the words of the writer, the mind of the reader and the words of the speaker. It is in all of us.

I am an upstate, eastern and central New Yorker. I have no ancestors who fought in the Civil War, haven't been in the military, or have interest in the GAR.

But I am an historian who has lived these last 3 years in the 19th century, studied it, read widely and written several published books. I formed Southern Heart Publishing to assist my publications. Partly that name was chosen because you cannot live the 19th century without sympathy for the South.

I have only visited Antietam and just the greeting center at Harper's Ferry. But I reflected sadly at Andersonville and was moved by it. I cannot know about all the battles. I have just compiled a list from the American Battlefield Protection Program and the Civil War Sites Advisory Commission. They list only 384 battles but believe there were 8,000 hostile conflicts. Shelby Foote believes there were 9,000.

Estimates vary, depending on which account you read. There were about 2 million Americans who participated in it. About 80,000 to 100,000 freed blacks fought bravely in it the last year to year and a half of it after the Proclamation. About 600,000 or 620,000 or 650,000 or just under 700,000 Americans of all arms were killed. Less than 2% of Southern whites owned as little as one slave, yet 20% of the male population (service age 17 to 45) of them were killed. The South was demolished of infrastructure. For the South, this was The War of Northern Aggression.

Reconstruction was not focused on repairing any of this. It was focused on creating opportunity for freedmen. This is the only part many late 20th and early 21st century modern historians care about.

I care about all of it. It was the pivotal moment in all of American history. For good or bad or whatever reason, Shelby Foote says it was its own thing. It was its own thing he said, but it was not one thing; it was many streams of things coming together into an unstoppable river.

The events that led up to it were the broken promise of The Northwest Ordinance of 1789 by the Missouri Compromise of 1820, the Compromise of 1850, the Kansas-Nebraska Act of 1854, "Bleeding Kansas", John Brown's rampage of violence and killing in the Pottawatomie massacre, the sacking of Lawrence, the raid on Harper's Ferry, the Dred Scott case and finally the firing on Fort Sumter from Charleston.

And yes, it was about slavery and tariffs and states' rights versus a central government, two different economies, cultures and geographies. It was about John Adams' view versus Thomas Jefferson's; two different visions for a new country from its inception, two powerful factions that would fulfill George Washington's worst nightmare that he shared with us and warned us about in his kindly farewell address.

Our ideals were just spoken about and written down when our nation was formed, but were not yet realized. In one way, the Civil War's conclusion began to realize those ideals for some of us in reality, while for others of us, it was a loss of those ideals.

Either way, it forged the country we would become, one with few states rights and a powerful central government.

The Scots-Irish in America

Originally written in 2014

The Scots-Irish southern people got the rawest deal in the post-Civil War failed reconstruction.

If you read our history, you will understand why we always rebel against authority and we never suffer fools gladly. With few exceptions, we have never made good salesmen, but we were historically phenomenal engineers and military generals. As with other groups of settlers, we arrived in America with our own unique history, culture and aspirations.

Do not confuse us with the potato famine Irish - a larger group - who came to Boston and New York in the 19th century and were conscripted to fight for the North in the Civil War. Do not confuse us with the many great Scottish immigrants, like Andrew Carnegie, who immigrated to America throughout its history.

The Scots-Irish came to America as immigrants in the 17th century as the third, the largest, and the only non-English of the original three waves of colonists – the Massachusetts Puritans, the Jamestown Virginian Anglican Royal Cavaliers, and the Ulster Scots. When they arrived in Philadelphia and other northern colonial areas, they did not fit in with the mercantile society there and were not particularly welcome. Land was scarce and expensive, so they migrated to remote areas in modern-day Maine and out to the Ohio territory. They settled in the backwoods and in the hills along the spine of the Appalachian Mountains from Tennessee and down through the Carolinas and Georgia. They were the American frontiersmen – fiercely independent and self-reliant, clannish, and suspicious of outsiders.

James Webb, in the conclusion of his book, wrote:

But to be sure, the Scots Irish are people filled with many offshoots and derivatives, with common threads that join them while strong differences obviate any thought of "ethnic purity" or even complete philosophical unity. We are related to those who stayed behind in Scotland in the border areas in the north of present-day England. We count as cousins those who remained in Ulster, not only Protestant but many Catholics as well. We ourselves are those who remained in the rough north of New England and especially along the mountain ridges that stretch from Pennsylvania to Georgia and Alabama; those who settled the backcountry and farmlands of the South, the Ohio Valley, in the Midwest; those who went north to the factories, west of the Rocky Mountains, and farther still to the farmlands and new freedom of the Pacific Coast. Some continue to marry among themselves, and some did not. Some are wildly prosperous, and some are not. Some remember at least pieces of this journey, and some do not. Some care, and some do not. Some think it matters, and some do not.

Who are we? We are the molten core at the very center of the unbridled, raw, rebellious spirit of America. We helped build this nation, from the bottom up. We face the world on our feet and not on our knees. We were born fighting. And if the cause is right, we will never retreat. [1]

Our people include Andrew Jackson, Davy Crockett, Johnny Cash, John Wayne, Dolly Parton, Elvis Presley, Ulysses S. Grant, Thomas "Stonewall" Jackson, George S. Patton, Mark Twain, John Steinbeck, Edgar Allen Poe, Jack Dempsey, and numerous other entertainment and sports celebrities, authors, politicians and military leaders.

When the southern states seceded from the Union, and the Civil War broke out, the Scots-Irish, having mostly settled in the South, fought for their way of life. Do not confuse this with the aristocracy of the South who broke away to preserve their way of life – the institution of slavery and states' rights. Scots-Irish were on the bottom rung of southern, stratified society and a class apart from the aristocrats.

It is estimated that 20% of the adult male population of the South was killed in the Civil War. Very few of these were the plantation owners. The southern Scots-Irish did not fight in the war to protect the southern landed aristocracy or their institution of slavery. They fought to defend themselves from outside invaders. The war preserved the Union and abolished slavery. It also established the supremacy of the federal government over the states forever. States' rights would be a hollow issue from that time on.

After the war, the South was devastated. The emphasis for reconstruction was directed in three areas:

- Republicans in the federal government were reluctant to readmit the southern states to the Union because the participation of the southern Democrats in Congress would dilute their power.

- The North wished to punish the South for the loss of life suffered by Union soldiers and the assassination of Abraham Lincoln. There was no sympathy for loss of southern life of the Confederacy. Robert E. Lee's property was seized in Arlington, Virginia to build the Arlington National Cemetery for the Union dead.

- There was concern for what would become of the black freedmen released from the plantations. There were considerations for confiscating land from the plantation owners and allotting it to the freedmen.

There was no consideration for the plight of poor Scots-Irish backwoodsmen and southern farmers. Characteristically, these Americans had fought for their beliefs and way of life and expected no quarter from the victors. With no assistance from their government, they struggled for their very survival for about 70 years until Franklin D. Roosevelt offered them relief in his programs for recovery during the Great Depression. Finally, at long last, electrification, roads, and infrastructure were provided for the people in the rural Appalachian regions. Today many, not all, are prospering. It is better.

But even today, these distant descendants of William Wallace are scorned as being rednecks and ignorant; not worthy of respect or consideration from the modern, elite intelligentsia.

When I remember the historical American Scots-Irish, and particularly the southerners, it is with sadness for their loss and respect for their grit, their contributions, and our forgotten values that originated with them. As a northerner, I most certainly would have been an abolitionist and fought for the end of slavery. However, I can never contemplate the horrific loss of life in the Civil War with the satisfaction that we won and they lost.

Given the historical and political circumstance in the aftermath of the Civil War, I would not expect that there would have been an outpouring of concern and financial support for the devastated poor white backcountry people and small farmers of the south. What is discouraging however, is that they were not worthy of a mention. Perhaps there are some books in print on this subject. I hope to find them. In any case, this finally gives me closure for the aspect of failed reconstruction overlooked in the chronicles of our history.

Notes

1. James Webb, *Born Fighting - How the Scots-Irish Shaped America*, (Broadway books, New York, year unknown), 327 (e-book)

Bibliography

Webb, James, *Born Fighting - How the Scots-Irish Shaped America*, New York: Broadway books, year unknown

Author's comments

For more historical detail, reference my related articles and essays previously published on this subject-

Celebrating White History
http://awlos.wordpress.com/2012/04/02/celebrating-white-history/

Failed Reconstruction
http://awlos.wordpress.com/2014/06/10/failed-reconstruction/

The Missing Narrative
http://awlos.wordpress.com/2014/06/10/the-missing-narrative/

Brigadier General Joshua L. Chamberlain's surrender ceremony at Appomattox

---

May, 2017

On April 9th, with General Lee's meager forces surrounded in the Village of Appomattox Court House by the overwhelming forces of Grant's generals, and with all escape routes blocked, he decided to end the fight. When Sheridan saw Lee's defenseless forces huddled together, he asked Grant to permit him to ignore the fragile cease fire and for the order to annihilate them. He said it would only take five minutes.

Grant angrily told him, "No, that would place our names in infamy forever."

Lee waited in the home of Wilmer McLean for Grant's arrival. They met to discuss the terms of surrender as gentlemen and with dignity. They drafted brief documents and, through their attendants, exchanged them. Lee's final letter addressed Grant as commander of all the armies of the United States, including his own, and awaited his orders.

Grant would have nothing of Lee surrendering his sword. That would have brought no honor to the ceremony and would have only served the newspapers and politicians.

He remembered the words in the Old Testament of the Holy Book, and thought, 'The prophet Micah reminds us: *He has showed you, O man, what is Good. And what does the Lord require of you? To act justly and to love mercy and walk humbly with your God.*'

He paroled the men and permitted them to leave and go back to their homes. He required they surrender and stack up their arms and ammunition. Officers were permitted to keep their side arms. All cavalry soldiers could take their personal horses and mules back

237

to their farms. The terms were as generous as Lee could have hoped for.

Grant ordered Sheridan, "Provide food rations to the beaten Confederates. They have been starved for many months. Take care of them. That is my order. See to it." Sheridan obeyed.

Across the fields, a spontaneous celebration of cannon and musket fire broke out from the Union forces. Grant ordered it to cease immediately.

He expressed his belief, "There is no dignity or honor in humiliation. The enemy knows full well they are beaten. The Confederates are now our countrymen."

Both Lee and Grant knew that there was no glory in war, but there was dignity and respect between its combatants. For war's leaders, the purpose was to inspire men to march and face the enemy across the killing field - to fight for their country. They were trained to believe that and had lived their whole lives with that code. They had learned the meaning of duty and that guided all their actions and conduct. They understood the meaning of honor better than others ever would.

After Lee's farewell address to his army on April 10th, Union Brigadier General Joshua L. Chamberlain was charged with leading the ceremony for the formal surrender on April 12th. Chamberlain reflected on what he had observed and wrote a moving tribute containing these words:

Before us in proud humiliation stood the embodiment of manhood: men whom neither toils and sufferings, nor the fact of death, nor disaster, nor hopelessness could bend from their resolve; standing before us now, thin, worn, and famished, but erect, and with eyes looking level into ours, waking memories that bound us together as no other bond;—was not such manhood to be welcomed back into a Union so tested and assured? Instructions had been given; and when the head of each division column comes opposite our group, our bugle sounds the signal and instantly our whole line from right to left, regiment by regiment in succession, gives the soldier's salutation, from the "order arms" to the old "carry"—the marching salute. Gordon at the head of the column, riding with heavy spirit and downcast face, catches the sound of shifting arms, looks up, and, taking the meaning, wheels superbly, making with himself and his horse one uplifted figure, with profound salutation as he drops the point of his sword to the boot toe; then facing to his own command, gives word for his successive brigades to pass us with the same position of the manual,—honor answering honor.

No expression could have captured the common bond of esprit de corps for the soldiers of the North and South better than this.

Excerpt from *After Bondage and War*, David Claire Jennings

The Presidential Election of 1912

Originally written in 2014

The presidential election of 1912 was not typical in that it did not merely pose two candidates of different parties running against each other with a clear choice in ideology for the electorate. While the candidates did include Woodrow Wilson, a professorial progressive Democrat against William Howard Taft, a conservative Republican, Theodore Roosevelt, joined the race for his own purposes. The result of the contest served Roosevelt's purposes even though he did not win. Perhaps the most interesting aspect of this election was the back-story and intrigue between Roosevelt and Taft.

Theodore Roosevelt, during his term in office as president from 1901 to 1909, had been a Republican who had expended most of his efforts on natural conservation, regulating the large business trusts, and providing some consumer protections. Late in his career, his views of progressivism began to focus more clearly in his mind. When out of office, he viewed himself as a relevant national voice and important advisor. In 1912, while William Howard Taft was president, Roosevelt formed the Progressive Party.

An event occurred in 1909, which became known as the Pinchot-Ballinger dispute. President Taft had replaced Roosevelt's Secretary of the Interior, James R. Garfield, with Richard A. Ballinger, a conservative corporate lawyer. Many progressives had been unhappy with Taft's replacement of Garfield with Ballinger. Roosevelt's good friend, Gifford Pinchot, was the first Director of the National Forest Service and became involved in the ensuing dispute.

Suspicion of Ballinger grew when he attempted to invalidate Roosevelt's removal of nearly 1,000,000 acres of forest and mineral reserves from private development. In the midst of this mounting concern, Louis Glavis, an interior department investigator, charged Ballinger with having once connived to turn over valuable public land in Alaska to a private syndicate for personal profit. Glavis took the evidence to Gifford Pinchot, still head of the forest service and a critic of Ballinger's policies. Pinchot took the charges to the president. Taft investigated them and decided they were groundless. However, Pinchot was not satisfied, particularly after Taft fired Glavis for his part in the episode. He leaked the story to the press and asked Congress to investigate the scandal. President Taft discharged him for insubordination. The congressional committee appointed to study the controversy, dominated by Old Guard Republicans, exonerated Ballinger. However, progressives throughout the country supported Pinchot. The controversy aroused as much public passion as any dispute of its time, and when it was over, Taft had alienated the supporters of Roosevelt completely and, it seemed, irrevocably. Animosity grew between Roosevelt and Taft.

Roosevelt decided to assume leadership of Republican reformers. He outlined a set of principles, which he labeled the "New Nationalism", that made clear he had moved a considerable way from the cautious conservatism of the first years of his presidency. The campaign for the Republican nomination had now become a battle between Roosevelt and Taft. The nominating convention selected Taft as the Republican nominee. Roosevelt responded by launching the new Progressive Party (nicknamed the "Bull Moose" Party) nominating himself as its presidential candidate. It was notable for its strong commitment to a wide range of progressive causes.

The election results declared Wilson the victor with 435 electoral votes and 41% of the popular vote. Roosevelt placed second with 88 electoral votes and 27% of the popular vote. Taft placed third with 8 electoral votes and 23% of the popular vote. Wilson won the presidency. Roosevelt did not weaken him by splitting the vote. The victory for Roosevelt was the crushing defeat of Taft and perhaps the hope that Wilson would adopt some of his progressive ideas.

Bibliography

Brinkley, Alan *American History - Connecting with the Past*, New York: McGraw-Hill, 2012.

Author's comments

For this essay, I have referred to the instructor's lecture notes from the Columbia College HIST 122 American History since 1877 course and referred to its text, *American History - Connecting with the Past* by Alan Brinkley. The essay's detailed language does not require primary source note citation or bibliography since it contains common historical knowledge, has been published numerously, and is in the public domain.

US Foreign Policy – 1920 and 1941

Originally written in 2014

United States foreign policy was markedly different in 1920 than in 1941. The reason for this was due to the different circumstances associated with these two years in our American history. This paper will describe those circumstances and the reasons for our foreign policy change.

In 1920, Woodrow Wilson was our president. The United States had entered into World War I late, and reluctantly, but contributed to its success and conclusion mostly for the benefit of our allies - Great Britain and France. Our intent before the war had been to remain neutral, but we ultimately became involved. While our ocean vessels were attacked and American lives were lost, our shores were not threatened by German aggression. In the aftermath of World War I and during the inter-war period, our government and society remained isolationist. This foreign policy posture continued throughout the 1920's and 1930's. Woodrow Wilson's philosophy was one of promotion of world peace through his idea for the League of Nations. His Fourteen Points at the conclusion of the war made recommendations for adjusting boundaries, creating new nations, and general principles to govern future international conduct. The United States was not directly threatened by world events. Our society was inwardly directed and focused on societal issues like prohibition and women's suffrage.

In 1941, Franklin D. Roosevelt was our president. The country was dealing with the Great Depression and beginning to emerge from it. The Japanese had directly attacked our soil at the Pearl Harbor Naval installation. This precipitated America's immediate entry into World War II. We declared war on Japan and Germany. At that point, most of Europe had been ravaged by Hitler's German army aggression. Germany had invaded Poland and France in 1940.

It had invaded Russia in 1941. The British had retreated from Dunkirk. The United States was directly threatened by world events. This war required deep commitment to our defense and the defense of our allies. We were compelled to become involved throughout Europe and the Pacific Rim. Our policy was directed toward internationalism and global interest.

The circumstances of American history and international events were different in 1920 than in 1941. Foreign policy reflected these differences and was in response to them. In 1920, we saw the aftermath of World War I and naturally responded with isolationism. In 1941, we saw the beginning of World War II and naturally responded with international participation.

Bibliography

Brinkley, Alan *American History - Connecting with the Past*, New York: McGraw-Hill, 2012.

Author's comments

For this essay, I have referred to the instructor's lecture notes and the text used for the Columbia College HIST 122 American History since 1877 course.

The essay's detailed language does not require source note citation since it contains common historical knowledge, has been published numerously, and is in the public domain.

Recollections of the 60's

Originally written in 2014

As a child of the 1940's, I came of age in the 1960's. In 1962, I moved to Syracuse with my young wife and baby on-the-way to begin my career. I went to work for Syracuse University Research Corporation to help develop electronic countermeasures for the Defense Department to combat Communism. After a few years, students on the SU campus began protesting that we were building bombs or doing some other dark, nefarious, deeds. The University responded by requiring that we remove their name from our corporate name. We became Syracuse Research Corporation.

So much happened in this tumultuous time filled with youthful exuberance, bitterness, violence, tragedy, and rapid social change. Led by our generation of young people, this was an inflection point where the country changed direction. Early 20th century progressivism had become institutionalized liberalism by mid-century. The post war prosperity, peace, and quiet "happy days" of Eisenhower were replaced by a noisy time when activism dominated our society. While civil rights became a legal reality, the decade ended with great poignancy and sadness. This resonates with me as reminiscent of the time after the Civil War.

Cold war

The Cold War dominated this period. The ideological conflict was fought with words, threats and brinksmanship to determine whether American style democracy or Soviet style communism would prevail.

Cuban Missile crisis

John Kennedy's CIA-sponsored invasion at the Bay of Pigs in Cuba was his greatest recorded failure. He later prevailed against the Soviet Union and caused them to remove their missiles from Cuba.

Berkeley

At the University of California students protested and demonstrated for free speech, academic freedom, students' rights and representation. Ironically, decades later, most of academia ultimately has responded with "political correctness" as a liberal suppression of free speech. Don't worry. It won't happen here in Jim's classroom. The positive good of PC is that it teaches us to be respectful, kind, and tolerant to each other, even when we are confronted with uncomfortable truths. Open-mindedness is left to the individual.

San Francisco

Haight-Ashbury. Sex, drugs and rock-and-roll. Flower children, free love, and women's liberation. No more needs to be said.

Vietnam War

With the rationale to halt the "domino effect" of spreading Soviet style communism, we replaced the French and entered the Cold-War proxy war in Vietnam in 1956. At first, the effort was minimal but gradually escalated. It culminated in 1975 with our failed effort and the fall of Saigon. An estimated 58,000 U.S. Service members died in the conflict.

Peace protests

Many of my generation were demonstrating against the Vietnam War at college campuses and in the streets all across the country. Anti-war sentiment reached intense levels. The country was sharply divided over the Vietnam War. Many protested and evaded the draft. Some went to jail and some fled to Canada. While few fervently believed in the cause, most reluctantly served.

The vitriol and emotions ran so high that some of us took it out on the returning soldiers. They were welcomed home by protests where they were called baby killers and spit upon. This has left these veterans with resentment, depression and mental issues for generations since. We have not responded to the sacrifice and service of our servicemen in this shameful and disrespectful manner since.

Celebrated actress, Jane Fonda visited North Vietnam and posed for the famous photo-op on the NVA anti-aircraft battery. She denounced American political and military leaders as "war criminals" and was called "Hanoi Jane". While she publically apologized to American veterans in 1988, she claimed her actions and the situation were misunderstood, but many believed she should have been tried for treason. This did not happen and she was recently given a lifetime achievement award for her acting career and lifetime of activism. I am not one of her fans.

Just to clarify this a bit. I agreed that the war was unjust and should not have occurred. It was Fonda's actions that were disgraceful. At a minimum, her harsh insensitivity caused a great amount of hurt for our troops. At a maximum, she provided aid and comfort to our enemy. American servicemen have despised her for her actions ever since that time. But these events occurred in the early 1970's and I don't want to let Jane Fonda or Richard Nixon dominate this narrative.

Civil rights movement

Jack and Bobby Kennedy did not come early to the Civil Rights cause. Jack was drafting civil rights reforms when he died. Bobby was influenced by the charismatic leader, Martin Luther King, Jr. and became impassioned with the cause. After JFK's assassination, Lyndon Johnson formalized the Civil Rights Act of 1964 and after Bobby and Martin were assassinated in 1968, the Civil Rights Act of 1968. These laws ended segregation in public institutions and accommodations, ended unequal voting rights and practices, and assured equal housing opportunities.

Folk Music

Many of us, including myself, expressed our beliefs and feelings by following folk music as a revived musical and social form. Soloists like Joan Baez and groups like Peter, Paul and Mary were eloquent voices for the cause of peace and even the emergent environmental movement.

Assassinations

Saddest of all, we lost three great, young men in a short time:

John F. Kennedy in 1963 at age 46 in Dallas, Texas

Martin Luther King, Jr. in 1968 at age 39 in Memphis, Tennessee

Bobby Kennedy in 1968 at age 42 in Los Angeles, California

I'll end with this poignant tribute to the memory of these men. It is a simple song you may have not heard before. It may strike you as corny and overly sentimental. For those of us who were there, it captured a sadness of our time. It ties the death of Abraham Lincoln in with the deaths of JFK, Martin Luther King, Jr. and Bobby Kennedy.

I hope this song has meaning for you and that some of these personal reflections have given you more insight into the 60's.

Play song - "Abraham, Martin and John"

Attacks on the United States

Originally written in 2014

In modern American history, during the 20th and 21st centuries, there have been two major attacks on our soil. The first was the attack on Pearl Harbor in Hawaii on December 7, 1941. The second was the attack on New York City and Washington DC on September 11, 2001. These attacks were perpetrated by different aggressors, with different motives, by different means and under different circumstances. While both were aerial attacks based on surprise, and caught us unprepared, they were strikingly different in nature. Both events shocked the American people, undermined our sense of security, and changed us forever. The differences, and some similarities, as well as our response, will be described further in this paper.

On Sunday morning, 7:48 AM, December 7, 1941, the aerial strike began at our Pearl Harbor US naval base on the island of Oahu, west of Honolulu in Hawaii. This was a military strike and an act of war by Imperial Japan motivated by the desire for military domination of the Pacific. Fortunately, our aircraft carriers were out on maneuvers or else our entire Pacific Fleet would have been destroyed. The Japanese government had been negotiating peaceful arrangements with our government immediately prior to this planned attack. The Japanese deployed 420 fighter-bomber airplanes launched from all 6 of their aircraft carriers at sea. There were approximately 2,400 military deaths and 1,300 wounded as a result of the attack. The damage to our naval installation resulted in 5 battleships, 3 destroyers, 3 cruisers, and 188 planes being destroyed. The United States responded by declaring war on Japan. Japanese citizens, and their families, were removed from their homes on the West Coast and interred in camps throughout the country for the remainder of the war.

On Tuesday morning, 8:46 AM, September 11, 2001, the first of four commercial airplanes struck World Tower One in lower Manhattan, New York City. Four United Airlines planes were hijacked departing Boston, Massachusetts. The hijackers were Al Qaeda operatives who were part of an Islamic terrorist group under the direction of Osama bin Laden. The attack was planned by Khalid Sheikh Mohammed as part of a retribution for perceived US imperialism in the Middle East. This act of terrorism was one of many intended to punish American society and its institutions for its sins against Islam. Ultimately, two of the airplanes struck the two tower buildings, one flew into the Pentagon, and one was overtaken by American passengers and forced to crash in a field in rural Stony Creek Township, Pennsylvania. It is believed that this last plane was intended to crash into the White House. The events resulted in the deaths of approximately 3,000 American innocents and a massive loss of property infrastructure. The United States responded by declaring a War on Terror. A military initiative began in Afghanistan to find Osama bin Laden. Several Muslims, who were suspected of 9/11 involvement and other acts of terrorism, were captured at various locations throughout the world, and were arrested and imprisoned in the US facility at Guantánamo Bay, Cuba.

In the case of the Pearl Harbor attack, the enemy was clearly defined and could be pursued under an immediate declaration of war and military mobilization. In the case of 9/11 however, the enemy was more dispersed and more difficult to locate. The so-called War on Terror could not be conducted or consummated in the same manner as conventional warfare. World War II was successfully concluded by the defeat of Japan and Germany, whereas the war against fundamentalist Islam may never be. Appeasement will likely not dissuade this enemy, but will likely embolden him from that action which he would perceive as weakness. Our continued military efforts to date however, both covert and overt, have been moderately successful.

Bibliography

Brinkley, Alan *American History - Connecting with the Past*, New York: McGraw-Hill, 2012.

Author's comments

For this essay, I have referred to the instructor's lecture notes and the two texts used for the Columbia College HIST 122 American History since 1877 course.

The essay's detailed language does not require source note citation since it contains common historical knowledge, has been published numerously, and is in the public domain.

Dut Leek Deng Biography (A New American Story)

———◦———

Originally written in 2013

INTRODUCTION

My story is essentially the same as all the Lost Boys of Sudan. All of them are my age-mates and brothers in the broadest sense. Together we struggled for our very survival through ten years of our childhood. Our relationship, and Christian faith, kept us going and was deeply rooted in love, respect, and trust for one another. We kept going with the hope that someday we would be delivered from our trials and suffering. Many thousands of us died while about 2,800 of us were fortunate enough to seek and be given refuge in America as unaccompanied minors. We were given a new chance for life all across the United States in cities like San Diego, San Francisco, Chicago, Kansas City, Atlanta, Tempe, Rochester and Syracuse.

I arrived in Syracuse, New York, on December 4, 2000 at age nineteen accompanied by my two cousins, Sami (now Dr. Samuel) Gai Alony, and Moses Khoor Joh. There were about 100-200 of my brothers who began a new life in Syracuse. Since I had no overcoat, my first impression of America was that it was very cold. It felt like I was thrown into an alien place where everything was surreal.

Some of us settled in the Village Apartments in the Eastwood area of Syracuse. The Interfaith Council of Churches assisted with our settlement and our basic needs of food, water, shelter, and clothing. We were assisted with job and school search and instructed in necessary life skills like shopping, driving, cooking, how to use toilets in the bathrooms, refrigerators and stoves in the kitchens and all the technology and machinery "peculiar" to American life.

SUDAN AT WAR

Our shared experience is the modern history of Sudan at war. What is now northern Sudan was formerly known as the Kingdom of Kush and was an area along the Nile River connected politically with ancient Egypt over several historical periods. Due to its proximity to Egypt, the Sudan's history participated in the history of the Near East. It was Christianized by the sixth century and Islamized in the seventh. As a result of Christianization, the old Nubian language stands as the oldest recorded Nilo-Saharan language with its earliest records dating to the 9th century.

The modern Republic of Sudan was formed in 1956 and inherited its boundaries from the Anglo-Egyptian Sudan established in 1899. Since its independence in 1956, the history of Sudan has been plagued by internal conflict, beginning with the first Sudanese Civil War (1955-1972).

The second Sudanese Civil War (1983-2005) resulted in the secession of South Sudan on July 9, 2011 and on that date, South Sudan became an independent country. The war in Darfur (2003-2010) also occurred during this time period.

The former federal government located in northern Sudan was based on Arabic Islamic fundamentalism. It subjected the southern black society of Christian and animist faiths to a holocaust of jihad military attacks to force conversion to Islamic Sharia law and protect newly discovered large oil reserves in the region. The largest tribes in southern Sudan are the Dinka and the Nuer people. They are the tallest and blackest people of Africa. They were slaughtered, and their villages destroyed, by the northern Arabic Islamic forces. Adults were killed and young girls were sold into slavery or also killed. In all, two million southern Sudanese were killed in the war. Many of the young boys were often outside the villages tending herds of goats, sheep, and cattle during the attacks and were able to hide in the bush and escape.

The federal forces deployed Soviet supplied Antonov high-altitude bombers. The young boys said, "They poured fire on us from the sky." They deployed shooting helicopters, troop convoys in trucks transporting soldiers with automatic weapons, and land mines. They even deployed Arab Murahilin jihadists on horseback. This was a modern day holocaust.

The southern rebel forces were called the SPLA (Sudanese People's Liberation Army). Dr. John Garang De Maboir served as a Colonel and led the SPLA forces from 1983 to 2005. He assisted the boys on their trek from Bor to the refugee camp in Ethiopia. He was a Dinka from Wangulei village and was educated in the United States and Africa. He briefly served as First Vice President of Sudan in July 2005 until his death in a helicopter crash. His political and military rival was Dr. Riek Machar, a Nuer.

On November 15, 1991 the event known as the "Dinka Massacre" (or Upper Nile Dinka Massacre) commenced in South Sudan. Forces led by the breakaway faction of Riek Machar deliberately killed an estimated 2,000 civilians in Dinka villages of the Jonglei State and wounded several thousand more over the course of two months. It is estimated a 100,000 people left the area following the attack. Famine followed the massacre, as Machar's forces had looted and burned villages, as well as raided their cattle. An estimated 25,000 more people died as a result of hunger, according to Amnesty International.

FLIGHT FOR SURVIVAL

It was during this second Sudanese Civil War that the diaspora of young boys from the Sudan occurred. Having lost their elders, parents, and relatives to war, these orphaned young boys migrated, mostly on foot, across the southern Sudan to the Pandu refugee camp in Ethiopia.

After a few years, the current Ethiopian government leadership was deposed, the refugees were no longer welcome in Pandu, and they had to evacuate quickly. To escape immediately, they did not wait until night as was their habit, but instead left during the day. Pursued by the Ethiopian soldiers, many were slaughtered crossing the Gilo River back into Sudan. After they crossed a portion of the Sudan, they finally arrived at the Kakuma refugee camp in Kenya.

Throughout their entire journey from Bor to Pandu to Kakuma, they struggled to survive. In total, they walked barefoot for months across a thousand miles where they encountered dangers of land mines, snakes, crocodiles, and lion. Without sufficient food, they ate wet mud and tree leaves to fill empty stomachs and stave off hunger when a small handful of grain was not available. They sometimes drank their own urine when water was not available for sustenance. They suffered foot and leg injuries, infections, malnutrition, and diseases like malaria and meningitis.

The boys were caught up in military battles between the federal military forces and the SPLA. When they encountered the SPLA, they were often well received, and the older ones were recruited and trained to protect themselves in case of any emergency along the way. Sadly, boys as young as 12 years old were encouraged to take up arms to support the rebel effort.

Ultimately, the fundamentalist jihad of the northern government drove an estimated twenty thousand boys from their families and villages in southern Sudan. They wandered for years, first fleeing to the temporary refugee camp in Ethiopia where they were treated poorly, nutrition was insufficient, and schooling was inadequate. Organizations like the American Red Cross, churches, world food programs, and the UNHCR helped the best they could. Without help from the Ethiopian government, and with limited budgets, they brought in basic supplies - food stuffs like grain, water, writing stationary, medications and tents.

Half of the boys died before others found sanctuary in the Kakuma refugee camp in Kenya.

As many as 98,000 refugees of all ages and many countries gathered and lived in Kakuma. Eventually, permanent schools were built in Kukuma that were safer and staffed with professional teachers. The unaccompanied young boys who had survived to this point grew up in Kakuma and received their knowledge of English and primary education in schools established by world humanitarian organizations. The heroic stories of the young boys' survival are almost beyond comprehension. These homeless orphans became known as the Lost Boys of Sudan.

INHUMANITY COMPARED

If we compare the American history to the story of the Lost Boys of Sudan, some similar themes from shameful periods come to mind. Our history of forced African enslavement resonates with this modern story in one way. However, perhaps a closer parallel would be our treatment of native peoples during the periods of our westward expansion. One event stands out. Cherokee peoples from Georgia were force-marched during the winter of 1838 to new Indian Territory in what became the state of Oklahoma. Thousands perished in what would be called the "trail of tears".

Most certainly the evil that came to our shores on September 11, 2001 is also a close parallel to the story of southern Sudan. The evidence continues to grow around the world that the broadest intent toward non-believers of Islam is both intolerant and merciless.

While we must not expect the many good Muslims in our country to bear guilt or responsibility for those unspeakable acts, they should acknowledge and condemn them. Not enough of them have done that. In much the same way, modern Americans are not bound to guilt or responsibility for the evil of slavery here in our country during the 18th and 19th centuries, but they must acknowledge it and condemn it. In 1865, Thaddeus Stevens rightfully condemned it as an unspeakable offence to God.

In consideration of the above, nothing short of the Jewish holocaust can compare in magnitude to the experience of the Sudanese holocaust.

Fortunately, there is exceptionable good in what America has offered to its people and the peoples of the world. It has always provided a refuge and safe haven for displaced peoples. It has provided an opportunity, beyond mere survival, to pursue individual happiness. Immigrants have always come here from countries like England, Scotland, Ireland, Poland, Germany, Cuba, Haiti, Mexico, Japan, China, Korea, Vietnam, Thailand and many other countries, to create a new and better life for themselves. With honest intent and through proper means, all are welcome.

MY AFRICAN LIFE

The village of Bor is located in the region of Jonglei, south of the Unity State, along the White Nile River in what is now the new country of South Sudan. It is the place of my birth. My name is Dut Leek Deng. Following tradition of the Dinka people, my middle name comes from my father and my last name from my grandfather. Without a birth certificate, my birth date is given as January 1, 1980 since the exact date is unknown. In fact, even the year 1980 is an estimate based on the recollection of a distant uncle. My first papers of birth were created at the Kakuma refugee camp in Kenya. The night before my Christian baptism, the name Abraham came to me in a dream. I chose it as my Christian name.

My father was Leek Deng Leek and my mother was Yar Mach Yuot. They were not educated and could not attend school since Bor village and South Sudan did not have schools.

However, my parents were successful and very well established in the community since they had many cattle, sheep, goats, and other animals. In an instant my mother, father and sister were killed, along with so many others, when the war came to Bor one fateful day.

As young boys, we were tending our animals in the bush when we witnessed all our worldly riches destroyed, the lives of our loved ones perish, and life, as we had known it, disappear. We fled and wandered aimlessly until we were advised to make the brutal journey on foot to the Pandu refugee camp in Ethiopia.

My personal journey for survival and its history is the same as my age-mates, whereby our collective experience was equally horrific for us all. We did not know if we would survive, but we relied on each other and told each other to never give up. Sadly, we watched many of our fellows, unable to walk another hour or mile, fall on the roadside and die.

I must never forget my other family members alive and deceased:

Brothers - Majok, Mach, and Majier Leek Deng (pastor and deacon of Episcopal church in Bor)

Sisters - Atong and Amer Leek Deng

Cousins - Abuot Manyang Deng, Khoor Joh Riak, Dr. Samuel Gai Alony, and Moses Khoor Riak

Aunts on my father's side - Amer Jongkuch Riak, Apiel Deng Leek, and Yom Riak Leek

Uncles on my father's side - Jur Arou, Manyang Deng, Joh Riak, and Ajak Kurwell Jok

Aunts on my mothers's side – Angou Mach, Ajier Mach, yell Mach, Lou Ayuel, Aluel Yuot, Yar Yuot

Uncles on my mother's side - Mabil Yuot, Jok Mach, Majok Yuot, Mach Ajith Mach, and Mach Majak Mach

THE PROMISE OF AMERICA

Our immigration to America was organized by the UNHCR, IOM and churches. When I arrived in America, I settled in the Village Apartments in the Eastwood area. Since my arrival, I have been busy with jobs, school and activism for the South Sudan cause. In the thirteen years, I have become a U.S. citizen, completed a 2-year degree in criminal justice and am currently working on a Bachelor's degree. With the future goal of a graduate degree in law accomplished, I hope to become effective with my South Sudan Initiatives foundation's efforts as a means to help my home country. My childhood lessons and experience taught me to never give up, to always hold a stern resolve, and to face hardships and situations with perseverance and courage.

My Episcopal Church has sponsored my participation at many workshops and conventions all over the country. I have traveled to fifteen states and cities like San Diego, San Francisco and Kansas City. I have been to New York City and Washington, DC many times and have spoken at the Library of Congress for a dedication ceremony of the Lost Boys of Sudan. I have told our story to schoolchildren in many classrooms. I speak well of America and have come to think like an American regarding world affairs. I am grateful for the opportunity America has given me and feel a need to not let down the many good people who have helped me along the way.

I hold President George W. Bush in high regard. After the September 11, 2001 attack on the United States, political attention was given to the Sudan. The Sudan Peace Act was signed by President Bush on October 21, 2002. This set aside $100M for 3 years assistance to the Sudanese population for peace and governance, support for civil administration, communications infrastructure, education, health, and agriculture.

When I am asked what I like best and least about America, I always answer pizza and the way you treat your old people. Compared to my childhood in Africa, pizza is special and so delicious. One of my work experiences was as an orderly at St. Joseph's Hospital. There I talked to and cared for many elderly patients. When Americans become old and sick, they are often ignored by their families. In African village life and pastoral culture, all the generations live together and interact every day. The elders are revered, respected and looked to for guidance and wisdom. They are a valued asset and never a burden. In America, old people are not treated as well. With urban based life, children grow up and move away, leaving the older generation behind and often ignored. Many families are scattered apart by the nature of American society.

DREAMS AND PRAYERS OF ABRAHAM

While I am striving to succeed in America, my own family still lives in Africa. Sadly, I may not know what it is like to see my children grow up, but pray that someday my grandchildren will live all around me. My wife (Debora Nyibol Garang), my son (Leek Dut Deng), and my daughter (Yar Dut Deng), live in Kampala, the capital of Uganda. Debora works as a government customs official there and I send her support and visit when I can. While they are dearly missed and our separation has been very difficult, I have been trying to bring them to America.

I have great hopes and dreams, as well as a vision, to re-unite with my family and help my young, free country through my foundation - South Sudan Initiatives, Inc. Pray for all of us and both of my beloved countries.

Footnote: Since we arrived in 2000, so many Americans that have met us have been inspired by our story, our courage and our spirit. They have been compelled to help us, befriend us, write about us, and love us. We, in turn, have been inspired by the way God has worked through them to give us succor, peace and a safe haven upon which to build our adult lives.

EPILOGUE

When I first met Dut in a college history class, I was intrigued by the things he said and his background, and was immediately drawn to him. There was a charisma, spirit, and strong heart about the man that was compelling. In a short time, through much conversation, I came to know him better and came to learn and care about him, his story, the history of his country, and the Lost Boys of Sudan. I have never known a person or history like this, or as closely as this, before. We have developed a deep friendship with each other and I have been honored that he has let me be his friend, supporter, and biographer.

As we have enjoyed each other's companionship, and our mutual affection has grown, I have asked myself what is so unique about this man, his history, and its obvious importance to me. The answer lies in Dut's values and the value system of his young countrymen.

As an old man and a new history student, I have become passionate about the history and development of America. Consider the waves of immigration to America from ethnic groups at the end of the 19th and beginning of the 20th century, long after the original English colonists and founders. They came from nations like Ireland, Italy, Germany, and Poland. They came to escape poverty, religious persecution, and war. They were welcome to come but often treated poorly by American "nativists". They had to start at the bottom of American society and its economic strata. Most, with the strength of their personal faith and strong self-reliance, have worked hard, achieved a higher education, and rose to create and populate our vibrant middleclass. This is the story of our core, traditional, American value system. Sadly, it has devolved over the last few decades, and I grieve for that.

Dut and the Lost Boys have come to America in the early 21st century in just the same manner and circumstance as our earlier, humble immigrants. However, their story of hardship and struggle has been even greater than their predecessors. Likely, due to that, their strength and values are even more in the spirit of American tradition. Likely, because of that, but not out of pity, we have loved them and accepted them more than those before. I am heartened and inspired by them, and through Dut, am dedicated to support their efforts to succeed in America and give back to their struggling native country. Dut has asked me to serve on the Board of Directors for his South Sudan Initiatives foundation. Within the limits of my abilities and energy, I am honored to help and serve.

- Dave Jennings

"There is no passion to be found playing small - in settling for a life that is less than the one you are capable of living."

- Nelson Mandela

Section 4 – Law

Article I. of the U.S. Constitution

Originally written in 2013

Article I., and the Constitution as a whole, is based on English Law (Magna Carta, English Parliament), our own historical documents (Mayflower Compact, Articles of Confederation) and our own experiences with legislation (The House of Burgesses in Virginia and town councils in Massachusetts and throughout New England). Finally, it was devised by the framers after discussions and deliberations before and during the Constitutional Convention in Philadelphia in 1786. It was ratified and became the law of the land in 1788.

James Madison has been called "the Father of the Constitution" and has been credited for devising the system of checks and balances and with most of its writing. He, along with Alexander Hamilton and John Jay, wrote the Federalist Papers during the two-year debate. Many earlier events led up to the development of the Constitution, and it was viewed as a compromise by the many conflicting parties involved.

Article I., as the first article of the U.S. Constitution, describes the definition, function and authority of the Congress. To accomplish this, it is partitioned into ten sections. A brief, paraphrased summary of these sections is as follows:

Section 1:

All powers are vested in Congress, which consists of a Senate and House of Representatives.

Section 2:

House - Two year terms; elected by the people. Members must be age 25 (originally), a resident of state represented, and a citizen for 7 years. It defines the number of representatives per state and chooses its speaker and its body, which has the role of impeachment of any public official, and establishes the census.

Section 3:

Senate - Six years terms, rotating 1/3 of body every two years, two members for each state, elected by the people. Members must be age 30, a member of the state represented, and a citizen for 9 years. Its President is the Vice President of the U.S., and its body has the power to try impeachments.

Section 4:

Each state chooses time, place and manner of holding election, subject to alteration by Congressional legislation, except for election place. Must assemble at least once per year.

Section 5:

Each house judges its elections, returns and qualifications of its members. A majority quorum is required to do business. Each house determines its procedural rules, punishes its members for disorderly behavior including expulsion, and keeps a journal of proceedings.

Section 6:

Defines compensation for both houses paid by the Treasury and immunity for arrest (with limitations) during attendance.

Section 7:

The House originates all bills for revenue. The Senate may propose or concur. Both houses must concur on every bill, and every bill must be presented to the President before becoming law. Rules are defined for actions if he vetoes a bill.

Section 8:

Congress has power to lay and collect taxes, to borrow money, to regulate commerce, to coin money, to establish standards of weights and measures, rules for naturalization and bankruptcy, to punish counterfeiters, to establish roads and post offices, to promote science and arts, to establish patents, to create lesser courts, to define and punish piracy and felonies, to declare war and raise armies, to provide a navy, and to call forth a militia.

Section 9:

Congress shall not prohibit or control- Migration or importation of slaves prior to 1808; but may impose a tax or duty, suspend Habeus Corpus (evidence of accusation), deny a person the right to a trial, make ex post facto law, tax interstate commerce, regulate commerce or ports, draw money from the treasury without law, grant no title of nobility.

Section 10:

States power prohibitions - States may not make treaties, grant letters of reprisal, coin money or bills of credit, lay import or export duties, keep troops or ships, engage in war without imminent danger.

The earlier Articles of Confederation, ratified in 1787, was viewed as inadequate since it defined an impotent central government with no power for taxation, and perhaps more significantly, a unicameral (one body) legislative body which did not solve the critical issue of proper representation of the States. The bicameral (two bodies) legislature defined in the Constitution resolved this in the minds of the framers.

Has our history proven that the design of our legislative process is correct? Is it still relevant in the 21st century? Its intent was to make the lawmaking process fair and just by being deliberative and difficult. In my opinion, while the legislative structure has checks and balances and no better design has been achieved, it appears we have created such a multitude of laws that many are unenforceable by the Executive branch's Department of Justice, or challenged sufficiently by the Judicial branch for constitutionality in case law. Therefore, the deliberation often does not adequately foresee the unintended consequences. Furthermore, our freedoms were to be protected by our laws, but our sovereignty was to be guaranteed by only passing laws prohibiting behavior. This means that anything is permitted if there's no law against it. Regrettably, we have passed many laws permitting behavior, thus losing our sovereignty by relinquishing it to our government and requiring permission for a behavior.

Many of us have believed that the government that governs least, governs best. Based on the framers' views, our founding principles, we believe that the creation of laws should be difficult and deliberative and that fewer laws would be better than too many laws.

In conclusion, the founders likely began the constitution with the legislative branch of government since much of their earlier history was directed in that area. Despite the frequent occurrence of "gridlock", Article I. is likely the most workable design for a legislative body. To crudely paraphrase Ben Franklin, there is no Plan B. Most of the time, even in our 21st century, this legislative process can still be effective.

Notes

1. U.S. Constitution, art. I.

Author's comments

Quotation from, and paraphrased reference to, detailed language in the U.S. Constitution does not require primary source note citation or bibliography since it is common knowledge, has been published numerously with identical text, and is in the public domain. For this article however, I referred to two publications:

Cullop, Floyd G., *The Constitution of the United States - An Introduction*, New York: New American Library, a division of Penguin Group, 1999

and

Author undisclosed, *The United States Constitution and Other American Documents*, New York: Fall River Press, 2009

I have compared these two sources in the original language so that when I paraphrased the text, it would be my own and not that of someone else.

Article II. of the U.S. Constitution

Originally written in 2014

Articles I., II., and III. of the U.S. Constitution define the legislative, executive, and judicial branches of the federal government, respectively. Of these, the legislative role of government was best known to the framers of the Constitution based on their previous experiences. The judicial role was also familiar to them from their colonial history. The executive role however, was relatively unfamiliar and required that the founders use more imagination, thought, and faith in their definition of this branch of government. For this reason, Article II., and the response to it from each of our presidents, is perhaps the most interesting of the first three articles of the Constitution. It is amazing how men of differing personality and skills have matched the demands of their times to their individual abilities to fulfill their duties and responsibilities as president. It has been fortuitous that the right man has very often come along at the right time.

The key features describing the executive branch of the federal government in Article II. of the U.S. Constitution are as follows:

Section 1.

- The President's term is four years.

- The states shall appoint Electors who in turn will place voting ballots to elect the President. The Senate and the House of Representatives participate in the vote counting. The majority of ballots will determine who is elected President.

- Whoever receives the minority (the lesser, second number) of ballots shall be Vice President.

- To qualify for President, the candidate must be a natural born citizen, at least 35 years old, and a resident of the US for 14 years.

- In case of death or removal from office, the order of succession for the presidency shall devolve to the Vice President, and thereafter be an appointment of the Congress.

- The President's compensation may not change during office.

Section 2.

- The President is Commander-in-Chief of the military.

- He shall have the power to grant pardons.

- He may call upon his executive departments for opinion.

- With the advice and consent of the Senate, he may make treaties.

- With the advice and consent of the Senate, he shall appoint ambassadors and other ministers, Judges of the Supreme Court, and all other officers of the US.

- The President shall have power to fill all vacancies that may happen during the recess of the Senate.

Section 3.

- The President shall from time to time give a State of the Union address to the Congress and recommend measures necessary and expedient.

- Under extraordinary occasions, the president may convene both houses of Congress.

- The President shall receive ambassadors and other public ministers.

- The President shall take care that the laws are faithfully executed.

Section 4.

- The President, Vice President, and all civil officers of the United States, shall be removed from office on impeachment for, and conviction of, treason, bribery, or other high crimes and misdemeanors.

Historians have ranked the presidents based on how each of them rose to the challenges and situations of their respective time in US history. The accepted criteria has been to rate them based on the degree of difficulty of the problems they faced coupled with how successful they were in resolving them.

On that basis, Abraham Lincoln is almost unanimously regarded as the first ranked president. This rating is easily understood based on his challenges of preserving the Union while abolishing slavery. The second ranked president is most often Franklin D. Roosevelt, whereas he is occasionally ranked third. George Washington is ranked close to FDR with numbers ranging from first to fourth, but usually third.

Lincoln agonized about the rule of law - the Constitution - while he generally used executive authority to accomplish his purposes. Congress was generally agreeable with his decisions.

Franklin D Roosevelt had to deal with a financial crisis followed by a world war. Woodrow Wilson faced the same circumstances as FDR but of a much lesser magnitude. Roosevelt chose to drastically increase the size of the federal government by creating a vast number of agencies, loosely organized under the executive branch, to address the problems posed by the Great Depression. He was partially successful in solving the immense problems he faced.

Washington, while a magnificent figure of courage, integrity, wisdom, and humility, did not face severe crises after he took office. His greatest challenge was likely that everything was new and lacked precedents. His greatest legacy is perhaps his symbolic value to our country.

Given the general guidelines of Article II., each president has deployed his own style to serve his office to the best of his abilities and with honest concern for the good of the country.

Bibliography

Brinkley, Alan *American History - Connecting with the Past*, New York: McGraw-Hill, 2012.

Authors comments

For this essay, I have referred to the instructor's lecture notes from the Columbia College HIST 122 American History since 1877 course and referred to its text, *American History - Connecting with the Past* by Alan Brinkley. The essay's detailed language does not require primary source note citation or bibliography since it contains common historical knowledge, has been published numerously, and is in the public domain.

Article IV. of the U.S. Constitution

Originally written in 2014

James Madison, and his colleagues, devised the U.S. Constitution as the plan for a government that would fulfill the founding principles established in the Declaration of Independence. This would provide the structure and mechanism, as a basis of law, for the United States of America following the successful conclusion of its war for independence from Great Britain. The idea was to form an indirect democracy through representation - a Republic. The system of government was devised horizontally to have three branches governed by a system of checks and balances. It further was devised vertically as a system called Federalism, whereby the power of the federal government would be limited and enumerated, whereas the states would have all powers not designated for the federal government. All powers, in terms of rights and law, not defined specifically for the states would default to the citizens. Sovereignty would reside with the citizenry and be granted to the state and federal levels of government.

Article IV. of the U.S. Constitution defines the relationship between the states and the federal government in four sections as follows:

Section 1: describes rights and duties of the states-

The federal government will assure that the states respect each other's laws. Full faith and credit shall be given in each state to the public acts, records and judicial proceedings of every other state. Congress may, by general laws, prescribe the manner in which these acts, records and proceedings shall be proved, and the effect thereof.

Section 2: describes rights and liabilities of citizens-

The citizens of each state shall be entitled to all privileges and immunities of citizens in the several states. A person charged in any state, who shall flee from justice, shall be delivered back to the state having jurisdiction of the crime. Escaping slaves from one state shall be returned to the state from which they escaped. This clause became obsolete with the 13th amendment.

Section 3: describes creation of new states-

New states may be admitted by the Congress into the union; but no new state shall be formed within another state, nor any state be formed by joining two or more states, or parts of states without the consent of the legislatures of the states concerned, as well as of the Congress.

The Congress shall have power to dispose of and make needed rules and regulations respecting a territory or other property belonging to the United States. Nothing in this Constitution shall be construed as to prejudice any claims of the United States, or any particular state.

Section 4: describes guarantee to states-

The United States shall guarantee to each state a Republican form of government. It shall protect each of them against invasion and, on application of the legislature or of the executive, against domestic violence.

Throughout US history, the issues of States rights versus federal authority have arisen many times. As American society became more complex, these issues have caused contention. The secession of the South at the onset of the Civil War was an instance, among other things, of states asserting their rights over the federal government. In modern times, states bordering with Mexico, particularly Arizona, have asserted their state's right to protect their border, in defiance of the federal government's prerogative

280

in this area. In many cases, the federal government, through Congress, has invoked the Interstate Commerce Clause (article 1, section 8, clause 3) and the Necessary and Proper Clause (article 1, section 8, clause 18) in order to assert its authority over a state or states by declaring an issue a national matter. In reality, over time, the role of the federal government versus state governments, and the balance of their respective powers, has become obfuscated.

Notes

1. U.S. Constitution, art. IV.

Author's comments

Quotation from, and paraphrased reference to, detailed language in the U.S. Constitution does not require primary source note citation or bibliography since it is common knowledge, has been published numerously with identical text, and is in the public domain.

Article V. of the U.S. Constitution

Originally written in 2013

"The Congress, whenever two-thirds of both houses shall deem it necessary, shall propose amendments to this constitution, or on the application of the legislatures of two-thirds of the several states, shall call a convention for proposing amendments, which, in either case, shall be valid to all intents and purposes, as parts of this constitution, when ratified by the legislatures of three-fourths of the several states, or by conventions in three-fourths thereof, as the one or the other mode of ratification may be proposed by the Congress: Provided, that no amendment which may be made prior to the year 1808, shall in any manner affect the first and fourth clauses in the ninth section of the first article; and no state, without its consent, shall be deprived of its equal suffrage in the Senate." [1]

Note: the two provisos written at the end refer to restrictions that 1) barred amendments that would have outlawed slave trade before 1808 and 2) assurance that no amendment can end equal representation of all states, regardless of size, in the Senate.

From our 21st century lens, the Constitution is regarded from two viewpoints, that of the "absolutists" and that of the "relativists". The "absolutists" believe that the Constitution is permanent and its truths are eternal. The "relativists" believe that it is a "living document" subject to change with the needs and issues of the times.

President Woodrow Wilson, as an academic political thinker, founded the progressive movement. Refer to his book: *The New Freedom: A Call for the Emancipation of the Generous Energies of a People* (New York: Doubleday, Page and Company, 1913). [2] In all fairness to Dr. Wilson, I have not had an opportunity to read his book. But perhaps that emancipating of those generous energies of the people had something to do with either taxation or philanthropy. Wilson believed that the original form of the Constitution had become obsolete and should be regarded as a "living document" in the sense that it is "organic" and must evolve as Darwin's theory of evolution, popular at the time, would dictate. It is not clear what mechanism Wilson had in mind for this evolution. Presumably, he was justifying excessive use of power by the Executive branch.

In any case, the framers provided one means of perpetual clarification of the Constitution for the interpretation of any situation that might arise in the future- the body of case law written by the Supreme Court.

They also provided one means to modify the Constitution itself for any situation that might arise in the future - Article V. The Constitution has been amended 27 times. An interesting example of the amendment process is the 18th amendment banning manufacture, sale, or transportation of intoxicating liquors (prohibition) ratified January 16, 1919 and repealed by the 21st amendment ratified December 5, 1933.

Perhaps most interesting are the first ten amendments known as the Bill of Rights ratified on December 15, 1791. These were selected from twelve that were proposed and were intended to explicitly articulate basic principles of human liberty not expressly stated in the Constitution as it was written and ratified on June 21, 1788. As an aside, note that Rhode Island ratified the Constitution later on May 29, 1790 but New Hampshire's earlier ratification provided the sufficient nine votes for it to become the supreme law of the land.

In conclusion, many Presidents throughout our history have sought a "work-around" for the Constitution in order to accomplish their objectives. The solution has always been there, albeit an intentionally designed arduous one - Article V.

1. U.S. Constitution, art. V.

2. Woodrow Wilson, *The New Freedom: A Call for the Emancipation of the Generous Energies of a People* (New York: Doubleday, Page and Company, 1913).

The Bill of Rights

Originally written in 2013

The first ten amendments to the new U.S. Constitution were called the Bill of Rights since they enumerated individual rights and liberties not specifically stated in the articles of the body of the U.S. Constitution. The Constitution was signed in 1787 and ratified in 1789. The Bill of Rights was proposed later in 1789 and was ratified thereafter by the end of 1791. Of the twelve amendments discussed and approved, ten were finally adopted by state ratification.

George Washington was directly involved in the process of developing the Constitution. He was elected president of the Constitutional Convention of 1787. As the first U.S. President, he was inaugurated in April 1789 and was involved in the controversy surrounding the proposal and adoption of the Bill of Rights. The issue was that the Federalists, like Washington and John Adams, did not see a need to enumerate individual rights and liberties, whereas Republicans like Thomas Jefferson saw a need for specific protection of the individual. James Madison was concerned that by enumerating individual rights, rights would be limited to only those written down, and other rights would be disavowed.

Over our history, the U.S. Supreme Court has built a body of case law by deliberating specific cases brought before them that have challenged the various rights outlined in the Bill of Rights. Over time, and with specific situations, their rulings have provided clarity and have defined limits and bounds as refinement of law.

As to the need for the Bill of Rights, I disagree with Madison's view and hold that our rights must be enumerated or else they will be ignored. The constitutional process, under article V., provides for amendments to further define our rights, and therefore, they are not limited.

While all ten of the adopted rights are important for our protection as individuals under constitutional law, a few have been proven to be critically important and have been tested and scrutinized throughout our history. These are:

The 1st Amendment defines the five freedoms of religious practice, speech and press, peaceful assembly, protection from libel and damaging lawsuits, and the right to petition the government for redress of grievances. Many cases have been presented and some resolved on issues such as: protests in the streets, the limitation of speech to not cause danger (like falsely shouting "fire" in a theater), pornography, impingement of religious practice in schools, religious displays on public property, criticism of current administrations by factions of the media, and delaying approval of tax benefits for certain charitable but political organizations. I generally side with the people and their 1st amendment rights.

The 2nd Amendment defines the right to bear arms and is written in terms of providing for a well-trained militia. It has come to mean the right of citizens to own firearms for lawful purpose and the right to self-defense. This issue has been historically contentious and several Federal and State laws have been appropriately enacted to limit the types of firearms permitted, registration and permits required, and the nature by which they may be carried or displayed. Guns rights advocates have argued that gun ownership provides means to defend our persons and property from a domestic threat and protects individual sovereignty in the event of tyranny imposed by our own government or from foreign threat. I fervently agree with and hold that position.

The 4th Amendment provides protection from unreasonable search or seizure. Specific warrants must be issued for each circumstance. It protects us from "Writs of Assistance" which would allow search or seizure anytime and anyplace. Many have argued that The Patriot Act of 2001 is in clear violation of the 4th amendment. They hold that, in order to protect us from potential foreign threat, the government has conducted certain practices which invade our privacies without acquiring appropriate warrants. More recently, the government practices of electronically acquiring data on individuals have been challenged as coming very close to being unconstitutional. The debate has been about the balance of security versus liberty. I hold with Ben Franklin who said: "Those willing to give up liberty for security deserve neither and will lose both." I'll go with liberty almost every time.

The 10th Amendment defines that powers not exclusive to the U.S. government, and not denied to states by the Constitution, are the powers of the states and further of its people. These provide for state taxation, laws about education, marriage, divorce, inheritance, corporations, state courts, regulating health, and other matters. One could argue appropriately that the creation of the federal Department of Education is therefore unconstitutional. I agree with that position and more broadly that the federal government has systematically and illegally taken away power from the states and individuals in violation of the constitutional requirements of the 10th amendment.

Further amendments have been proposed and debated subsequent to the original ten. Several have been incorporated into law, while some have been dropped or held in abeyance. The Equal Rights amendment has been proposed to eliminate discrimination based on sex and was originally written in 1923 by Alice Paul. It has been introduced in every Congress between 1923 and 1972. The seven year time limit was extended, but at the deadline it was narrowly defeated for ratification. Thirty five states ratified it, just short of the required thirty eight. It has been brought up in every Congress since that time. I would certainly support that this right of equality be enumerated and incorporated into law.

Over time, as our government and laws have "progressed", the federal government has assumed more power at the expense of the states and individuals. Many of these events and activities might have been called into question for their constitutionality. Some have, but some remain unchallenged. In any event, I hold that the Bill of Rights has always been critical to protecting our freedom and liberties and are as important now, or even more important, than the moment they first became law.

Bibliography

Brinkley, Alan *American History - Connecting with the Past*, New York: McGraw-Hill, 2012.

Author's comments

For this essay, I have referred to the instructor's lecture notes from the Columbia College HIST 121 American History to 1877 course and referred to its text, *American History - Connecting with the Past* by Alan Brinkley. The essay's detailed language does not require primary source note citation or bibliography since it contains common historical knowledge, has been published numerously, and is in the public domain.

Is it Legal or Illegal?

Originally written in 2011

This article will make only one point and that will be about how our laws are written. The "it" in the title is not important. How our laws are written is not only important, it is everything.

Americans rightfully enjoy freedoms and are bound by the laws of our land. Whether our rights, freedom and liberty are God-given or come from some core definition of humanity is of less consequence than that they should not come from our government, sovereign or state. That is the point of the founding of our country.

Webster's New Encyclopedic Dictionary defines freedom as the quality or state of being free; as the absence of necessity, coercion, or constraint, or constraint in choice or action; liberation from slavery or restraint or from the power of another; **independence**; **exemption** , **release** (freedom from care); **ease, facility** (freedom of movement); the quality of being outspoken; unrestricted use (the dog had the freedom of the yard); **privilege, right**; esp one guaranteed by fundamental law; **syn freedom, liberty, license** mean the power or condition of acting without compulsion. **Freedom** has a broad range of application from total absence of restraint to merely a sense of not being unduly hampered or frustrated. **Liberty** suggests release from former restraint or compulsion. **License** implies freedom specially granted or conceded and may connote an abuse of freedom.

It is a given that laws necessarily restrict freedom. The key point to this article is to question whether laws should be written in the negative sense or the positive sense. Does a law prohibit or permit a freedom? Does our government give us license?

We have many laws that prohibit some thing or activity; making it illegal. This is good. It means that if it is not prohibited, it is legal. Freedom is not granted from the state but comes from us.

We have many laws that permit some thing or activity; making it legal. This is bad. It means freedom is granted by the state and does not come from us.

We have had many laws that prohibited something and were then not simply rescinded; but were superseded by new laws permitting what was previously prohibited. This approach is the most pernicious of all since it means that once freedom came from us but now it is granted by the state.

Should there be a law making abortion legal? No; that would permit it. No law regarding abortion is necessary. It is legal by default if not prohibited by law. If it is decided that it is considered under certain circumstances to be murder, as held by some, then pass a law prohibiting it and making it punishable as murder. Until then, it is legal.

Should there be a law making gay marriage legal? No; that permits it. There should be no law regarding gay marriage. It is legal by default if not prohibited by law. Do you see where I am going with this?

Whenever I hear about a proposed law permitting something, I cringe. Hopefully, from this article, you can see why. It means the state is granting a freedom.

The laws banning smoking in public places are appropriate and written in the correct sense. I may do anything I wish as long as it does not do harm to others. Smoking has been proven to do harm to others.

The laws banning marijuana are written in the correct sense but may not pass the "harm to others" criteria. Unless proven otherwise, the law prohibiting smoking pot should be rescinded. A new law permitting the use of pot would be wrong.

Footnote: Reference my article "Political Ideology Matrix" in this blog. E.J. Dionne Jr's book "Why Americans Hate Politics" brilliantly traces our political ideologies from the 1960's to the present. He concludes that there are four definitive ideologies. In an effort to make them more understandable, I have put them into a 4 by 4 matrix. Since this is about the government intervening on economic and social issues, the definitions cannot make sense unless the "sense" of intervention is consistent and understood. It does not compute if our laws are a hodgepodge of prohibition and permission. I must conclude that it is dealing with the laws that prohibit.

E.J. is a prominent liberal and Senior Fellow in Governance Studies at the Brookings Institution who writes for the Washington Post and has written many insightful books. As a libertarian, I agree with much he has to say on social issues.

What Gun Control Advocates Need to Know

Originally written in 2011

Recognizing that gun control advocates know far less about the mechanics and types of firearms and gun control legislation than gun owners, I wrote the blog article "Gun Control and Gun Violence" last February. It was an attempt to provide some basic information about attitudes, firearms and related laws to anyone who has little or no knowledge of the subject. It barely scratched the surface.

Regarding the 2nd amendment, I have heard the "militia" argument from gun control advocates countless times. If you have read the amendment, you know what this means. This argument will never win over a single gun owner. It will not prevail in the courts or legislature either.

If your father never took you out in the woods or to a gun range when you were an adolescent and taught you the basics of firearm use and safety with a .22, you have missed out on an important learning experience. As an adult, you have formed your views about guns based on emotion, fear and ignorance. With this background, you are not prepared to prevail in your anti-gun movement.

If you believe that guns kill people and that no one should possess them except the military and police, you may believe that the 2nd amendment should be repealed. If you take this naïve, head-on approach, I promise you that you will never win.

If you believe that guns kill people and that no one should possess them except the military and police, but you own an old hunting rifle or a family heirloom, you are a hypocrite. Turn your guns over to the local authorities and request that they destroy them as I did a few years ago. As an aside, local authorities will likely not destroy them but will take them home for themselves. They will remain in circulation but you will not have one.

Purge the hypocrisy from your ranks. Contact NYS Senator Charles Schumer and tell him that since he is an anti-gun advocate, he should relinquish his handgun permit and surrender any handguns he owns. Contact other congressmen who are anti-gun advocates and also gun owners and ask them to do the same.

Involve yourself in gun control advocacy groups to increase your knowledge on the subject; not just to contribute money. Gun owners know who these are. If you don't, shame on you. You will not prevail.

Advocate for enforcement of the laws we have. Detect, apprehend and prosecute violators of our gun control laws; starting with our own Department of Justice- BATFE. I agree with Michael Bloomberg, the Mayor of New York City on his statement "There are lots of gun control laws. We have enough gun control laws. We need to enforce the laws we have and that will require that we fund the enforcement."

You may be aware that President Obama has operated under the radar, for political reasons, to further his gun ban agenda during his first term. If he is elected for a second term he will operate overtly. Gun owners know most of what he has been doing and so far have blocked his efforts. Do you?

As a footnote, I generally agree with Ayn Rand's philosophy about the roles of government and our nation's citizenry. She believed that government should be severely limited and bound by controls since government is force. I agree with that. She also believed that the citizenry should be prohibited from ownership of firearms since no counterforce would be needed under her terms.

I think she was very naïve on this point and strongly disagree with her.

Gun Control and Gun Violence

Originally written in 2011

Before you think you know what this article is going to say and go running away, give it an open-minded read. I promise for many of you this will be informative.

Daniel Patrick Moynihan said "You are entitled to your own opinions but you are not entitled to your own facts". Unfortunately, Senator Moynihan didn't live long enough to witness the vagaries of our modern, digital information age. In the ascending progression from data to information to knowledge to wisdom, we often go no further than the data stage either for reason of ignorance or cunning. By this I mean there is more and more data out there; mountains of it for us to discover and believe. It's all facts skewed every which way. The numbers can be manipulated to prove or disprove any assertion.

So how do we actually learn something and gain wisdom through knowledge obtained from the information in the raw data? That's a tough one! All I can come up with is we need to apply the left brain to process information in an analytical and sequential way, looking first at the pieces and then putting them together to get the whole. The creative, emotional right brain doesn't help. So what does this have to do with gun control?

I watched Lawrence O'Donnell interviewing a congressman from Arizona shortly after the shooting in Tuscon, Arizona. He obviously knew the correct answer to the question he asked the congressman before he asked him. He asked with an aggressive demeanor if the congressman thought we should pass a law limiting the capacity of gun magazines as that would have saved lives in Tuscon. The congressman hemmed and hawed and beat around the bush but did not directly answer the question. In rapid succession, and now more angrily, O'Donnell asked the question again. He would not be denied his answer. Again, the congressman did not give the satisfactory answer. Now O'Donnell was livid and apoplectic as he asked a third time and got the same response. That was the entire interview. The solution to tragedies like this one requires more comprehensive, less simplistic answers; certainly not O'Donnell's emotional kneejerk one. This was the right brain response – visual, processes information in an intuitive and simultaneous way, looking first at the whole picture and then the details.

Certainly a clip limited to ten rounds, as compared to thirty, would have slowed Jared Loughner down. Such laws are already in existence in Federal and State statutes; more about that later. The important point here is about O'Donnell's attitude, emotion and smug confidence that he had the answer to the problem. I couldn't help but recall a routine Howie Mandel used to do as a standup comic. He would heckle (harass) an audience member in the front row by asking him 3 times in succession- "What's your name?" "What's your name?" "What's your name?" He would intentionally ask the question so fast that the guy had no chance to answer. Then in mock anger Howie would say- "I asked you three f**cking times, what's your name?"

Most legal gun owners and NRA members are necessarily knowledgeable of Federal and State gun laws, the mechanics of gun design and the safe operation of firearms. Many who possess firearms illegally may not be as knowledgeable. Many gun control advocates and Brady Campaign supporters may have good knowledge of gun laws but probably little or no knowledge of the mechanics or operation of firearms. You can glean this from their obvious fear of guns and emotional focus on the guns rather than the perpetrators.

O'Donnell is not a recognized arms expert so I don't know whether he knows he's talking about semi-automatic weapons or not. Fully automatic weapons fire repeatedly as long as you hold the trigger until the magazine is empty. They are banned in the United States except for police and military. A semi-automatic fires each time you pull the trigger in rapid succession until the magazine is empty. Manually operated rifles (repeaters) require that you cycle the rounds between firings by use of a bolt, lever or pump. Many of these have magazines, typically tubes below the barrel, that hold more than 10 rounds but these higher capacity magazine tubes are typically in rifles chambered for small caliber ammunition like .22's since more short bullets can fit in a given length tube than longer bullets which are of higher caliber. Manually operated handguns are typically revolvers that are either single action (you have to cock the hammer) or double action where you can optionally repeatedly pull the trigger. The revolving cylinder classifies them as repeaters, not semi-automatics.

In any case, O'Donnell's posture was typical of the emotional reaction to a terrible tragedy followed by the kneejerk, quick solution of narrowly crafted legislation. I don't disagree with him but know that this law already exists and that the Federal and States gun control statutes are sporadic, inconsistent and not a cohesive solution. I also know that the Brady Campaign supporters intentionally will not discuss gun violence perpetrated with illegal guns. They just won't discuss it. It's like they know the answer is to eliminate all guns by legislation and the problem will be solved. They won't discuss enforcement of gun laws either. Once the law is passed, we are all done. Honestly, the process includes strong but fair (I won't even go into the 2nd Amendment thing) laws that are **enforced**. Enforcement involves detection, apprehension, prosecution and sentencing.

Michael Bloomberg, the Mayor of New York City has offered to come to Arizona and help them with improvement of their gun control laws. While I think this offer is very arrogant, I do give him kudos for recently saying (to paraphrase him) "There are lots of gun control laws. We have enough gun control laws. We need to enforce the laws we have and that will require that we fund the enforcement."

Ok, so what do we know about gun control laws? There is a baseline of Federal laws and then a layer of State laws on top. The state laws vary a great deal from pro-gun states to anti-gun states. Arizona, Texas, Florida and Vermont are very lax. California, New York and Massachusetts are very strict. There are laws that deal with hand guns and laws that deal with rifles (long guns).

The Brady Background Check Act of 1994 defines the FBI Instant Criminal Background Check and applies to the purchase of a firearm in every store (and gun show) everywhere in the United States without exception. I am familiar with this process since I have completed it 10 times purchasing long guns in New York State. First the sales clerk has the authority to refuse selling to you if he has any concern about you. Jared Loughner should have been refused.

To proceed with a purchase, you give the sales clerk your driver's license and fill out a form as follows. You include basic information like your name, address, height, weight, date of birth and Social Security number. You must be over 18 years old and certify that you are a U.S. citizen and include the city and state of your birth. You certify that you are not a convicted felon or currently indicted for a felony, are not a fugitive from justice in any state, have not been dishonorably discharged from military service, are not an unlawful drug user or convicted drug addict or dealer, have not been involuntarily committed to a mental institution or legally declared mentally incompetent, are not an illegal alien or legal alien admitted to the United States on a non-immigrant visa, are not a person who has officially renounced their American citizenship, are not a person convicted of misdemeanor domestic violence offences, and not someone under certain domestic violence restraining orders (stalker).

Then the sales clerk phones into the FBI instant background check number and gives them your full name, Social Security number and (in my case) that you are purchasing a long gun. They run their database searching for your name. If your record is clean, they give the sales clerk the OK. Here is the rub – the quality of the data in the FBI database; ie. the completeness of the list of criminals. Some states have been very good about reporting the data to the FBI and some (for their own reasons) have not. While Jared Loughner's mental problems were well known, he was presumably not in the FBI database.

In New York State, you cannot purchase a handgun or even touch one in a store without a handgun permit. To obtain a handgun permit is a very lengthy and costly process involving fees to various local and state agencies (New York State's way of life), multiple hurdles of forms, background checks, character references and certified safety training. Then, based on a judge's ruling, you can get a sportsman's or travel permit. The judge's decision is subjective and varies from county to county within the state. While New York State is technically a "right-to-carry" state, it is virtually impossible to get a "concealed carry" permit from a judge. After you receive your permit, you can go to a store and buy a handgun. You pay for it but cannot take possession of it until that firearm's serial number is registered to your permit. So, you come back to the store a few days or weeks later to get your weapon.

In New York State you cannot buy an ammo clip with a capacity greater than 10 for any semi-automatic weapon- a .22 rifle or a 9mm handgun. Due to a loophole in the law (I don't know whether Federal or New York State) some stores will sell "pre-ban" magazines with capacities of 20 or 30 rounds. These are essentially used and old magazines manufactured before the ban prohibiting magazines with greater than 10 rounds that lapsed in 2004. These magazines are for semi-automatic rifles.

In Massachusetts, you need a gun permit to buy ammunition. You cannot carry a bullet in your pocket without a gun permit. If you are caught with a bullet in your pocket and without a gun permit on your person, you and any companions with you are subject to arrest and a one-year prison sentence. That was for a bullet in your pocket with no firearm in your possession.

In Vermont, if you are a Vermont resident, you can walk out of a gun store with a handgun following the FBI instant background check. No gun permit is required. Apparently, the same is true for Arizona.

As stated by the second amendment which was written down by the founding fathers of the United States, each citizen is given the right to keep and bear arms. There is a huge controversy on its interpretation and whether or not we should take the statement literally.

One thing is for sure, all of us have a right to bear arms, but like all our other rights, there should be boundaries and limits. This is where sensible gun laws come in.

Here is some reference information for sites regarding existing Federal gun control laws:

- National Firearms Act (1934)

- Omnibus Crime Control and Safe Streets Act of 1968

- Gun Control Act (1968)

- Firearms Owner's Protection Act (1986)

- Brady Handgun Violence Prevention Act (1993)

- Federal Assault Weapons Ban (1994 – 2004) **(now defunct)**

- Arms Export Control Act (1976)

- Protection of Lawful Commerce in Arms Act (2006)

Like any controversial subject, there can be no dialog moving toward resolution without reasonableness. If a person maintains the position that all guns should be banned and no one should be permitted to possess one, then no meaningful dialog is possible with that person. If a person maintains the position that everyone should have the right to possess guns with no restrictions, then no meaningful dialog is possible with that person.

My intent was to write this article in such a way as to provide its information evenhandedly and without bias to the best of my ability. It is just information derived from data. If wisdom is profound knowledge, that must be formed within you. I would invite comments from fair minded and reasonable people.

Section 5 – Politics

Political Parties in Historical Perspective

Originally written in 2011

From The Life of the Parties – A History of American Political Parties by A. James Reichley

This book, without point of view, details the entire history of our political parties and political leaders from the beginning to our contemporaries in the late 1980's. Beyond our familiarity with the founding of our country, the revolutionary war and the civil war, the rest of our history is especially fascinating when you read about the constantly changing political labels used at various times and the way the parties' ideologies shifted and combined in almost every conceivable way. There are strains of similarity with today's politics; but also significant differences. The politics continuously evolved with almost every election cycle.

What follows are a smattering of Reichley's historical accounts and some of my interpretations.

We are all familiar with how it started with George Washington- the reluctant Federalist, John Adams- the Federalist, Alexander Hamilton- the uber Federalist and Thomas Jefferson- the Republican (Antifederalist). The Federalists were something like today's Republicans BUT were for a strong central government to protect property rights of the landed gentry and sovereignty over the states. They followed the British authoritarian style of government. Remember this was before the Bill of Rights – the first 10 amendments to the Constitution.

The Jeffersonians were something like today's Democrats BUT were for a loose union with states rights and more individual freedoms. Jefferson liked the French and their "burn-everything-to-the ground" revolution leading to anarchy but freedom (temporary until the vacuum allowed Napoleon Bonaparte to sweep in as dictator and emperor). It is difficult, maybe impossible, to match these ideologies up with today's Republicans and Democrats.

The secession of seven southern states before Lincoln's inauguration, and four more when the President resorted to arms to put down the rebellion, directly challenged the Republicans' concept of nationalism. The nation, Lincoln maintained, was anterior to federation and took precedence over even the Constitution. "Was it possible," he asked, when the constitutionality of some of his wartime measures was challenged, "to lose the nation and yet preserve the Constitution?"

The progressive era began under Theodore Roosevelt's Republican administration and expanded under Woodrow Wilson. Roosevelt described himself as a centrist conservative. At that time progressivism meant reforming the corruption in government. It meant revisions in electoral procedures to circumvent the stranglehold that political machines and the "bosses" in the cities and states held over the process. Their goal was to weaken the political parties.

The populists of the early 1890's had aimed to form a party capable of breaking through the existing party system. But they had no particular objection to the party as a political institution. In contrast, the progressives, their successors as advocates and agents of political reform, set out not only to supplant one of the major parties but to reduce drastically the role and power of party institutions.

The progressives, who won control of many state and local governments around the turn of the century and established broad influence in Congress and in several national administrations, had almost as low a view of parties as the Founders. Government inefficiency and political corruption, they argued, grew almost inevitably from the party system. Parties of the kind that had evolved by the end of the nineteenth century, Herbert Croly, a leading progressive ideologist and publicist, claimed, were concerned chiefly with the pursuit of patronage, which produced "enfeeblement" of government. "Overthrow of the two-party system," Croly wrote, was "indispensable to successful progressive democracy."

The sources feeding progressivism pursued differing, in some cases incompatible, social goals. But they had in common certain assumptions and themes: government should play an active role in promoting the public good: political life is best seen as a moral struggle between good and evil; public confidence requires honest elections and effective government: the existing party system is a major barrier to political reform; and government should serve the public interest rather than advancing particular interests to the exclusion of others or acting chiefly as broker between competing special interests. All these themes came together in the pronouncements and personality of the charismatic leader who became the progressive movement's virtual embodiment: Theodore Roosevelt.

What the progressives, like the Founders, overlooked was that democracy without strong parties, particularly when government authority is constitutionally divided, is likely to be short on means to pose significant policy choices to the voters, to coordinate governmental decision-making, or to implement ideological or policy shifts among the electorate.

In the 1920's the term liberal in American political discourse usually represented, as it still does in Europe, opposition to all forms of collectivism. Liberals defended civil liberties, opposed an established church, favored limited and decentralized government, and championed the market as the fairest and most efficient means of organizing the economy.

In the political struggles from the 1890's to the 1920's, progressives and liberals, though allied on some issues, were politically distinct. Progressives were governmental activists, though the goals of their activism were often conservative. Liberals, in contrast argued that government, because of its inherent inefficiency, intrusiveness into private life, resistance to change, and tendency to reinforce the socially strong against the weak, should be turned to only as a last resort, except for a few specified purposes such as keeping up national defense and maintaining a stable national currency.

Jefferson, John Stuart Mill, and William Ewart Gladstone were the patron saints of liberalism, as Hamilton and Lincoln were of progressivism. In the great debate of 1912 Wilson and Brandeis were liberals and Theodore Roosevelt and Croly were progressives. These differences were by no means clear-cut or consistently applied, but they were meaningful within the political community.

So, liberals and progressives are distinctly different. We should keep this in mind when we use the terms interchangeably today.

Lincoln's Storytelling

Originally written in 2013

According to the new movie *Lincoln*, starring Daniel Day-Lewis, Abraham Lincoln had a penchant for obsessive storytelling. His colleagues in his cabinet would groan and beg him to stop. He would smile wryly and respond with the telling of another story. This was his way of teaching a lesson.

When asked to explain my political beliefs, I like to answer this way:

In 2006 Edie and I took a wonderful 21-day, motor coach excursion covering over 3,300 miles of the UK. At one point we stayed overnight way up in the highlands on the northwest coast of Scotland. In the Isle of Skye, there was a lady folksinger who entertained us in the lobby of our old hotel.

She said "Half of me is Irish and half of me is Scottish; so I really want a drink, but I don't want to pay for it!"

Well, "Half of me is liberal and half of me is conservative." I am a libertarian.

This position is often misunderstood. Think of it this way. With respect to our liberties, make a list of all the freedoms and rights that liberals believe in. Next make a list of all the freedoms and rights that conservatives believe in. These lists are very different. Now make a list containing all the items from both of these lists. In the case where there is a direct conflict (pro-choice versus pro-life), we will make a personal decision. That is what libertarians believe in.

Conservatives hate us because we have the liberal stuff on our list. Liberals hate us because we have the conservative stuff on our list. This does not dissuade us.

We believe in a small, limited government that provides us the basic protections of our rights and of law and order, but no more. Madison's famous words "If laws are required by the fact that men are not angels, controls on the government are required by the fact that angels do not govern men" apply. Beyond the appropriate necessity of government, leave us alone to pursue our happiness, provided we are law abiding and do not cause harm to others. Our individual moralities and personal beliefs are our own and should not be imposed on us by others.

We reject the dual tyrannies of socialistic-democracy and rigid conservative ideas and thought. We will not willingly accept either or willingly live under either.

We can eat what we want, drink what we want, smoke what we want, lawfully shoot with what we want, work where and how we want, love whom we want, marry whom we want and we own our own bodies. We respect the right of others to do the same. Liberty values individualism and this is all about individualism.

We do not believe in imposing our beliefs on other persons or countries. We do not accept the impositions of conservatives or liberals on our rights and freedoms. If there is no state or place where these liberties can be accommodated, we will live within ourselves.

Looking inwardly, the libertarian idea would be about self-rights. John Locke outlined the principles of natural rights and government by consent. He had much to say about our inherent rights and our interactions with others - ".... that being all equal and independent, no one ought to harm another in his life, health, liberty, or possessions."

Looking outwardly, it would be a view of tolerance. From Emerson's Transcendental view, it would be about independence from society.

Ralph Waldo Emerson's *Self-Reliance* contains the most thorough statement of one of his recurrent themes, the need for each individual to avoid conformity and false consistency, and follow his or her own instincts and ideas. It is the source of one of his most famous quotations: "A foolish consistency is the hobgoblin of little minds."

We believe our beliefs are quintessentially American.

Sorry this wasn't more about Lincoln's storytelling. Would you have read it if it had a title about my political beliefs?

What Liberals Won't Admit

Originally written in 2013

There's a reason why conservatives think that liberals are a special kind of stupid. Believing that they are the better ones by providing their brand of loving-kindness, tolerance, and goods and services to their neighbors, liberals are weakening peace and stability at home and around the world.

As secularists with no tolerance for Christianity, liberals cannot accept the uncomfortable truth that Islam is proving more and more around the world that their intent is intolerant and merciless. They don't understand that they are complicit in killing innocent black Christians in Africa and threatening the existence of Israel. Their notion of tolerance, and their view that to get along, we must go along, emboldens forces of hate and greedy self-interest.

They don't understand what it means to be an exceptional nation, or that there is good in hegemonic power asserted competently as needed, or that to abdicate it is to descend into decline and mediocrity.

Liberals are also a special kind of arrogant. They believe that because they know best how to do good, the outcome will fall into place just as they have determined it. There will be no unintended consequences or overlooked considerations. It is a naïve belief that all factions are inherently good and well-meaning. James Madison wisely knew better. That allusion is left understood by those with a more complete education.

While these uncomfortable truths are harsh, they are also broad concepts that require enough understanding about reality that the inclusion of details is unnecessary. To include those details would require volumes – volumes that would not be read, understood, or agreed to. I've wasted years of my life trying to do that to no avail. This article is not an attempt at reeducation, but simply a condemnation. Stupid and arrogant cannot be reeducated.

_____

My Priorities

Originally written in 2011

To the Organizing for America grass roots movement e-mail I received from its director, Mitch Stewart asking for my input on Obama's budget I wrote:

I visited your form but couldn't express my priorities there.

My priorities would be:

1) Eliminate the Departments of Education, Energy, Agriculture, HUD and Fannie Mae and Freddie Mac. Send everybody home and sell the buildings.

2) There are 3 million Federal employees. Layoff 1 million of them and freeze the wages of the remaining 2 million. Reduce their pension and health care benefits going forward to match the more realistic norms of private industry.

3) Eliminate all subsidies (corporate welfare) to all industries, corporations and farmers. Let the free market do what it claims it can do.

4) Raise the Social Security retirement age to 67. Do it now. Raise the income cap for payroll tax contribution to increase revenue.

5) Stop the importation of foreign oil. Eliminate the ethanol program. It is an embarrassment. Put a muzzle on the EPA and permit drilling domestically for oil and natural gas onshore and offshore as well as coal mining and the construction of new nuclear power plants. Let the free market invest in this, as well as develop alternative energy, by staying out of the way.

6) Cut the defense budget by 50%. Bring the troops home from Korea, Germany, Japan, Iraq and Afghanistan. Let the Predator drones loose on the Afghan-Pakistan border and anywhere else they are needed. Post troops on the U.S.-Mexico border and have them shoot all illegal immigrants entering our country.

7) Do not raise the budget deficit limit. Pass a constitutional amendment requiring a balanced federal budget every year starting next year.

8) Eliminate the IRS and replace the tax code with a flat tax.

9) Lastly, and by all means, repeal Obamacare and start over on a smaller, more sensible scale.

That is change I can believe in.

David Jennings

Footnote:

To the Democratic Senatorial Campaign Committee (Guy Cecil) and AFSCME (Gerald W. McEntree) e-mails I received asking me to weigh in on the radical Republication agenda in Wisconsin, I responded:

It sounds to me like public employees are catching up to the economic realities that private employees have been experiencing for years - wage freezes, layoffs, reduction in benefits. It seems fair to me.

See my blog "Americans With A Lick Of Sense" at:
http://awlos.wordpress.com

_____

What is Everything?

―――――――――――⇒○⇐―――――――――――

Originally written in 2013

Some in the congress and administration have said that with respect to cutting the federal deficit and national debt, "Everything is on the table; including entitlements". There are two problems with their statement. First, they are disingenuous about the use of the word "everything". From their differing perspectives, they don't mean it. Secondly, the use of the word "entitlements" is a falsehood. While this word has been used extensively (ad nauseum) in recent years, technically there is no such thing. If this needs explanation, it is suggested you read more and with a goal of comprehension. See footnote.

So, in order to assist their sincere efforts to improve our economy, I am offering for their consideration the following, partial list of what everything includes:

- Reduction in the military budget to eliminate all non-essential expenditure while fully supporting the use of special forces. The philosophy and practice of nation building shall cease.

- Reduction in the foreign aid budget including elimination of all of our military defense forces in Germany, South Korea, Japan and elsewhere such that these counties may begin paying for their own defense.

- Elimination of fraud and abuse in the food stamp program.

- Elimination of fraud and abuse in the Medicare and Medicaid programs.

- Actuarial correction in the Social Security program – simple adjustments to raise the payroll tax salary limit and raise the retirement age for those under 55.

- Separation of the retirement and disability portions of the Social Security system.

- Elimination of fraud and abuse in the disability portion of the Social Security system.

- Elimination of the ethanol subsidy.

- Elimination of all the longstanding farm subsidies.

- Elimination of tax subsidies to the oil industry and any other applicable energy producing industries.

- Elimination of subsidies to large corporations including mortgage banking and green energy related businesses.

- Elimination of Fannie Mae and Freddie Mac.

- Elimination of the federal Department of Education.

- Replacement of the tax code with a simple flat tax for all wage earners supplemented by a small national sales tax.

- Elimination of the Internal Revenue Service.

- Replacement of federal expenditure for interstate highways and related infrastructure with a toll system based on use. Retain all state and local systems based on state and local taxation.

- Elimination of subsidies to the arts – National Endowment for the Arts and PBS.

- Elimination of all federal programs, agencies and departments not specifically required as defined in the U.S. Constitution.

- Reforms in the salary and benefit structure for all elected public officials and all unelected federal public service employees.

- Creation and institution of a balanced budget amendment to the U.S. Constitution.

- Campaign finance reform.

- Elimination of PACs and lobby groups.

- Term limits.

While this is not a complete list, it is a good start.

Footnote: Bill O'Reilly has just coined a new term called "no-thinkums". It refers to a large segment of the electorate who are either too stupid or too intellectually lazy to become informed. Their brain is not in gear and they are unconscious. They have no clue what is going on. Since they cannot, are not or will not use their rational mind for reasoning, they cannot see objective reality. So for example, when the Democrats incredulously squirm out of their complicity for our current economy by blaming the Tea Party, there are millions who will believe them and will vote for them.

The Good and Evil of Environmentalism

Originally written in 2014

In the 1970s, I was directly involved, as part of my career, with statewide air pollution monitoring for the states of Massachusetts, New York, Texas, and California. I was also involved with health and safety monitoring of coal mines in West Virginia. At that time, the states had strong environmental monitoring agencies and the federal EPA was a less significant entity. The coal mining industry however, was directly monitored by the federal agency - MSHA (Mine Safety and Health Administration).

At that time, much positive good was accomplished in reducing noxious gas pollution from stack emissions and to a much lesser extent, automobile tailpipes. The standards for coal mines also mandated a higher degree of protection for the miners.

Now, in 2014, our professor has given us a lecture on the economic plight of farmers in view of expansive industrial development in the late 19th century. Attention was given to this concern and the federal government began to get involved in support of farming. He asked if any of us had ever visited Washington DC. He mentioned that one time when he was there, he noted the size of the Department of Agriculture building. He said that it was four blocks long and four blocks wide and he wondered what all the people in the building were doing. I wondered if he had noted all the other buildings of comparable size for other federal agencies and what the people in those buildings were doing.

As the size and power of the EPA has grown, it has become a hegemonical force with the ability to independently affect all of our lives. It is a self-contained government unto itself that can administer, legislate, and adjudicate. If congressional oversight and the courts aren't paying attention, the EPA can pretty much do whatever it wants.

It can autonomously close down the last lead smelting plant in the United States and eliminate production of lead in ammunition, thereby impacting Second Amendment rights of law-abiding gun owners as a fulfillment of an unrelated political agenda.

As another minor example of the EPA's power, but a pointed one, it has mandated that we are required to replace 60 cent light bulbs with 6 dollar light bulbs that don't work as well. This will reduce the amount of current required to produce the same luminous output. That, in turn will reduce the amount of generated electrical power, and resultant energy consumption, required for lighting our homes and offices. Ultimately, the belief is that this will reduce the amount of pollution from the energy producing power plants. This is also a small, but pointed, example of our government causing our expendable income to be diminished and the effect of this on the economy of our society as a whole. Most often there is more than one solution to a problem.

So if you believe that absolute power corrupts absolutely, and you believe, with a healthy amount of cynicism, that most motivations are political, then you must start to become alarmed. To place blind faith in the progressive goodness of our government would be foolhardy.

Neocentrism

Originally written in 2010

For what it's worth, my political position has been changing the last couple years and is coming into focus as what I can best describe as neocentrism. Who cares what I believe? My friend Carl told me that the reason I am compelled to write down my views is so that when I die, people can read them and say "This is what Dave believed". Ha Ha.

In any case, as one would expect, neocentralism draws from the good (in my view) ideas of both the right and the left and is positioned in the ideological center. There are very few of us. The ideology is fiscal liberal and social conservative. The core values are precisely those outlined by the founding fathers of our country. They include the preservation of individual freedoms, tolerance and respect for the beliefs of others and respect for the law of the land.

Illuminating information

Naomi Klein's "The Shock Doctrine – The Rise of Disaster Capitalism" chronologues government activities since the mid 1970's. It details the collaboration of the government, the military and large corporations to take advantage of political regimes and natural disasters. It documents a consistent string of historical cases in South America, Eastern Europe, Asia and finally the US itself where capitalism, in collaboration with government policy, has taken advantage of situations in a predatory manner. It follows the economic principles established by Milton Friedman at the University of Chicago. The methodology is to privatize public institutions, including the government and military, by outsourcing all functions possible to profit making companies, leaving the public institutions hollowed out. This was very evident in the Iraq war where the government basically acted as a purchasing agent spending taxpayers' money to outsource all that it possibly could.

So when the Tea Party and other anti-government groups get incensed about out-of-control government spending, I agree with them. When they become outraged about the debt inherited by the middle class taxpayer, I agree with them. When they believe that funds can be better managed by smart, savvy capitalists than by feckless, incompetent bureaucrats, I disagree with them. The predatory capitalists are running the store and the government is the conduit for the money.

Joe the Plumber (the tool of the conservatives) said he did not want redistribution of wealth – its socialism. He was thinking about middle class wealth flowing to the poor. There has in fact been a reverse socialism going on for decades. Make no mistake; there has been a redistribution of wealth. Middle class wealth has been flowing to the rich.

More recently, we have learned of former AIG partner, Phil Heilberg who is now one of the largest private landowners in Africa. He has "invested" in global warming and is betting that overpopulation, floods, droughts, political unrest and food riots will turn him a huge profit. He says of Africa "The whole place is one big Mafia – and I'm like a Mafia head." Phil's moral code is that of Ayn Rand – Place yourself above all else; get in no one's way, and let no one get in yours; give no charity, and expect none.

Arrogance and self-interest are not the private and sole domain of capitalists however. Prominent liberal Michael Bloomberg, mayor of New York City, has made it his personal mission to trod on the rights of individuals. He has decided what is best for us by banning transfat, smoking and guns in his city. He has pushed hard in Washington to make his rules the law of the land. He says that he wants to enforce prosecution of ILLEGAL gun owners; but he is actually legislating the elimination of LEGAL gun ownership by law abiding citizens. Brady Campaign advocates say that the NRA wants to put a gun in everyone's hand. The NRA says that the Brady Campaign wants to take away all guns from everyone. A rational discussion is needed to clarify and distinguish the difference between the prosecution of criminals using illegal guns in the commission of criminal acts versus the lawful right of law abiding citizens to possess and use firearms.

Neocentrist Core Principles:

While these lists may appear incongruous on the surface, the beliefs fit together consistently if thought through. They are about pro-choice applied broadly.

Social conservative-

• Gays shall have equal rights in every regard- marriage, property law, openness in the military, the workplace and all walks of life.

• Women, on an individual basis, shall have the right to choose termination or completion of their pregnancy. There is no such thing as being for abortion or against abortion. It is a personal moral choice based on the individual's beliefs. The government has no place in this matter.

• Immigration laws shall be enforced vigorously. Violators shall be prosecuted to the full extent of the law. The only path to immigration shall be the legal one followed by the Europeans in the past. English is the written and spoken language in the United States of America. No more "press 1 for English".

• Law abiding citizens shall continue to have the right to keep and use firearms.

- The government shall not define social behavior and legislate "politically correct" social norms.

- The government shall not legislate food and nutrition laws dictating what the citizens can or cannot eat.

Fiscal liberal-

- Unfettered capitalism shall be rigorously regulated to protect the economy and the people. Violators shall be prosecuted to the full extent of the law.

- The rich shall bear the cost of caring for the poor.

- The middle class shall have the opportunity to regain its former economic stature.

- All citizens shall have access to affordable health care.

- The systematic destruction of unions by the government's Department of Labor shall cease. Union members are entitled to fair wages and benefits. However, unions must continue to sacrifice alongside fair and honest management in difficult economic times.

Footnotes:

1) Many of our politicians have stated their principles and beliefs in broad terms without any thought or mention of practical implementation. I have done the same in my principles stated above.

2) I realize that both extreme conservatives and extreme liberals have no margin for discussion or compromise of their views. Therefore, each will pick their specific offensive parts, find those parts unsatisfactory and reject the whole neocentrism ideology.

3) How can full equal rights for gays be considered a social conservative position? Simple; it fits perfectly with the core values of the founding fathers of our democracy.   Don't confuse the realities of our country's history with its founding principles.

4) How can a woman's right to choose be considered a social conservative position? Same answer.

5) I was asked recently during a telephone survey from a Democrat organization if I was for or against abortion. I said that the question was offensive and inappropriately phrased and refused to answer it as worded. I was being kind. The question was stupidly worded. No one is for abortion. That would mean one would go up and down the streets admonishing pregnant women to abort. Personally, I am against killing fetuses and I am against killing 18 year olds by sending them off to war. Sometimes both are necessary. The question is are you for pro-life or pro-choice. To be for pro-choice still does not mean you are for abortion. It means you leave the decision to the pregnant lady. It's a matter of respecting the individual's moral or religious beliefs. Again, this fits with our founding principles.

Facts, Truth and Logic

Originally written in 2009

There are a limitless number of "facts" out there. You choose to believe the ones that fit your ideology and so do I.

As a still practicing engineer, I am compelled to seek irrefutable logic to arrive at "truth" from "facts". As with everyone, I am biased by my personal values and sense of morality.

When I hear "truth" arrived at from "pretzel" logic, I am disturbed. I have observed both the smart, as well as the stupid, twist the "facts" and make illogical connections to draw absurd conclusions to form their "truth". Some may not even believe their own words but are trying to convince others. Among these, I include Sarah Palin, Nancy Pelosi, Sean Hannity, Rush Limbaugh, Glen Beck, Jim Demint, Eric Cantor and John Boehner.

Based on my attempts at logical reasoning, I have many questions:

What is wrong with universal health care?

Why is gay marriage a threat to anyone?

Why isn't adoption a viable alternative to abortion in most cases of unwanted pregnancy?

Why is it wrong to abort fetuses but OK to send young people to unnecessary wars?

Why isn't stricter enforcement a more viable alternative than stricter gun registration laws to reduce gun violence?

333

What is wrong with racial profiling as a statistically valid approach for law enforcement and security forces?

Why is government "bad" and corporations "good"?

What is wrong with government regulating free market capitalism?

Why are captains of industry competent while government bureaucrats are not?

Why are deferred compensation retirement plans being replaced by deferred contribution retirement plans?

Really, why?

What's in a Name-calling You Idiots?

Originally written in 2011

As you can tell from the facetious title, we are all guilty of name calling and labeling. Even open-minded, gracious and kind hearted individuals like Joy Behar. Even myself and members of my family. Of course, when we do it, it's with intelligence and cynicism toward all. If I could, I'd be P.J. O'Rourke. But how does it help? It's how we express our displeasure; especially when we feel powerless. But enough psychoanalytical justification.

I recently did due diligence and tried to read through an article in the blog publication "Natural Born Citizen – Respecting the Constitution" (http://naturalborncitizen.wordpress.com/) called "Multiple Instances of Historical Scholarship Establish The Supreme Court's Holding in Minor v. Happersett as Standing Precedent on Citizenship – Obama Not Eligible". The Constitution states that only a "natural born citizen" qualifies a person to be president, a much more stringent requirement than simply being "born a citizen". Several readings of the case are evaluated and the opinions go back and forth in this interminably lengthy presentation.

I tried to read this but became confused. I guess the issue is that while Obama was born in the USA and one of his parents is a U.S. Citizen, the other is not. This apparently satisfies one of the two legal definitions of citizenship requirement for POTUS but not quite the other. It's about the law. Yeah, right! What is the end goal of this hair splitting? Do we want to throw Obama out and have Joe Biden as our president to complete this one-term presidency? We have more concerns than this to worry about with Obama and our country's economy, debt, and unemployment problems.

This is like all the nonsense circulating around that Obama is another Hitler while at the same time another Mao. Who cares?

Throughout history effigy hangings have made some feel better but have not solved a single problem. Who needs these labels and name calling; only childish minds. All that matters is that Obama is a big government spender and a collectivist. We need to vote him out.

A recent joke circulating around demonstrates the low road many are taking based on their frustration with the President and his administration:

A black guy, an illegal alien, a muslim, and a communist walk into a bar.

The bartender asks, "What can I get you Mr. President ?"

Mr. President, you are just a poopy head. What are we; in 3rd grade?

And then there is the vicious name calling circulating the media demonstrated by Hank Williams, Jr's recent remarks. I am not a northeastern snob and have nothing against rednecks but I really don't like this cocky, ignorant guy. As Jon Stewart recently said, Williams once fell off a 400 foot cliff and survived despite holding his oozing gray matter in his hands and that you could smell the Jack Daniels on his breath through the television.

We have plenty of rednecks in upstate New York. They are everywhere. Why can't we all just get along? I strongly identify with working people and I particularly like southerners like Will Hayden, owner of Red Jacket in Baton Rouge, for his values rooted in liberty, patriotism and our history. I only know his public persona from the Discovery channel on cable TV, but he seems to be one of the least sanctimonious men I have seen. I certainly would enjoy meeting him.

So, applying all my intelligence and erudition, and with no sanctimony, I will call them as I see them.

I Can See Clearly Now

Originally written in 2010

This is not to be critical of anyone or tell them how to think or what to believe. It is just to tell of the infancy of my path to understanding, enlightenment and consciousness.

In the beginning, I listen to MSNBC and FOX. I read the supposedly humorous hate mongering circulating on the internet. I am taught who to hate and why. Depending on who I listen to, I am supposed to hate Barack Obama, John Boehner, John F. Kennedy, George Bush, Franklin Delano Roosevelt, Nancy Pelosi, Al Franken or Ann Coulter. This teaches me nothing. I am not enlightened or any wiser. I am unconscious. The view is too narrow; too microscopic. I have no perspective.

I step back and try to look more macroscopically. In truth I can learn something from the stories and beliefs of all the persons above and many others.

I try to understand the circumstances of the creation of our democracy, what the people thought, how our republican form of government was born. I understand that our present day government takes our property, tells us how to live and does not give us representation. Are we more free? Is our system broken and in need of reform?

I listen to the concerns of George Washington and John Adams who warned that political parties would cause great harm to the development of our country. I reject our two-party system and the virtue, correctness or wisdom of either party to govern our people. The answer might be a strong, independent third party untethered by the ideologies of the other two. Perhaps a smaller federal government would serve us better. I know that man living in his natural state with no government is anarchy.

I step back further and try to look at an even bigger picture. I have read some Adam Smith but need to read John Locke, Jean-Jacques Rousseau, Pericles, Aristotle and Socrates for more perspective. I am beginning to see more clearly and understand. I am awakening.

Section 6 – Economics

Federal Income Tax Structure

Originally written in 2010

Here is a brief history of personal income tax in the United States:

The Act of 1862 established the office of Commissioner of Internal Revenue. The Commissioner was given the power to assess, levy, and collect taxes, and the right to enforce the tax laws through seizure of property and income and through prosecution. The powers and authority remain very much the same today.

In 1868, Congress again focused its taxation efforts on tobacco and distilled spirits and eliminated the income tax in 1872. It had a short-lived revival in 1894 and 1895. In the latter year, the U.S. Supreme Court decided that the income tax was unconstitutional because it was not apportioned among the states in conformity with the Constitution.

In 1913, the 16th Amendment to the Constitution made the income tax a permanent fixture in the U.S. tax system. The amendment gave Congress legal authority to tax income and resulted in a revenue law that taxed incomes of both individuals and corporations.

In 1981, Congress enacted the largest tax cut in U.S. history, approximately $750 billion over six years. The tax reduction, however, was partially offset by two tax acts, in 1982 and 1984, that attempted to raise approximately $265 billion.

On Oct. 22, 1986, President Reagan signed into law the Tax Reform Act of 1986, one of the most far-reaching reforms of the United States tax system since the adoption of the income tax. The top tax rate on individual income was lowered from 50% to 28%, the lowest it had been since 1916. Tax preferences were eliminated to make up most of the revenue. In an attempt to remain revenue neutral, the act called for a $120 billion increase in business taxation and a corresponding decrease in individual taxation over a five-year period.

Following what seemed to be a yearly tradition of new tax acts that began in 1986, the Revenue Reconciliation Act of 1990 was signed into law on Nov. 5, 1990. As with the '87, '88, and '89 acts, the 1990 act, while providing a number of substantive provisions, was small in comparison with the 1986 act. The emphasis of the 1990 act was increased taxes on the wealthy.

On Aug. 10, 1993, President Clinton signed the Revenue Reconciliation Act of 1993 into law. The act's purpose was to reduce by approximately $496 billion the federal deficit that would otherwise accumulate in fiscal years 1994 through 1998. In 1997, Clinton signed another tax act. The act, which cut taxes by $152 billion, included a cut in capital-gains tax for individuals, a $500 per child tax credit, and tax incentives for education.

President George W. Bush signed a series of tax cuts into law. The largest was the Economic Growth and Tax Relief Reconciliation Act of 2001. It was estimated to save taxpayers $1.3 trillion over ten years, making it the third largest tax cut since World War II. The Bush tax cut created a new lowest rate, 10% for the first several thousand dollars earned. It also established a slow schedule of incremental tax cuts that would eventually double the child tax credit from $500 to $1000, adjust brackets so that middle-income couples owed the same tax as comparable singles, cut the top four tax rates (28% to 25%; 31% to 28%; 36% to 33%; and 39.6% to 35%)

The Jobs and Growth Tax Relief and Reconciliation Act of 2003 accelerated the tax rate cuts that had been enacted in 2001, and temporarily reduced the tax rate on capital gains and dividends to 15%. In 2004, the U.S. was forced to eliminate a corporate tax provision that had been ruled illegal by the World Trade

Organization. Along with that tax hike, Congress passed a cornucopia of tax breaks, which for individuals included an option to deduct the payment of whichever state taxes were higher, sales or income taxes.

Two tax bills signed in 2005 and 2006 extended through 2010 the favorable rates on capital gains and dividends that had been enacted in 2003, raised the exemption levels for the Alternative Minimum Tax, and enacted new tax incentives designed to persuade individuals to save more for retirement.

So this means that we may have started out with a flat income tax where everyone, at all income levels, paid the same percentage rate. Then we modified the tax structure to become graduated or progressive. This meant that the low-income wage earners paid a lower percentage rate than the higher earners. For example, earners of $5,000 per annum might pay 5%, earners of $50,000 – 15%, $500,000 – 30%, etc. This was intended to help out the people at the bottom. Is this socialism? If so, we have had it since before 1986 under President Reagan.

Currently, the Republicans are asserting that the tax structure is too progressive. If, for the top 2% of wage earners, the temporary Bush tax cut is allowed to lapse and the incremental tax rate reverts from 35% to 39.6%, they portray this as the highest tax increase in history. See above; not true.

Currently, the Democrats are asserting that the tax structure is too regressive. If, for the top 2% of wage earners, the temporary Bush tax cut is reinstated and the incremental tax rate remains at 35%, they portray this as a large tax cut. See above; not true.

In any case, this monumental decision will be made by the legislature very soon. It will be the reaction to the decision that will be so telling of our system.

If the decision is to reinstate the existing 35% for the highest wage earners, this status quo will set off jubilation in our underdamped, open loop (engineering control terms), perception driven financial markets. The DOW will rise to unchartered heights. Corporations and small businesses will release the floodgates of withheld cash, hire new employees and the economy will begin a robust recovery. Yeah, right. Over at MSNBC, snarky Rachael Maddow will bitch about the unfairness of it all every night for a month. Obama and Pelosi will bemoan this loss for the American people.

If the decision is to revert to the former 39.6% tax rate, this mighty change will set off devastation in the financial markets. Petulant investors will have a hissy fit and sell out. The market will plummet. Cautious businesses will take this as a very discouraging sign and hold their cash. Over at FOX, the spittle will be flying out of righteous Sean Hannity's mouth at this outrage. Obama and Pelosi will revel in this great victory for the American people.

Neither makes a lick of sense. Spin the facts; ignore history; leave out perspective; create perception; convince the electorate. Am I cynical? You bet. Could I be more cynical? Maybe. Do you see how ridiculous we are?

And Then There's The Other Middle Class

Originally written in 2011

Who work for a private sector employer.

Whose salary is based only on the fiat of the boss's perception of their value and market forces.

Whose salary has no cost-of-living escalation.

Who may experience years of wage freezes.

Who may experience reduced income from reduced hours.

Who, unbelievable but true, may experience temporary wage reductions in extreme circumstances.

Who, unbelievable but true, may experience no pay for some periods of work under special circumstances.

Whose bargaining power with their employer for any benefits is only their perceived value.

Who work on the government holidays.

Who work 40 or more hours per week for 52 weeks of the year.

Who may receive 6 paid sick days and 2 weeks paid vacation per year.

Whose job security is directly affected by the economy and the employer's success.

Who have no tenure or seniority.

Who must work until they are 65 and eligible for Social Security and Medicare.

Whose only pension is their deferred contribution plan with the possibility of partial matching by their employer.

Whose health insurance premium cost is substantially borne by themselves and coverage may be compromised to hold down cost.

Who, along with their employers, pay taxes into the public coffers with no control over the taxation amount, no wage protection, no guaranteed wage increases, no benefit increases and no job loss protection.

Who are not considered by society as special, exceptional or entitled.

This is the middle class that you don't hear anything about in the media.

This is the middle class that, with their sacrifice, is paying for the other entitled middle class.

Section 7 – Literature as Art

What is an Essay?

Originally written in 2016

An essay is a short written article or piece to express and develop one thought or idea. Its topic may be a warm or melancholy personal memoir, an observation of an external event or people, an exegesis of what one writer thinks about another writer's writing, or a strong expression of a view or perspective.

LENGTH

Typically an essay is short, containing 3 to 20 pages and 500 to 10,000 words. It has no chapters or table of contents.

STRUCTURE

It follows a typical school paper structure with an introduction, a body and a conclusion. The introduction is usually a brief one or two paragraphs which states a premise or hypothesis declaring what is to be said or proven. The body presents and develops the main information, facts or evidence to prove or disprove the hypothesis. The conclusion briefly states that the essay has proven or disproven its premise.

This is the classical structure of an essay. It may literally identify the introduction, body and conclusion with headings or merely imply them without captions through the flow of its writing.

This is in contrast to a pure memoir that merely tells a story without any of this formal structure.

TOPIC

This may be anything that strikes the writer's passion, and in his mind, that must be said and shared by his readers.

351

MARKETING AND DISTRIBUTION

The essay may be written just for one's own edification, shared with friends or family, or offered to a newspaper, magazine or internet vehicle for public consumption.

The Life of a Writer

Originally written in 2016

Writers love to talk about writing with anyone, but enjoy it most with other writers. It is like being with your own kind who understand the trials and tribulations, the purpose, the expectations, the glory and the shame – the glory of the well-crafted sentence and the shame of not writing enough.

First of all, it is a job. It isn't about writing a great book, or an article or poem. It is about going to work, picking up your tools and building what you can every day. If it doesn't fit or sit straight, you can fix it. But build something first.

It begins with a thought, an idea or a dream. That's all the material you need to start. You have a vision of a story you want to tell. Begin speaking.

Find an anchor – a central idea about which everything hangs or pivots. Put a picture to it in your mind. After a while, a title will come when the muse has visited you.

Do not outline. That is a computer program that does not leave you any wiggle-room to wander and explore and develop. Write your whole story almost all at once from beginning to end. At first it will go fast and you will have 5,000 to 10,000 words in a hurry. Maybe you will see, as Faulkner always bragged, you will know exactly how it will end and have an idea how it should begin.

This book you have written quickly is no book. It is your outline. But it is too short and pitifully thin. You only have a few chapters and none of them are finished. Strengthen the end and the beginning, or the beginning and the end and ponder the middle. You need more characters to meet your characters. You need to develop their personalities and their experiences. You need more scenes. You need the muse to come back.

Listen to music, watch movies, read books, look at art or nature or the world events around you. Learn history. Learn history. The muse will come back.

Fatten the middle of the book. Your rate of progress may begin to slow down. Do what you can.

If you are waiting for something to happen, start another book. You have chosen the life of a writer, so one book is not your whole life. The muse will come back and you can bring the first book to life once more. Keep building. Go to work every day.

How will you know when it's done? You won't. Read what you have written. Does it completely fulfill your idea of the first place? Is there more to say? You will know the moment the story is done.

This story is done (for now). There are 462 words here excluding this sentence. I have been writing for about 30 minutes. I will go back to work tomorrow morning and type it later after the muse has left. I'll add more to it and edit it after that if she stays away awhile. A book has begun.

This morning I am continuing from last night and coasting along on the ideas the muse has left me. I do not have one chapter or one character yet.

A writer writes because he has to. A runner runs because she has to. She looks for longer trails, higher mountains, greener pastures to conquer. It is the same for a writer. Your shoes may be the third person omniscient or first person personal voice – active or passive. It really doesn't matter. Both take practice. In the conversational style, it is impossible to avoid, I, me, my. But after a while, these can be minimized. (Now there are 618 words and I have been writing for about an hour, accumulatively. Do not dwell on word count unless you are waiting.)

The Path to a Novelist

Originally written in 2016

I do not know what I do not know. None of us does. But I do know what I have learned, seen, read, practiced and done.

We all learn our grammar and build our vocabulary in primary and secondary school, maybe not so much as we used to. We read some examples of literature and write book reports.

We may go on to college and study English Comp. 101 and creative writing. We read fine literature and write exegesis – more thoughtful diagnostic analytical book reports. We practice writing about writers and the process of writing itself. There is a steep learning curve and the lifting is heavy.

We may read William Strunk's classic *The Elements of Style* and maybe other writing help books like William Zinsser's *On Writing Well*. With an eye to studying style, we try to copy and emulate fine writers we admire.

This can become contrived, awkward and unnatural. But we see that fine writers have put aside many of the grammatical rules we have learned for a number of good reasons. They may write long sentences with more than one idea and with too many independent and dependent clauses. They make use of split infinitives effectively. They may make up descriptive adjectives that do not exist in the English language like Joyce's "soot bleakened".

We learn that writing dialog, spoken by our characters, must most often be grammatically incorrect.

After much practice and thoughtful absorption of all this knowledge and influences, we find our own unique voice and write with it. It becomes natural for us and likely the most effective we can be for our readers.

Maybe our voice is simple like Hemingway's, some say at a 4th grade writing level, but full of meaning. Or maybe it is like Faulkner, full of brilliant enigma and sardonic bitter irony. Perhaps it will be like Joyce, though doubtful, with incomprehensible out-of-the box lunacy and literary gymnastics, taking the English language and using it as his own personal property, even inventing fictitious languages. Or it might be like Fitzgerald, just heartfelt lush and elegant words painting pictures from the page to your mind.

If you want it, do it. The work is hard but the reward is beyond imagination.

A 15 Minute Writing Exercise

Originally written in 2017

In a Writers Ring meeting, we did an exercise to take seven unrelated words, or short phrases, and spontaneously burst-write a paper in fifteen minutes. Most of us used six of the seven words with little difficulty. The words written on the blackboard were "cute kittens", "a half-eaten piece of pizza", "existential angst", "magicians", "empty sleeve of saltine crackers", "telepathic" and whatever the one was that I did not use and have forgotten. To make it work for me, I abruptly changed the subject while using the required word to start. Here it is:

Kittens are cute but not as loving as dogs, I say. You might believe otherwise. I think a dog can do a better job on a fallen, half-eaten piece of pizza on the floor.

But here's the thing. I may not know much of anything about cats, but I can give testimony that dogs are telepathic, at least about food. They can smell that bit of pizza going by in a car on the thruway when its window is down.

You can't fool them with an empty sleeve of saltine crackers either.

They suffer no existential angst. They are merely geniuses of using their winsome ways to coax your food away from you. We call that love for us humans. I'm not certain but I will settle for their love.

That are not magicians but they think they are. They hide their treasured treats in plain sight, assured you can't see them. The only angst they suffer is if they think you spot their deception. Then they will move their treasure trove to another silly spot.

Speak of existential, you know DOG is GOD spelled backwards. Did you think that was an accident?

Ideas

March 2017

All that we read and write is to express ideas. Whether recognized or not, that is its purpose. All of it has perspective – the perspective of the writer and the interpreted perspective of the reader.

Whether to entertain, inform or convince, ideas are the purpose of writing. The paper or the screen convey the output of the expresser to the input of the receptor.

Since verbal expression is extemporaneous, if spoken the perspective may be clear but the ideas may be not. It is necessary to temporize, take some time, to formulate ideas to a cogency and clarity. That is the reason for thinking and the written form. That is the value and the need for reading.

I chose to write in a period two centuries removed from my contemporary period. This was intentional in order to avoid the noise and confusion, lack of clarity and cogency of the ideas too close to the moment. It is a necessity, and a metaphor if you will, to express ideas better.

The form as themes does not matter but the themes themselves do, especially if they are universal. In most cases this means themes that are human. After all, humans are the only species that can communicate at this level. The form may be a fictional story or a historical account or a blend of both. It may be a technical instruction or the great old verities of humankind. It may be prose or poetry, spiritual, religious, secular or scientific.

All that is written and read is history whether we recognize it or not, whether it is fantasy, true, current or past. All of it has perspective whether from a primary source voice or a second-hand interpretation of that voice. It is our expression of our ideas we desire to write or enjoy to read.

Conversation alone is too limiting – both in the magnitude and breadth of its perspective of ideas.

Without reading there is no basis for thinking. Without writing our thoughts there is no ability to process our thinking to its best level.

Read. Think about it. Write about it.

Shelby Foote's Monumental Civil War Narrative

Originally written in 2016

Shelby Foote (1916-2005) is in the American lexicon of the great southern writers. He spent most of his early career as a novelist. He was not trained as an historian. Foote was not known then as a writer in the same league as fellow Mississippian William Faulkner. But when celebrated editor of Random House, Bennett Cerf asked him in 1951 if he would write a narrative of the Civil War, he agreed to undertake the task.

The result must have both overwhelmed and tried the patience of Bennett when the book took twenty years to produce. It was undoubtedly Shelby's greatest life's work. There are three volumes of The Civil War: A Narrative – Fort Sumter to Perryville (840 pages), Fredericksburg to Meridian (988 pages) and Red River to Appomattox (1106 pages). Shelby said in an interview that this 1.2 million words represented more than half of the approximate two million words he had written in his lifetime – a 30 year writing career.

When Ken Burns produced his noted PBS Civil War documentary in 1990, he asked Shelby if he would serve as a moderator or maybe more, the soul of the series. Shelby again agreed. After that participation, Foote gained national renown and respect for his masterwork and novels.

His writing in The Civil War: A Narrative is strenuous in detail for the reader, and it must have been for him as well. He said that he produced merely 500 words per day on average. The only fault I found with it was that while it was organized with a table of contents and chapters, it lacked headings to keep the reader on track with the timeline and the battles. It is easy to get lost, even with keen attentiveness, and lose track of which general is referred to, which battle is taking place and who is doing what to whom.

There were indeed over 9000 battles in the Civil War, including major skirmishes and excluding picket fire. There were indeed hundreds of generals, more in the South than the North, coming and going in participation with the war. Every man, whether a West Pointer or a politician who raised a local militia, was made a Brigadier General, again more so in the South, which was the lowest rank of General. Oddly, the highest rank of General, below the Commanding General, was Lieutenant General while that sounds like a junior general.

As far as any potential bias Shelby may have had for the Confederacy, because of his beloved Mississippi Delta, he did his best to be even-handed and nearly succeeded. He kept advisors and editors to help him watch out for that potential problem.

Here is a paragraph from Shelby Foote's 3rd volume of his monumental Civil War Narrative I particularly enjoyed. His tongue-and-check humor shines through it.

"For once, by dint of hard marching on rural roads and steady pressure on the rebel rear, execution matched conception; the convergence would be offered by midday tomorrow, May 19, on schedule and with each of the three component armies in its assigned position for the final thrust, Schofield left, McPherson right, and Thomas center. The trouble was that Sherman, for all the speed and precision of his approach, was converging on a vacuum. Johnston was not at Kingston; he was at Cassville, five miles east, preparing to spring an ambush that would eliminate, or at any rate badly mangle, a solid third of the blue force whose commander had at least afforded him the opportunity he had been awaiting ever since the campaign opened, two weeks and better than forty miles ago."

Note that the paragraph is just two sentences. He wrote, as he contemplated, in long streams.

Time and again, Shelby tells how the battles rarely, nearly universally never, came off as the generals had carefully planned them. Unplanned rain and deep mud foiled marches and factions of brigades and corps were delayed to show up at the right place and time. Occasionally, a subordinate commander would get caught up in an unplanned skirmish or even disobey orders and set out in a different direction to follow his own smaller plan. It was most often pure happenstance that determined the outcomes of many battles. It is extraordinary that the war ever concluded. While the North was always the clear dominate power, it looked like the South would hold out forever.

Shelby is often quoted now because his quotes are interesting and insightful. To paraphrase him, he said that (despite the issue of slavery) this war was its own thing and that the truth is the facts we love.

Art and Awe

Originally written in 2016

Don't you admire artistic talent when you see it; that ability of others, whether God-given or honed from years of passionate practice and study, to create something out of nothing and make you feel something deeply when you see it or hear it? What a joy and blessing they bring to our lives by entering our minds through our senses.

I am fortunate, like many of you, to have friends, family and acquaintances who can do that and it enriches our lives. They may not be the very best in the world, but they exceed that journeyman level. They have mastered an art.

My people (I know all their names and some are related to me) can paint, sculpt, create and perform dance, sing with a beautiful vocal instrument, play a guitar or a horn instrument, compose a piece of music, or conduct an orchestra. How great they are. Some can teach, and that is wonderful, but it is a greater thing that they can do.

The word that comes to mind is awesome. That word today has lost almost all its meaning because of the way we have come to use it. It meant to be filled with awe, so filled with awe that you were awestruck. It meant your jaw fell slack, your mouth was open and you were in a state near rapture.

For whatever reason, I longed to be able to play the guitar, but I never could. I am tone deaf and without rhythm. For years I played my guitar left handed without restringing it, so I played with it upside down and backwards. It was difficult to form the chords with my fingers and the strumming of the strings was in the reverse

367

order. As much as I loved the sound of a voice singing, mine didn't work or have barely one octave range. That is fine, just how it is.

Now I appreciate how a master can write. I struggle to reach a journeyman level and am improving. For my own intellectual reasons, I have focused on fictional literature and history, and narrowed in on American history and further in on the Civil War period and our late 19th and early 20th century.

This may mean nothing to you, but I admire these words. They are representative of a certain rich narrative style, skillfully executed by the late Shelby Foote, and I find them to be awesome:

"Now both rested from their injuries and exertions. Wrapped in their blankets, those who had them, the soldiers of both armies huddled close to fires they had kindled against orders. The waxing moon set early and the wind veered and blew coldly from the north; the screams of the wounded died away with the singing of the bone saws. Unlike the night before, on the eve of carnage, there were no serenades tonight, no mingled choruses of "Home Sweet Home," for even the bandsmen had fought in this savage battle, and expected to have to fight again tomorrow, bringing in the new year as they had ushered out the old.

So they thought; but they were wrong, at least so far as the schedule was concerned. Though there were tentative skirmishes, fitful exchanges of artillery fire, and some readjustment of tactical dispositions on both sides, New Year's Day saw nothing like the carnival of death that had been staged on New Year's Eve. In point of fact, the two armies were rather like two great jungle cats, who, having fought to mutual exhaustion, were content – aside, that is, from the more or less secret hope on the part of each that the other would slink away – to eye one another balefully, limiting their actions to licking their wounds and emitting only occasional growls and rumbles, while storing up strength to resume the mortal contest."

These are just a few of the 1.2 million words he wrote in 3,000 pages and 3 volumes, taking 20 years to complete his Civil War Narrative when Bennet Cerf, the celebrated editor at Random House, asked him if he would write a book about the Civil War.

First he was a Southern novelist and then became an historical narrator. That great Mississippi son-of-a bitch could write. And I think he would want us to remember him with just those words.

The Bonafides of History Writing

May 2017

History writing can be done as historical non-fiction which includes survey level textbooks, printing of primary sources (letters, memoirs, speeches, etc.) or biographies. It can also be written as historical fiction such as novels. There is a stigma that historical fiction is not valid as historical account.

Some writers, like Shelby Foote begin as novelists and turn to non-fiction narrative. Others like myself begin as non-fiction academic history students and turn later to novels.

For students, papers and essays must be meticulously cited with Kate Turabian's Chicago Style of footnotes, endnotes and bibliography. Failure to do so, and using another's words as your own is plagiarism and may be punished as a capital crime. For the professor, work must pass the muster of peer review. No wonder they dismiss historical fiction.

Historical fiction may not contain fantasy. That would be historical fantasy or alternative false history.

It must be a blend of authentic history and the stories of imaginary characters living in a historical period with its historical events. It is a blend of the two, but the history is valid. References and influences are often given, but citation is not required.

The mix of the two elements may vary. John Jakes uses about 10% history and about 90% fictional character stories. The Shaara's, father Michael and son Jeff, use about 90% history and about 10% fictional characters or fictional attributes of actual historical figures. I attempted to write my novels with a 50-50 blend.

Most importantly, one must understand what is truth. Some say there is no truth since accounts conflict. Others say the events and human figures are proven and the causes and effects are well understood to be true. Maybe. Bias, prejudice, viewpoint and perspective (all words mean the same thing) vary with the source, the writer and the reader.

There are errors of omission and commission and narrow focus on an agenda – the telling truthfully of the exceptional portion of the account without giving proportional justice to the whole. It certainly is permissible to tell the part of it but acknowledgment that this is being done would be more honest.

Accounts vary also from the perspective of the writer's time frame – the past written and re-written at different points of time. This is called historiography. It reflects the difficulty, the prejudice and the certain impossibility for the writer to have been there at the moment the history happened, but instead viewed through his contemporary lens. It is unavoidable.

Therefore historical fiction could be just as valid or sometimes more valid that historical non-fiction.

Stephen and Braveheart

Originally written in 2016

In the 1995 movie *Braveheart*, starring Mel Gibson, the time period is circa 1297 and the Scots peasants, not the nobles, are rebelling against Edward I (Longshanks) for his subjugation of Scotland. In this delightful scene William Wallace is being joined by Stephen. Stephen is from Ireland and he is joyous at the prospect to kill the English. But Stephen is a little bit insane and hilariously funny.

Stephen: [*starts laughing*] Him? That can't be William Wallace. I'm *prettier* than this man! [*to the sky*]

Stephen: Alright, Father, I'll ask him. [*to William*]

Stephen: If I risk my neck for you, will I get a chance to kill Englishmen?

Hamish: Is your father a ghost, or do you converse with the Almighty?

Stephen: In order to find his equal, an Irishman is forced to talk to God. [*to the sky*]

Stephen: Yes, Father! [*to Hamish*]

Stephen: The Almight says, "Don't change the subject, just answer the fuckin' question."

Hamish: Mind your tongue.

Campbell: Insane Irish.

Stephen: [*draws a dagger on Campbell; everyone draws weapons*] Smart enough to get a dagger past your guards, old man.

William Wallace: That's my friend, Irishman. And the answer to your question is "yes". You fight for me, you get to kill the English.

Stephen: [*grins*] Excellent! [*removes his dagger*]

Stephen: Stephen is my name. I the most wanted man on my island, except I'm not on my island, of course. More's the pity.

Hamish: "Your island"? You mean Ireland?

Stephen: Yeah. It's mine.

Hamish: You're a madman.

Stephen: [*nods and starts laughing, then Hamish does as well*] I've come to the right place, then.

_____

Faulkner's Writing Style

Originally written in 2015

Foreword Comments

Since this paper is concerned with William Faulkner's writing and his style, I thought it fitting to make a few opening remarks about writing as a general proposition. William Zinsser in his book, *On Writing Well* has given writers permission and encouragement to begin sentences with the first-person singular nominative pronoun "I" or the occasional "And" or "But" as preposition, adverb or conjunction where emphasis is justified. This makes writing in the active voice more convenient and natural. The conventions for college term papers coerce us to avoid this practice and fairly force us to write in the more contrived passive voice, or at least with perfect conventional grammar, while we are simultaneously encouraged to always write in the more interesting active voice. This writer will make his best attempt to avoid speaking of himself in the third person with the passive voice as was just constructed in this sentence.

Note also that William Faulkner wasn't concerned about run-on sentences and didn't bother to use commas with care to demark clauses - independent or dependent - since it didn't matter to him. William Strunk in his monumental work on grammar and style, *The Elements of Style* took great pains to explain to us in excruciating detail our proper use of commas. I don't think that Faulkner disliked commas, sometimes he used a lot of them and sometimes few; it just seemed he was unconcerned with them. He didn't want them to get in the way of his attention or expression.

And if you care much about the appearance of your words on paper - like a writer would - just how the line spacing, tab depth and type font looks and feels, how the first word of a paragraph is positioned at the beginning of a page and the last word of the last sentence of the last paragraph sits on the bottom of the page unbroken from the rest, how the thought ends perfectly before you turn the page, then you might not abide apostrophes on word contractions like dont, cant, wont and the rest.

For the great writers, too much obsessive attention to grammatical purity - not artistic appearance - would be a distraction from their creativity. Further, grammatical purity that dictates avoiding writing that uses split infinitives - "To boldly go where no man has ..." or "To quickly eat", "To deeply sleep .... " or "To vividly dream ... " - diminishes the breadth of opportunity for beautiful phrasing. I won't make a case for the use of dangling participles and would agree their use muddles writing. If I were (the correct hypothetical) William Faulkner, I would likely not see merit in the dangling participle either. These are just opinions based on observations. I am wrong 50 percent of the time. And finally, I can never know what I do not know.

For the rest of us pedestrian writers, and depending on our audience, there is a danger here. Closer adherence to conventional grammatical structure is likely the safer approach.

However, I will take some personal risk here and depart from my experiences writing non-fiction history papers in the acceptable manner for college history class purposes. As this is an American literature class, in contrast to history or economics or even English composition, and with adult students, I trust that a more creative, loose and open form of writing will be acceptable. I will attempt it.

I have read the notes and handouts provided for class discussion and understanding. They were invaluable, working with my diminutive intellect, to understand what the hell Faulkner was talking about. Some appeared as written by the literary critics of the newspapers, magazines, best seller list publishers, fellow writers and the like of Faulkner's day and later. Some were postured in the highest tone of passive voice, with an impressive plethora of comparative literary reference, and some far-fetched propositions for his motivations. Like Benjy's character in *The Sound and the Fury*, I could fairly smell the writers grasping for their publication and graduate degrees. Perhaps that was dismissive. In fairness, each has tried to understand him in their own way, as their own ideas have come to them. As an aside, I hold the view, along with others, than man is a sentient being above the beasts and below the angels. Sentience is awareness to the degree that a creature can feel pain, joy, frustration and love. I'm confident that since my dog is sentient, so is Benjy.

I have included several quotations in this paper at near full length since I felt them valuable in support of my assertions, enjoyable as literature, sometimes quixodical and confounding to the reader, and with value for a collector of such things as a keepsake. The page length of the paper will be adjusted above ten pages to compensate for this practice and comply with the assignment requirement.

Finally, I have asked my old friend Joan Austin - my contributing writer, muse and purely honest editor who lives in rural Athens, Alabama as a transplant Yankee forty years ago from New York - to visit Mr. Faulkner's grave if she passes by Oxford, Mississippi. She is instructed to greet him with a smile and with good cheer he would appreciate, "Thanks a lot you Son of a Bitch for writing books to confound us. No, really thank you Bill. Memory believes before knowing remembers. Believes longer than recollects, longer than knowing even wonders."

Introduction

What we refer to as literature is a high form of art expressed as fiction. It is not bounded by many of the grammatical rules and conventions that must be abided in non-fiction. It allows expression with imagination, intelligence and creative use of language. It leaves much also to the imagination and intelligence of the reader to resolve for himself. In some instances, a complete understanding of the author's meaning cannot be understood by the reader. The author does this purposefully for his own reasons and motivations.

As much as can be learned from Faulkner's writing, can be learned about Faulkner as the man he was and what he wrote about himself. His personal family background, incomplete formal education, the abject poverty and bigotry of his post-bellum rural southern culture prior to and during the Great Depression, his influences (or lack of influences) from his contemporary writers, his self-view - all contribute to our understanding of him and his writing. His greatness might be attributed to what he accomplished with the body of his work in spite of his circumstance.

Background

Born in 1897 in rural New Albany, Mississippi, Faulkner grew up just 21 years after the abandonment of failed reconstruction in the South. With scant education, he lived near there in Oxford most of his life, struggling to earn a decent living as a writer, caring and providing for an emergent dependent family, as a keen observer of the devastated South and its people.

Jim Crow laws were firmly in place from the southern governments and blacks were segregated from whites in public institutions. Many white families had fallen from former affluence but kept up the pretense of their past glories. This group, the chronically poor whites and the struggling poor blacks all living in the rural areas and small towns, dominated the scenes and characterizations of his fictional writings.

The relationships between whites and blacks were complex and conflictive. There was a carryover view of superiority, blatant and thoughtless racism, paternalism and affection from whites toward blacks and a self-effacing, while steadfast assertion of worth, from blacks toward whites. Faulkner exploited all of this cultural behavior, racism and hypocritical Christianity in his books and characters.

His writing accomplished in the 1930's, just prior to the cusp of the depression and thereafter, came to critical acclaim, but did not sell well or provide him good income. The hard- scrabble lives he wrote about were similar to his own.

His Acclaim and Self-view

In the literary world, much has been written about William Faulkner as a major member of its canon. Some have claimed that nearly as much has been written about him as has been for James Joyce and the Bible. The critics consider him the best southern writer in the American lexicon for the 20th century and place 4 of his books in the top 100 for that century. For his readers, he is an acquired taste. His books did not sell well for most of his life.

I would speculate that the reasons for his acclaim are varied but would include his powerful style of explosive writing filled with enigma. Perhaps equally important would be his unique and interesting self-view.

If you listen to William Faulkner give his Nobel Prize acceptance speech (You Tube video) and read some of his work, you will see that he wrote for lofty purpose, with profundity, without fear, without apology and without reservation. He wrote with dark cynicism and not with a warm heart. He didn't leave us much hope.

His works convey a mood - dark, pessimistic, devoid of warmth, love, hope for mankind, cynical of Christian faith, full of condemnation of racism, empty of much goodness found in his beloved Deep South. Yet he chose to live there most of his life. In his time, the interwar period of the early 20th century, he

379

expressed concern of his fear that the world would blow itself up. However, he did not chronicle much good in the world and one would wonder why he would be concerned.

He was self-assured and held himself in high regard, or so he presented himself in public interviews and in writing about himself. On the back flap of *As I Lay Dying*, he claimed:

> *I set out deliberately to write a tour-de-force. Before I ever put pen to paper and set down the first word I knew what the last word would be and almost where the last period would fall.*

He claimed to have written this work in one pass from 12:00am to 4:00am each night over six weeks. He implied there was no need for editing, but this is likely a fabrication on his part. The acclaimed novel is short, approximately 75,000 words and 260 pages on a 5 1/4" x 8" paperback format with single-spaced 10-12 pt. type. Faulkner wrote this short novel in the first person voice. This is challenging with multiple characters. He resolved this by selecting a different character for each chapter, with their name as the title. The story moves along with each character taking turns. His 15 characters present 15 points of view. There are 59 short chapters. With this complex writing task, I estimate he would have had to maintain a writing rate of 75,000 words / 168 hours, or nearly 450 words per hour - an exhausting marathon pace. Even if he knew exactly what the book was to be, as he had claimed, and didn't require spending time thinking or imagining what to write, his claim stretches credulity. And no editing was required as the result of this. It might have taken longer than he claimed.

Had he known about them, the corrections provided by Noel Polk for Faulkner's ribbon cutting copy made in 1985 would have been a great hardship for him to bear. Fortunately, he passed away in 1962.

His Style

His works have been categorized as southern Gothic, presumably because they were dark and cynical. They differ from his predecessor, Edgar Allan Poe however, in that they did not delve into the macabre or detective fictional aspects of the American-Gothic modern movement.

His writing followed three approaches to linguistic modalities of expression as suited to his plot circumstance:

- First person narration spoken by his characters in the thick southern idiom of the black and white poor, with their unique sensibility, religious beliefs and world view.

- Third person omniscient narrator describing the scene and action characterized by extremely long sentences using elegant descriptive language, with impressive vocabulary, often archaic today but appropriate to his time, and without concern for grammatical conventions of punctuation or run-on sentences.

- Stream of consciousness flow of thought without organization, linear progression or grammatical concern. In this mode, the readers can glean a feel for what is written but cannot hope to fully understand it.

His Influences

Sherwood Anderson, author of *Winesburg, Ohio*, is remembered as influencing Faulkner, Steinbeck and Wolfe. Faulkner took a job as an assistant in a New York City bookstore managed by Elizabeth Prall who later married Anderson. Anderson met him and advised that he write about his native region. Generally though, Faulkner claims he was influenced by reading the books of Flauberts, Dostoievsky and Conrad. To confirm his claims, in his introduction to *The Sound and the Fury* (Southern Review Version), he wrote:

I wrote this book and learned to read. I learned a little about writing from Soldier's Pay - how to approach language, words: not with seriousness so much, as an essayist does, but with a kind of alert respect, as you approach dynamite; even with joy, as you approach women: perhaps with the same unscrupulous intentions. But when I finished The Sound and the Fury I discovered that there is actually something to which the shabby term Art not only can, but must be applied. I discovered then that I had gone through all I had ever read, from Henry James through Henty to newspaper murders, without making any distinction or digesting any of it, as a moth or a goat might. After The Sound and the Fury and without heeding to open another book and in a series of delayed repercussions like summer thunder, I discovered Flauberts and Dostoievskys and Conrads whose books I had read ten years ago. With The Sound and the Fury I learned to read and quit reading, since I have read nothing since. (705-710).

With reference to his writing of *Light in August*, he referred to his angst in comparing himself to other writers:

.... since now I was deliberately choosing among possibilities and probabilities of behavior and weighing and measuring each choice by the scale of the Jameses and Conrads and Balzacs. I knew that I had read too much, ... (705-710).

Faulkner, like many of the highly regarded authors of the literary canon, did not use stock characters - Jungian archetypes. His characters do not all remain static. Some evolve, while some devolve. He does not present the reader with a protagonist to love that is simply all pure good. Nor can his reader hate an antagonist since there are none that are simply pure evil. It is often difficult to identify the protagonist and antagonist characters in his novels. Caddy, in *The Sound and the Fury,* changes from the self-sacrificing child-mother to the self-serving adult. Jason remains self-sacrificing throughout his life but never gains our love due to his bitter nature.

We tend to sympathize with him while he begrudges all the good he does for others. He has no good heart associated with his care for his family. We dislike him while simultaneously understanding him.

Additionally, Faulkner joined with Joyce, Hemingway and Fitzgerald in the literary canon. And certainly Sigmund Freud's theories of psychology, popular in Faulkner's time, influenced him and the other "Stream of Consciousness" method writers.

In terms of writing style and literary impression in the eyes of their readers, I will pursue parallels I have observed between Joyce and Faulkner, not on a high or deep intellectual plane, but more at a sensory level - what the language sounds, looks and feels like. In my view, to be able to read or write literature, it is necessary to be able to feel first in order to see meaning after.

While in France, Faulkner would sometimes go to the cafe that James Joyce would frequent, but the interminably shy Faulkner never mustered the nerve to speak to him. (William Faulkner: *The Mississippi Writers' Page*). Faulkner must have revered Joyce for many reasons. There are similar strains and aspects in their works and persons and, of course, notable differences:

- While Joyce built complex allegories of great mythic figures to reveal human characters, Faulkner told stories with enigmatically disclosed plots and revealed seemingly plain characters as complex, nuanced and human.

- Both had a strong writers tool box of vocabulary and poetic prose, and wrote passionately for their own edification.

- Both men made up words - often concatenations of individual real words - and treated the English language as their personal property.

- Like Joyce, Faulkner's narratives placed seemingly incongruous vocabulary and scholarly word choices out of character with their characters.

- Both were skilled at subtle humor - both dark and light.

- Both had elevated the craft in their time with believable voices spoken by their characters.

- Both often employed a stream of consciousness technique to give their characters voice.

- Like Joyce, Faulkner cherished enigma. The mysteries of understanding and meaning are left to the reader.

- Like Joyce, Faulkner's blended narrative-dialogue in the first person is styled age-specific. As an aside narrative-dialogue is where the writer speaks in the first-person voice. The narrative becomes the dialogue as well. It is an easier way to boost the desirable dialogue content in a fictional work. Only when the narrator requires another speaking, is he required to identify the character and use quote marks (ie, Frank looked over at the barn and said, "I'm going over there to check on the horse."). Using the more common third-person omniscient narrator voice is easier, but requires more effort to increase dialogue content.

- Both men relished forcing intellectual intercourse on their readers for their gratification, the smartest-guy-in-the-room syndrome.

- Both took a harsh view of Christianity's hypocrisy and criticized it unabashedly.

- Both men enjoyed imbibing in alcohol.

- While Faulkner engaged in extramarital affairs, he was more of a gentleman than the truly perverse Joyce (his love letters to Nora Barnacle - not for the feint of heart or morally upright).

To approach a substantive comparison between Joyce and Faulkner, it might be helpful to compare their literary characters and their approaches to writing their stories - their language.

Some of their iconic characters are children or mentally impaired adults who are presented as child-equivalent. For Faulkner, consider Vardaman in *As I Lay Dying* and Benjy in *The Sound and the Fury*. For Joyce, consider Stephen Dedalus in *A Portrait of an Artist as a Young Man*.

Vardaman says, "My mother is a fish." (*As I Lay*, 84) - perhaps the shortest chapter in American literature. As a young boy, Vardaman views the world in a child-like sensory way. His mother is dead, slimy and smelling bad. His narrative language is age-specific.

Similarly, throughout the book (*The Sound and the Fury*), Benjy does not speak, perhaps cannot speak, moans and thinks his sister Caddie, and others, smell like a tree. In *The Sound and the Fury*, section 1, Benjy is the narrator and an idiot. He views the world in a very direct way, based on his senses - sight (light and shadows), sound, feel (texture) and simplistic observations. That is all. We are told, he cannot grasp meanings and may have been autistic. That would mean that he could not articulate or relate in a conventional way, not proof that he was incapable of understanding.

Stephan Dedalus (*A Portrait of an Artist as a Young Man*) recounts a childish story of his father's hairy face, and the smell of the oilskin on his wet bed and does speak as a wee lad.

Joyce wrote:

Once upon a time and a very good time it was there was a moocow coming down along the road and this moocow that was down along the road met a nicens little boy named baby tuckoo...

His father told him that story: his father looked at him through a glass: he had a hairy face.

He was baby tuckoo. The moocow came down the road where Betty Byrne lived: she sold lemon platt.

O, the wild rose blossoms

On the little green place.

He sang that song. That was his song.

O, the green wothe botheth.

When you wet the bed, first it is warm then it gets cold. His mother put on the oilsheet. That had the queer smell.

His mother had a nicer smell than his father. She played on the piano the sailor's hornpipe for him to dance. ... (A Portrait, 195)

And from *Finnegans Wake,* Joyce referred to the old nursery rhyme of Humpty Dumpty:

The great fall of the offwall entailed at such short notice the pftjschute of Finnegan, erse solid man, that the humptyhillhead of humself prumptly sends an unquiring one well to the west in quest of his tumptytumtoes." (Finnegans, 3).

Stephen was not an idiot, like Benjy, but a young boy who thought and spoke from that perspective. Benjy did not speak but may have had thoughts about observations of visual scenes, textures, sounds, wetness in this manner. We don't know. Certainly both characters were attuned to smell.

Take note of the esoteric vocabulary that both authors were fond of using. In these examples, Joyce's writing is humorous. He, as well as Faulkner, took liberties with the use of language.

Regarding their approaches, both Faulkner and Joyce brought imaginative innovation and their own unique elegance to the writing of the English language. It is debatable which writer strived harder to make his work less understandable for his ordinary readers or relished the joy of experimenting with language more.

Consider Faulkner's words in *Light in August* here:

Memory believes before knowing remembers. Believes longer than recollects, longer than knowing even wonders. Knows remembers believes a corridor in a big long garbled cold echoing building of dark red brick sootbleakened by more chimneys than its own, set in a grassless cinderstrewnpacked compound surrounded by smoking factory purlieus and enclosed by a ten foot steel-and-wire fence like a penitentiary or a zoo, where in random erratic surges, with sparrowlike childtrebling, orphans in identical and uniform blue denim in and out of remembering but in knowing constant as the bleak walls, the bleak windows where in rain soot from the yearly adjacenting chimneys streaked like black tears. (Light, 119)

Or Faulkner's words in *Absalom, Absalom!* here:

He seems to hover, shadowy, almost substanceless, a little behind and above all the other straightforward and logical even though (to him) incomprehensible ultimatums and affirmations and defiances and challenges and repudiations, with an air of sardonic and indolent detachment like that of a youthful Roman consul making the Grand Tour of his day among the barbarian hordes which his grandfather conquered, benighted in a brawling and childish and quite deadly mud-castle household in a miasmic and spirit-ridden forest. (Absalom, 74).

387

This refers to the dramatic character, Sutpen and the concern viewed about him from his community.

And Joyce's imaginative and elegant approach in *Finnegans Wake* here:

The book <u>ends</u> with "A way a lone a last a loved a long the" (628), and <u>begins</u> with "riverrun, past Eve and Adam's, from swerve of shore to bend of bay, brings us by a commodius vicus of recirculation back to Howth Castle and Environs." (3)

Joyce meant to portray both the meandering river and his love of Viconian (Roman historian Vico) cyclical history with this passage.

And Faulkner again in *As I lay Dying*:

Yet still she could watch his mind darting and darting as without pity, without anything at all, she watched him with her grave, unwinking, unbearable gaze, watched him fumble and flee and tack until at last all that remained in him of pride, of what sorry pride the desire for justification was, fled from him and left him naked. (*As I Lay*, 429)

And:

She just didn't hope. Didn't know how to begin to hope. I imagine after thirty years the machinery for hoping requires more than twentyfour hours to get started, to get into motion again. (As I Lay, 445)

And in Hugh Ruppersburg's book, *Reading Faulkner: Light in August*, he references William Faulkner's clarification of his title choice for *Light in August*. Faulkner's states that his choice came from the scene where Gail Hightower looks out his study window awaiting a recurring vision of his grandfather's last raid. The descriptive portrayal of light is vividly conveyed there where

Faulkner's words convert written language to a visual picture for the reader:

> . . .in August in Mississippi there's a few days somewhere about the middle of the month when suddenly there's a foretaste of fall, it's cool, there's a lambence, a soft, a luminous quality to the light, as though it came not from just today but from back in the old classic times. It might have fauns and satyrs and the gods and---from Greece, from Olympus in it somewhere. It lasts just for a day or two, then it's gone. . .the title reminded me of that time, of a luminosity older than our Christian civilization.(Ruppersburg, 3)

Faulkner's writing is elegant, lush and gorgeous. This is some of the most beautiful writing - descriptive imagery of light and ancient myth - I can imagine.

And in Joyce's *Araby*, an example of descriptive sensory elegance:

> The career of our play brought us through the dark muddy lanes behind the houses where we ran the gauntlet of the rough tribes from the cottages, to the backdoors of the dark dripping gardens where odours arose from the ashpits, to the dark odorous stables where a coachman smoothed and combed the horse or shook music from the buckled harness. When we returned to the street light from the kitchen windows had filled the areas. (Dubliners and, 24).

And also from *Araby*:

> The light from the lamp opposite our door caught the white curve of her neck, lit up her hair that rested there and, falling, lit up the hand upon the railing. It fell over one side of her dress and caught the white border of a petticoat, just visible as she stood at ease. (Dubliners and, 25).

And from *A Portrait of the Artist as a Young Man* as a young man:

> Such moments passed and the wasting fires of lust sprang up again. The verses passed from his lips and the inarticulate cries and the unspoken brutal words rushed forth from his brain to force a passage. His blood was in revolt. He wandered up and down the dark slimy streets peering into the gloom of lanes and doorways, listening eagerly for any sound. He moaned to himself like some baffled prowling beast. He wanted to sin with another of his kind, to force another being to sin with him and to exult with her in sin. He felt some dark presence moving irresistibly upon him from the darkness, a presence subtle and murmurous as a flood filling him wholly with itself. Its murmur besieged his ears like the murmur of some multitude in sleep; its subtle streams penetrated his being. His hands clenched compulsively and his teeth set together as he suffered the agony of its penetration. He stretched out his arms in the street to hold fast the frail swooning form that eluded him and incited him: and the cry that he had strangled for so long in his throat issued from his lips. It broke from him like a wail of despair from a hell of sufferers and died in a wail of furious entreaty, a cry for an iniquitous abandonment, a cry which was but the echo of an obscene scrawl which he had read on the oozing wall of a urinal. (Dubliners and, 276-277)

And finally from *A Portrait of the Artist as a Young Man* as a young man:

> ... The yellow gas flames arose before his troubled vision against the vapoury sky, burning as if before an altar. Before the doors and in the lighted halls groups were gathered arrayed as for some rite. He was in another world: he had awakened from a slumber of centuries. (Dubliners and, 277).

Conclusion

Trying to grasp a sense of Faulkner's writing style and his meanings, not even a full sense, is like trying to climb a greased pole. But even the student with limited faculty and inadequate literary experience, can sense and feel his expression, at least at that level. He writes, as he speaks, imbued with a smooth southern charm, never to be misconstrued as anything less than brilliance. His high skill in the craft is beyond doubt at the genius level. His versatility to accomplish this is demonstrated by his agility to change voice and convey such a great range of characters. He re-invents himself with each writing enterprise.

Everything he writes appears on the surface to be all the same, when it really is new and original with his each re-invention. The plain folk, narrating so believably in their first person voice in *As I Lay Dying,* are not the archetypal caricatures they appear. Faulkner understands humanity. There are no Jungian archetypes. Nothing is either all good or all evil. Only thinking makes it so. (William Shakespeare, approximate paraphrase).

In *Absalom, Absalom!*, the characters and families depicted with his third-person omniscient voice are complex and nuanced. He confounds us with his 200 word sentences that defy the rule we have been so carefully taught: to not express more than one idea in a sentence. There is a 1,288 word sentence in *Absalom, Absalom!*, Chapter 6 the Guinness Book of World Records claims to be the longest sentence in literature. His sentences present and juggle four or more ideas at once. He juxtaposes and cross-fires them at each other, while arguing with himself with increasing intensity as they proceed. We see that there is a volume aspect as well as a tempo beat - a cadence.

Faulkner is deceptive. The smooth southern charm appears to flow along at the slow southern pace, but intensifies to a rate as voiced from a much colder climate. His arguments with himself are like a nested loop in a software program, so difficult to exit.

Perhaps the simplest aspect to grasp is his cadence like the ratta-tat-tat and the clippity- clop of the dialogue in *As I Lay Dying* - "So I say Dewey Dell - Dewey Dell I say". That wasn't a direct quote - just a fabrication of style. Note the interesting word symmetry.

And lastly, to attempt understanding Faulkner, or at least appreciate the beauty and skill he communicates in his use of descriptive language, cadence, temporal sense, voice and other aspects, I was reading *Absalom, Absalom!* - the fourth and last book assigned to us. I will explain my search for this understanding experientially.

I got to thinking that this was like the layers of an onion - a commonly used metaphor. This book read more like a normal book. At least, like in that idiot Benjy's reality, it smelled that way. It still had excruciatingly long sentences. The experience begins at first with your head spinning. Then you are shaking it, confounded; your mind fights to wander. Finally, you are smiling, laying down, taking it as he gives it to you, letting the words flow over you. To surrender to him is to enjoy. Maybe that was an allegory, maybe not. It doesn't matter. It expresses the solution I have found for enjoying William Faulkner's writing for the time being.

And so, truly finally, here are Faulkner's words as the narrator, waxing philosophical as he speaks of Bon and the New Orleans whorehouse:

But we save that one. God may mark every sparrow, but we do not pretend to be God, you see. Perhaps we do not even want to be God, since no man would want but one of these sparrows. And perhaps when God looks into one of these establishments like you saw tonight, He would not choose one of us to be God either, now that He is old. Though He must have been young once, surely He was young once, and surely someone who has existed as long as He has, who has looked at as much crude and promiscuous sinning without grace or restraint or decorum as He has had to, to contemplate at last, even though the instances are not one in a thousand thousand, the principles of honor, decorum and gentleness applied to perfectly normal human instinct which you Anglo-Saxons insist upon calling lust and in whose service you revert in sabbaticals to the primordial caverns, the fall from what you call grace fogged and clouded by Heaven-defying words of extenuation and explanation, the return to grace heralded by Heaven-placating cries of satiated abasement and flagellation, in neither of which - the defiance or the placation - can Heaven find interest or even, after the first two or three times, diversion. So perhaps, now that God is an old man, He is not interested in the way we serve what you call lust either. Perhaps He does not even require of us that we save this one sparrow, anymore than we save the one sparrow which we do save for any commendation from Him. (Absalom, Absalom!, 91-92)

It matters little whether Bon is speaking, or Henry speaking of Bon, or Judith speaking of Sutpen, or Faulkner is narrating. It is all Faulkner writing with profundity, philosophically, poetically, and vividly - using the old South and its people as a living laboratory to study the human condition - for himself but giving us the chance to see it, to understand it. I believe that this is why he stands at the pinnacle of the American writers.

I have enjoyed and appreciated most all that I have read of Faulkner's writing so far. Some of it has struck me much deeper than some other of it. I think he is at his best when he is writing as himself in third-person omniscient voice. There his most profound thoughts and the beauty and elegance of his skill with the English language comes through and touches the reader the most.

Thank you Mr. Faulkner. Even if you were alive today and could hear my gratitude, you could not know how much you have helped me in a very short time. I hope to learn and appreciate your work more.

Works Cited

Joyce, James. *Dubliners and A Portrait of the Artist as a Young Man*. New York: Barnes and Noble Books, 1992. Print.

Joyce, James. *Finnegans Wake*. New York: Penguin Books, 1976. Print.

Faulkner, William C.. *Light in August*. New York: Vintage Books, a division of Random House, Inc., 1990. Print.

Faulkner, William C.. *As I Lay Dying*. New York: Vintage Books, a division of Random House, Inc., 1990. Print.

Faulkner, William C.. *The Sound and the Fury*. New York: Vintage Books, a division of Random House, Inc., 1990. Print.

Faulkner, William C.. *An Introduction to The Sound and the Fury* edited by James B. Meriwether, *The Southern Review* 8 (N.S. 1972): 705-710. Print.

Faulkner, William C.. *Absalom, Absalom!*. New York: Vintage Books, a division of Random House, Inc., 1990. Print.

Ruppersburg, Hugh. *Reading Faulkner: Light in August*. University Press of Mississippi, 1994. Print.

The Verities

May 2017

Not to single out William Faulkner from all the great writers in the American literary canon including Twain, Steinbeck, Hemingway and Fitzgerald, but his life and his writing were instructive, especially when he spoke about his purpose. He was very serious minded, full of vanity and self-assured when he described himself or his books. But I respected his seriousness of purpose.

He said that he wanted to write about the old verities but he did not list them or explain which eternal truths he intended. The truths that mattered to Faulkner did come out in his work. Much has been written about that from critics in their exegesis.

Lawrence Thompson wrote that Faulkner's moral vision, those laws that have to do with the verities of the heart, would include courage, endurance, compassion, aspiration, sacrifice, pride and love.

My observation is that Faulkner drew from mythology or mysticism as a substitute for his personal lack of spirituality. His characters were metaphors for Diana, the earth mother goddess and he wrote often about the fecundity of the earth, the fire wheel of eternity and illumination. He believed in nature, the earth's nature, as it compelled human nature to act in an automatic and pre-ordained pattern. But that is not spiritualism; it is secularism at best or perhaps paganism.

So I believe he lacked spirituality. It needn't had to have been Christianity, but his concerns with Christian hypocrisy kept him from spirituality in even a broader way.

As for his trove of the verities, he therefore had little concern for grace, redemption and salvation, as a religious person might. While I learned some things from him, his work encouraged me to read more widely and deeply. Some of Faulkner's characters achieved a degree of redemption, though he often denied its possibility, and it was thin and not transcendent. He could have moved more of us had he held a belief in God.

So more on my own, without any ideas of the kind from him, I found more of these universal verities of humankind and included them in my writing. I saw that the verities include forgiveness which he seemed to have ignored in his work. It seems to me that forgiveness of one's self and others can lead to a peace and a happiness and joy beyond the mere achievement of endurance and survival. Forgiveness leads to hope and hopefully hope leads to grace and redemption. As a matter of perspective, I suppose Faulkner saw little of that in his time and place so that he did not feel it and could not write about it.

The Southern Psyche

Originally written in 2016

We have all learned about our 19th century American history to a greater or lesser degree. We know the causes of the Civil War, its horrific battles and the aftermath. We know about Reconstruction that began in 1863 in the middle of the war and ended when the Federal troops left the ten military districts in the South in 1877.

We know there was a brief span of years when the 13th, 14th and 15th Amendments (the so- called Civil War Amendments), reinforced by the redundant Civil Rights Act of 1866, meant something for freed slaves. They voted, held public office and began building schools with their allies in the strong AME churches throughout the South. The Southern governments had complied with Federal requirements to produce State constitutions prohibiting slavery and one by one were admitted back into the Union. Their Democrat politicians again participated fully in government in Washington, D.C.

We understand the exploitation of the Carpetbaggers from the North and the Scalawags within the South. We know that after the troops left, the Governments in the South produced the so-called Jim Crow laws to segregate blacks that could no longer legally be enslaved. We know all this.

We know that for many, maybe most, whites in the South, especially the formerly prosperous, there was a melancholy and bitterness of their lost cause, their fallen glory. It was somehow inconceivable to accept and impossible to reconcile.

Our modern history professors have studied it and produced works of specialized scholarship on these matters. They know the truth as immutable. Just ask them, they will tell you that this is so. They never lived there during that time, or ever, but they know.

But what they are missing, and we as students never learned, is the perspective of intelligent southerners who did live there and wrote about it some few decades, or a generation, later.

They were novelists like William Faulkner, and later Shelby Foote, who grew up in the Mississippi Delta during the early decades of the 20th century. They had insights about individuals and groups of peoples they expressed through their writing of imaginary characters and stories. There is more to learn from them. I know that some academic historians dismiss them, but I do not.

Having read many of these books, I am revisiting *The Portable Faulkner* published by the Viking Portable Library. It is bits, pieces and slices of his writing, some of which I have seen before, throughout his career. The editor is Malcolm Cowley and his introductions and reflections at the beginning of his selected sections of Faulkner's writing are as interesting as Faulkner's writing itself. They provide insights to reinforce my own understanding.

Sometimes someone's writing strikes a chord so strong we want to share. This is a great part of my motivation to write.

In his Editor's Note to The End of an Order, Cowley explains Faulkner's viewpoint about those southern times and its people.

"A recurring theme in Faulkner's novels is that the old South was defeated from within. After four years of fighting against hopeless odds, the landowners of Yoknapatawpha County had remained "the unvanquished," and they all had tried, as did Colonel Sutpen, to restore their houses, their plantations, and their social order to the image of what they had been before the war. Moreover, they achieved a partial success. There were years in Jefferson when the prewar standards prevailed; when a Sartoris was mayor, a Benhow was county judge, and Major De Spain was the local magistrate. But the heirs of the men who had withstood the Northern armies and defeated the carpetbaggers were driven from their posts of influence by Southern renegades, or rather by a coalition between Northern business and a new class of Southerners descended in part from the bushwhackers of Civil War days. Jefferson itself was overrun, infested by the tribe of Snopes: for a time there were Snopeses in the bank, in the power company, in politics, Snopeses everywhere gnawing like rats at the standards by which the South had lived.

The Snopeses and their allies are the destructive element in Faulkner's novels. The Negroes are an element of stability: they endured. Faulkner's favorite characters are the Negro cooks and matriarchs who hold a white family together: Elnora and Clytie and Dilsey and Aunt Mollie Beauchamp. After the Compson family has gone to pieces, in *The Sound and the Fury*, it is Dilsey the cook who is left behind to mourn. Looking up at the square unpainted house with its rotting porticoes, she thinks, "Ise seed de first en de last"; and later in the kitchen she says, looking at the cold stove, "I seed de first en de last."

Of the four stories in this section, "That Evening Sun," with its black heroine, is one of Faulkner's very best; it belongs to a cycle dealing with the Compson children. "Ad Astra" is part of another cycle recounting the adventures of Bayard Sartoris' twin grandsons in the Royal Air Force: John was killed, and Bayard, named for his grandfather, came home (in *Sartoris*, 1929) feeling that he too had died on the night of the Armistice. In "A Rose for Emily," often anthologized, Faulkner has found one of his most effective symbols for the decay of the old order. These three stories were included in *These 13* (1931) and reprinted in *Collected Stories of William Faulkner* (1950). "Dilsey" comes from the last part of *The Sound and the Fury* (1929), which describes the going to pieces of the Compson family and which remained Faulkner's favorite among his novels. For the early history of the Compsons and the fate of the survivors, see "Appendix: The Compsons," printed in the last part of this volume."

Hightower's Calling

———◦———

April 2017

In *Light in August* Gail Hightower remembers his days in seminary when God gave him his calling to minister to the town of Jefferson, Mississippi. His troubled reflections:

While at the seminary, after he first came, he often thought how he would tell them, the elders, the high and sanctified men who were the destiny of the church to which he had willingly surrendered. How he would go to them and say, "Listen. God must call me to Jefferson because my life died there, was shot from the saddle of a galloping horse in a Jefferson street one night twenty years before it was ever born." He thought that he would say that, at first. He believed they would comprehend. He went there, chose that as his vocation, with that as his purpose. But he believed in more than that. He had believed in the church too, in all that it ramified and evoked. He believed with a calm joy that if ever there was shelter, it would be the Church; that if ever truth could walk naked and without shame or fear, it would be in the seminary. When he believed that he had heard the call it seemed to him that he could see his future, his life, intact and on all sides complete and inviolable, like a classic and serene within which the hampered and garmentworried spirit could learn anew serenity to contemplate without horror or alarm its own nakedness. vase, where the spirit could be born anew sheltered from the harsh gale of living and die so, peacefully, with only the far sound of the circumvented wind, with scarce even a handful of rotting dust to be disposed of. That was what the word seminary meant: quiet and safe walls

F. Scott Fitzgerald's Language

Originally written in 2016, updated in 2017

Fitzgerald, like Hemingway, was an American writer in a time of angst and disappointment with America and life in general after World I. Many writers of the early 1920's had expatriated to France and cynically sat and stewed about their art and how awful a place the world was.

Hemingway was lauded for his phenomenal writing and the fact that his style was incredibly simple – some say written at the 4th grade level. But he is appreciated for the powerful messages and feelings behind his simple words. I have only read his *The Sun Also Rises* and believe I made a poor choice. The book was dreadfully boring and virtually without a plot. It was mostly about the social life of expatriated artists living in Paris who did not practice their art. They mainly loafed and slept, gathered together for food, drink and gossip all the while licking their wounds and whining about life as they saw it.

Fitzgerald also wrote about these themes but with an emphasis on poor little rich boys in the age of bootlegging and the Roaring 20's. His level of language was to me higher and more profound than Hemingway's. There is an elegance with a visual component as a way to convey deep melancholy so very well. His *The Great Gatsby* was my choice and it affected me as both a writer and a conscious, feeling human being.

Here is an excerpt from the end of the book, where the narrator of the story speaks about Jay Gatsby's Long Island eastern tip, that I thoroughly enjoyed-

"Most of the big shore places were closed now and there were hardly any lights except the shadowy, moving glow of a ferryboat across the Sound. And as the moon rose higher the inessential houses began to melt away until gradually I became aware of the old island here that flowered once for Dutch sailors' eyes – a fresh, green breast of the new world. Its vanished trees, the trees that had made way for Gatsby's house, has once pandered in whispers to the last greatest of all human dreams; for a transitory enchanted moment man must have held his breath in the presence of this continent, compelled into an aesthetic contemplation he neither understood nor desired, face to face for the last time in history with something commensurate to his capacity to wonder.

And as I sat there, brooding on the old unknown world, I thought of Gatsby's wonder when he first picked out the green light at the end of Daisy's dock. He had come a long way to this blue lawn and his dream must have seemed so close that he could hardly fail to grasp it. He did not know that it was already behind him, somewhere back in that vast obscurity beyond the city, where the dark fields of the republic rolled on under the night.

Gatsby believed in the green light, the orgastic future that year by year recedes before us. It eluded us then, but that's no matter – tomorrow we will run faster, stretch our arms out farther … And one fine morning –

So we beat on, boats against the current, borne back ceaselessly into the past."

Arthur Herman's masterwork, *How The Scots Invented the Modern World*, is filled with stories and countless names throughout Scottish history and particularly those who arose during the Scottish Enlightenment in the 18th century after the

Scottish wars of 1715 and 1745. There men were prominent in all fields of intellectual endeavor and invented an education system which was at the time the best in the world. For a time, an extended time actually spanning much of the 18th and 19th centuries, the Scots leap-frogged over all others in England, France, Germany and the western world in establishing modernity.

A portion of his book is allocated to the men of letters who set the standard for literature for the world to follow. He highlights Sir Walter Scott above these as the last minstrel, a romantic during the Highland revival. He would lead all those to follow with the invention of the historic novel- Austen, Dickens, Thackeray, Eliot, Trollope, Balzac, Hugo, Flaubert and Tolstoy.

Without all the detailed explanations and examples, Scott was complex and multi-dimensioned and saw the opposing tensions of the modern world and the divisions in himself as a reflection of the Scottish culture itself. He wrote a friend, "The Scottish mind was made up of poetry and strong common sense, and the very strength of the latter gave perpetuity and luxuriance to the former."

Herman wrote that the credit for defining the artist as a person who can hold two inconsistent ideas at once goes to F. Scott Fitzgerald. The credit for realizing that that is precisely what all modern men can do – indeed, must be able to do – belongs to Sir Walter Scott.

Mark Twain's – The Gilded Age and other works

April 2017

As good fortune would have it, I was left from someone in the generation past a series of beautifully bound old books of Twain's printed in the 1930's or 1940's. They are not dated and don't have a copyright page like modern books. The original publisher, when he had written them, was Nelson Doubleday in Garden City, New York. But in the 40's my copies were published by arrangement with Harper & Row under permission of S. L. Clemens trademark.

Of the set, I read *A Connecticut Yankee in King's Arthurs's Court* first. It was fanciful and I suppose in its own way a very early science fiction work. Twain's sardonic humor was skillfully deployed in this imaginative work. He, the Yankee, Sir Boss is the narrator and educates us about the absurdity of humanity using medieval "values" contrasted with his 19th century modernity. It was thought-provoking and hilarious at once. His 19th century thoughts about society, culture and humanity are not that much different than ours were up to the late 20th. The 21st century is a strange new thing and who knows where it's supposed values will lead the culture and the society.

Certainly I enjoy living in the past through literature and my own writing. It is there I find some evidence of grace and graciousness I cannot find in the present. Yes, our American history is a million stories of the good, the bad, and the ugly. That is no surprise to any adult with a developed pre-frontal cortex and the ability to reason. But I learn from the past more than the present, so I find myself there often, exploring and reasoning.

Currently I am reading *The Gilded Age*. I had previously written about many of its themes in my own third novel – *The American: A Man's Life*.

I guess I have become an exegesis writer in addition to my own work. That is because I admire so many of the writers in our American lexicon. I study them and examine the way they use language and put words together. It has helped me a little bit but I am comfortable with my limited abilities. The bar is too high for my talent. But I work hard and I have read writers who are worse than I am.

So here once again are some words from a great writer I admire:

"She sat long, with the letters in her lap, thinking – and unconsciously freezing. She felt like a lost person who had traveled down a long lane in good hope of escape, and, just as the night descends finds his progress barred by a bridgeless river whose further shore, if it has one, is lost in the darkness. If she could only have found these letters a month sooner! That was her thought. But now the dead had carried their secrets with them. A dreary melancholy settled down upon her. An undefined sense of injury crept into her heart. She grew very miserable.

She had just reached the romantic age – the age when there is a sad sweetness, a dismal comfort to a girl to find out that there is a mystery connected with her birth, which no other piece of good luck can afford. She had more than her rightful share of practical good sense, but still she was human; and to be human is to have one's little modicum of romance secreted away in one's composition. One never ceases to make a hero of one's self, (in private,) during life, but only alters the style of his heroism from time to time as the drifting years belittle certain gods of his admiration and raise up others in their stead that seem greater.

The recent wearing days and nights of watching, and the wasting grief that had possessed her, combined with the profound depression that naturally came with the reaction of idleness, made Laura peculiarly susceptible at this time to romantic impressions. She was a heroine, now, with a mysterious father somewhere. She could not really tell whether she wanted to find him and spoil it all or not; but still all the traditions of romance pointed to the making of the attempt as the usual and necessary course to follow; therefore she would someday begin the search when opportunity should offer."

Congress vs. the Press in the 19th Century

March 2017

Mark Twain's cynical and satirical genius shines through again and again. In this passage from *The Gilded Age*, he writes with hilarity about a fictitious bill brought to Congress, as reported in the papers, for a Knobs Hill University to benefit the Negroes. It is a sham and hypocritical Senator Dilworthy anxiously awaits the carnage coming from the newspaper reports-

"Senator Dilworthy was so anxious to know what the New York papers would say about the bill, that he had arranged to have synopses of their editorials telegraphed to him; he could not wait for the papers themselves to crawl down along down to Washington by a mail train which has never run over a cow since the road was built, for the reason that it had never been able to overtake one. It carries the usual "cow-catcher" in front of the locomotive, but that is mere ostentation. It ought to be attached to the rear car, where it could do some good; but instead, no provision is made there for the protection of the traveling public, and hence it is not a matter of surprise that cows so frequently climb aboard that train and among the passengers.

The Senator read his dispatches aloud at the breakfast table. Laura was troubled beyond measure at their tone, and said that that sort of comment would defeat the bill; but the Senator said:

"Oh, not at all, not at all, my child. It is just what we want. Persecution is the one thing needful, now – all the other forces are secured. Give us newspaper persecution enough, and we are safe. Vigorous persecution will alone carry a bill sometimes, dear; and when you start with a strong vote in the first place, persecution comes in with double effect. It scares off some of the weak supporters, true, but is soon turns strong ones into stubborn ones.

And then, presently, it changes the tide of public opinion. The great public is weak-minded; the great public is sentimental; the great public turns around and weeps for an odorous murderer, and prays for him, and carries his flowers to his prison and besieges the governor with appeals for his clemency, as soon as the papers begin to howl for that man's blood. – In a word, the great putty-hearted public loves to 'gush,' and there is no darling opportunity to gush as a case of persecution affords".

So much then is so much the same as today.

David Wexley's story

May 2017

No sir, I am not he. David Jennings is not present or familiar to me. Perhaps he will come by later, Captain.

This is a strange place not familiar to me either. This is the year 1892, is it not?

Hi Folks,

I'm David Wexley from Aspen, Colorada. I'm here tonight to tell you my story. But before I do that, I want to tell you that there will be a writer in the 21st century, your time, who will publish my story.

His name is David Claire Jennings, no relation to me. He will have been something called an Electronics Engineer and when he retired he began writing essays about our country – America. Then he went back to college – Columbia College of Missouri – as an old man to study American History and Literature. He will write three books about me he will call *After Bondage and War*, *Hanna's Promise: A Story of Grace and Hope* and *The American: A Man's Life*. Then he will bundle the three books together in a 19th century American trilogy he will call *Slaves, Saints and Soldiers*. I was the soldier in his story.

The short version of my life is pretty simple. I followed the fates placed before me in my time. I was born in 1832 in Baltimore, fought at Antietam in '62 and The Battle of The Wilderness in '64. There I was shot and taken to Richmond and then Andersonville. After the war I wandered and spent time with my new friend Joe who was just freed from a plantation. We visited Shiloh together in '65 and it broke my heart.

413

We settled in Ohio, but after some 20 years of troubled spirit, I struck out for the West. I wanted another chance for redemption and forgiveness and a happy life. It would be my last chance and it worked out as well as I could have hoped for. Finally I was killed and brought back on the train to Cincinnati where my best friend Joe buried me on his land. But that is another story.

Would you like to hear about my experiences that day at Antietam? Or The Battle of the Wilderness? Or Shiloh? It is beginning to get easier to talk about it.

You know men have said I look like Bobby Lee. I don't agree with that. I think I look more like Abraham Lincoln, only more handsome than he, maybe more like General Grant.

Would you like to hear what I found out about Presidents Abe Lincoln and Jeff Davis or the Generals - Ulysses Grant and Bobby Lee or Jeb Stuart, Uncle Billy Sherman, that killer Little Phil Sheridan, or Ambrose Burnside, George McClellan, George Meade or Nathan Bedford Forrest, Thomas (Stonewall) Jackson, or James (Old Pete) Longstreet?

There were almost a countless number of generals on both sides. Many were West Pointers who were graduated about the same time and fought together in the Mexican War, the Indian conflicts and "Bleeding Kansas", starting as Brevet Lieutenants. Of course Tom Jackson came from VMI where he was a professor of mathematics. He was a bit touched in the head.

Others were non-professional military men who were politicians and raised a regiment from their own region. They all became Brigadier Generals on the spot.

Both sides of my war fervently believed God was on their side. That has been one of the greatest causes of my troubled feelings all the years since then – God, the Generals, the Politicians, the truth about glory and honor. For me, it was more about mud, rain, misery, starvation and depravity.

I'm here to tell ya.

Seth Grahame-Smith's Creativity

March 2017

Anne Rice's books were enjoyable and well written. I read a couple of them and appreciated her visual imagery, fantasy and imagination about vampirism. But I found Seth Grahame-Smiths' books better in those regards. His genre is slightly different than Rices'. His is alternate history and he accomplishes it impeccably.

With his education in English and filmmaking, he is wired as a screenwriter, but began his career with novels first. Without any formal background in history, he writes in a screenwriter's visual way. I found his descriptive writing level even higher than Rice.

For me, I have always liked reading and writing about ideas, whatever the venue or genre.

Here is an excerpt from the early chapters of his latest book, *The Last American Vampire*:

Henry had wandered America in the years after Abe's fatal leap, watching with a sort of detached fascination as the young country rose from the ashes, brushed itself off, and began to move west by way of iron and ink. The purchase of Alaska in 1867; the golden spike of the first transcontinental railroad two years later. America had looked inward. It had gone to war with itself to decide what kind of nation it was going to be. And with that decision firmly and finally made, it pulled itself together and soldiered on, emerging from its near-death experience with a new vitality. A new spirit of progress.

Henry had marked his three hundredth year during America's Civil War. Three hundred years of motion. Of taking new names, making new homes, adapting to the world as it changed around him. In 1888, with the war long over and the greatest man he'd ever

417

known twenty-three years in his grave, he moved again. This time he swam against the westward tide of progress, leaving the Midwest and settling in New York City.

I'd heard it said that "when a man is tired of moving, he moves to New York, and the movement comes to him." I supposed it was partially this. The need to relax in the anonymity of large numbers. To let the movement of the world come to me for a change. And I suppose I also liked the thought of being closer to the headquarters of the Union. But looking back, more than anything, I think I wanted to be farther away from America. It had been a long relationship, fraught with discovery and upheaval and loss. To me, it was a nation of ghosts, you understand, whether it be Richmond or St. Louis or New Orleans, there were a hundred faded memories. The faces of a hundred friends lost to time.

Henry's home in St. Louis was put up for sale and a new one procured in New York. Arrangements were made via letter and cable. Furnishings were bought. A staff hired, sight unseen, based on recommendation from other well-to-do New Yorkers, human and vampire alike. Clothing, keepsakes, books, and artwork were packed up and shipped from St. Louis in advance.

Conclusion

The story of America is many stories as varied, diverse and great as the people who came to settle here on our great, vast land and our beautiful land itself.

America's story has been shaped by both internal and external forces, not completely within our control, that have swept us along through our history.

There have been watershed periods, like our great and horrible Civil War, that have changed us forever but were inexorably predicable from Washington's first warnings to the two views of our culture expressed by Adams and Jefferson.

The conclusion is that there is no one overriding conclusion but many conclusions because the more things change, the more they stay the same. There have been repeating patterns recognizable as the cyclical nature that is all of human history.

In this present age, where this is a scarcity of grace and graciousness, it may be particularly meaningful to search the past for understanding of our Americanism.

God bless America.